A HISTORY OF ARGENTINE POLITICAL THOUGHT

JOSÉ LUIS ROMERO

Introduction and translation by
THOMAS F. McGANN

STANFORD UNIVERSITY PRESS
STANFORD, CALIFORNIA
1963

Originally published in Spanish under the title of
Las Ideas Políticas en Argentina, in three editions, 1946, 1956, 1959

Copyright by Fondo de Cultura Económica, Mexico City

This book is a translation of the Third Edition, 1959,
with an Epilogue added by the author

Stanford University Press
Stanford, California

© 1963 by the Board of Trustees of the
Leland Stanford Junior University
All rights reserved

Library of Congress Catalog Card Number: 63-12042
Printed in the United States of America

PUBLICATION OF THIS BOOK WAS ASSISTED BY A GRANT FROM THE
ROCKEFELLER FOUNDATION AND THE LATIN AMERICAN TRANSLATION
PROGRAM OF THE ASSOCIATION OF AMERICAN UNIVERSITY PRESSES

ARGENTINA

Scale in miles
0   250   500

N

FALKLAND IS.
(Malvinas)

Drafted by B. Hartmann

A HISTORY OF
ARGENTINE
POLITICAL THOUGHT

CONTENTS

ACKNOWLEDGMENT

The translator gratefully acknowledges the assistance in the preparation of this book of Professors Michael G. Hall, George D. Schade, Jr. (who translated the poems), and David D. Van Tassel, all of the University of Texas, Miss Shirley Nelson of the Stanford University Press, and Mrs. Helen P. Travis, Mrs. Gretchen Blackmon, and Miss Colleen Kain.

INTRODUCTION

The history of Argentina, important in itself, is significant also as part of the history of the Americas. That there has been an American experience, or at least a number of common, profound American experiences, is a thesis that has aroused lively debate. The Mexican scholar Edmundo O'Gorman denies the existence of a uniquely American heritage, claiming that what seem to be mutually shared experiences in the Americas are in fact no more than aspects of universal human conduct; their paradigms can be found throughout history in many lands. The United States historian Herbert E. Bolton, on the other hand, insisted on the validity of what he called the "Epic of Greater America"—the identity of the major historical movements wherever they occurred, from Hudson Bay to Tierra del Fuego.

There are similarities that at times emerge from the enormous diversity of the American past, and it is likely that both the comparisons and the contrasts between Argentina and the United States are more marked than those that may be found elsewhere in America. There seems to be a common stamp imprinted on the two peoples, at times so light as to be nearly indistinguishable, at times deep and heavy. The nature of the first primitive settlements along the Río de la Plata and in New England and Virginia; the wars with the Indians; the struggle with oppressive royal officials—these are some of the experiences both peoples shared. In the eighteenth century the Europe-oriented eastern seaboards of both countries produced men imbued with European rationalism who led wars for independence and republicanism. In the nineteenth century internal expansion brought the age of the frontier, the pioneer, the gaucho, and the cowboy. In the twentieth century, despite its greater complexity, strong parallels between the two nations have appeared, again in political thought and economic activity. It is by examining such parallels, and also by giving at least equal weight to the diversity of institutions and ideas, that *norteamericanos* may better understand Argentina's history and increase their awareness of the history of the United States and of the other American nations.

A History of Argentine Political Thought, by José Luis Romero, is the work of a skilled historian who is also an Argentine citizen deeply involved in the contemporary condition of his homeland. Dr. Romero's interest in political thought is intimately connected to his concern for human liberty. Author, teacher, editor, university administrator, Professor Romero was among the Argentine intellectuals whom Juan Domingo Perón expelled from their university positions in the mid-1940's. No other book states so competently as *A History of Argentine Political Thought* the themes that have formed Argentina's political history; no other book gives the reader a better opportunity to perceive the shaping of a great American people. The book is not primarily concerned with formal political thought but with the political manifestations of social and economic forces. Therefore, Dr. Romero's analysis makes it possible for other Americans to compare and to decide how much the Argentine experience is unique, how much is shared, and how much is common to mankind.

One decisive fact lies at the root of any comparison of the British and Spanish colonial ventures in the New World. The Spanish conquerors were men of the fifteenth century; the English settlers were of a later age. Many of the Spaniards had fought in Renaissance wars in Italy, which were known only as century-old history to the men along the James River and Massachusetts Bay. Pedro de Mendoza, who made the first settlement of Buenos Aires in 1536, was born in Granada in 1487; John Smith of Virginia was born in Lincolnshire in 1579, and William Bradford of Massachusetts was born in 1590 in Yorkshire. Separating these men lay a century, a Reformation, and a continent—the breadth of land and sea between the sun of Sevilla and the gray mists of Bristol.

Formed in different epochs, imbued with distinct concepts of the individual and of Church and State, Spaniards and Englishmen went at the business of colonization in dissimilar ways. In human terms, the Spaniards regarded the Indians as persons possessing souls, as being fit for Christianization, and for wiving. In material terms, if the Spaniards were more exploitive in a pejorative sense than the English, this was perhaps because they had more to exploit than rocks, woods, and thin soil.

But Argentina is in many ways unlike other areas of Spanish America. The provinces of the Río de la Plata were not Peru or Mexico, rich in gold and silver and native people. Argentina was on the frontier of the empire, and life there was harsh. The fact that Buenos Aires had to be founded twice, the second time in 1580, long after the first settlement had disintegrated under the pressures of Indians and isolation, testifies to the hardships that the colonists endured. The Río de la Plata provinces were not only distant geographically from Spain; they were remote administratively and economically. Spanish monopolists in Spain and in Panama forced all trade with the Río de la Plata to go by way of Panama and Peru. And until 1776, the Viceroy in far-off Lima was responsible for the government of the Río de la Plata provinces.

Argentina was settled from the north and northwest, from Paraguay and Peru. As a result, the inland provinces and towns were older and for many years more important than the town and province of Buenos Aires. This situation became the basis for the fierce rivalry that divided Buenos Aires from the other provinces after independence was achieved in 1810. The conflict lasted until 1880, when the city of Buenos Aires became the federal capital of the nation, its power too overwhelming to be challenged by other parts of the country.

In the remote borderland that was Argentina, priests and royal officials, landowners and merchants, matched wits and strength in the interest of God, king, and self. Self usually won in the persons of the landowners. These men of great property were not freeman farmers, edging their way through the forests, who expanded their political rights as they advanced the line of settlements. The Argentine landowners were ranchers. They preferred in the Spanish way to live much in town, where they were close to affairs and to their other properties. They were men of rugged individualism that matched anything the British colonists could show. Spanish American individualism is perhaps even more rugged, since it is more complete, more focused. It does not extend to civic activities, neighborly cooperation, or philanthropy. The needs of society are supposed to be taken care of by the State and the Church; voluntary cooperation among individuals is achieved only in the most critical situations, as during a struggle for national independence. Yet as Romero shows, royal rule and Church authority were ever-present realities to the lords of the land, who often disobeyed but seldom disavowed their spiritual and temporal superiors. Thus, with the paradoxical capacity of the Spaniard, the colonists combined liberty and despotism, personalism and hierarchy, in a pattern of life that reached back hundreds of years into Spain's own past and was to endure in Spanish America for the imperial span of three centuries, and even beyond, to today.

The political end of the colonial age came with the War for Independence, which for Argentina began in Buenos Aires in May 1810 and did not end until the Spaniards were defeated in the high Andes of Peru in 1824. Inevitably, the war, too, was on an imperial scale, fought during many years and over a vast area. Argentina played a principal part in gaining victory for the *criollos*—the creoles, people of Spanish descent born in America. The continental scope of Argentina's efforts on behalf of freedom from the Spanish Crown, including San Martín's passage of the Andes with the army that helped liberate Chile and Peru, gave the Argentine people a continent-sized pride and faith in their national destiny.

The objectives of the Argentine and other Spanish American leaders of the War for Independence were not revolutionary; no more so than those of the North American colonists when they had fought for independence from Britain thirty years earlier. The aim of the creole leaders in Spanish America was personal power; they sought to replace the Spaniards as exploiters and administrators of the colonies. The social and economic structure remained largely unaltered; so did political thought, as Romero demonstrates. Secession involved the substitution of republicanism for royal absolutism. For the new Argentine State, which was for half a century to remain an inchoate confederation, the substitution proved to be desperately difficult. British America had faced no comparable problem, although both revolutions were conceived in much the same ideological matrix, the eighteenth-century Enlightenment. The Spanish colonial heritage endured in the forms of authoritarianism, personalism, an oligarchic social order based on an illiterate mass, and in intractable regionalism. These forces were stronger than any counterparts they may have had in the United States—too strong to allow Argentina to pass unmarked from the world of the eighteenth century into the nineteenth century. Political and economic democracy had been no part of the Spanish colonial order, and the new ruling creole class, especially in the interior provinces, had no intention of altering the status of the masses.

The land was a wilderness, for the unbroken pampa, like the western prairies of the United States, was a kind of wilderness. In 1810, fewer than one million people occupied a territory of more than one million square miles. Enormous distances conspired against national unity; the mounted plains Indians contained the weak thrust of the frontier. The hope for political stability was smothered by inexperience and lost in civil strife as the other provinces turned against the more liberal and economically aggressive port city of Buenos Aires. By the 1830's, when the United States had produced President Andrew Jackson and frontier democracy, Argentina had produced the dictator Juan Manuel de Rosas. Rosas led the feeble confederation back into the eighteenth century. He called himself the Restorer of the Laws: by "laws" he meant the imposition of the colonial system and the negation of the small gains in education, in the economy, and in political liberty that had been made in the first years of the republican experiment. Any parallels that may have existed between the young republics of the United States and Argentina disappeared during the Rosas dictatorship. Culture was paralyzed, the economy stagnated, and a generation of Argentine exiles fled to neighboring states.

When the exiles and internal opponents finally overthrew Rosas in 1852, Argentina adopted a constitution that was profoundly influenced by the Constitution of the United States. Argentina's economic and political life took on some of the pace and direction prevailing in "the Great Republic of the North," as the Argentines then called the United States. Argentina's rhythm was not always steady in the middle decades of the nineteenth century—but neither was that of the United States. Both countries engaged in civil war at the same time, in part for identical reasons, chief among which was the growing domination of one region of the country over another, less economically developed section. In the case of Argentina the two sections were the rich province-city of Buenos Aires, and the other provinces. The decisive battle in Argentina's war of sectionalism was fought at Pavón five months after the attack on Fort Sumter. The victory of Buenos Aires made possible the organization of an effective national government and the beginning of economic development patterned on Europe and the United States.

The last four decades of the nineteenth century and the first three decades of the twentieth century were for Argentina, as for the United States, the era of triumphant Liberalism. Professor Romero skillfully describes the influx of ideas, capital, immigrants, and technology—all coming chiefly from Europe—which converted Argentina from a colonial anachronism into an active force in the Atlantic world. He terms the period the "alluvial era," properly emphasizing the role of the hundreds of thousands of immigrants, who numbered more, proportionately, than those who entered the United States in the same period. The native-born Argentine leaders customarily viewed the newcomers with a mixture of contempt and selfish interest; they were welcomed as laborers, but were denied political rights. (It should be pointed out that the elite in the United States did not do much better by the immigrants in Boston or other cities.) And if among the plutocracy there was no figure exactly parallel to John D. Rockefeller, this was because Argentina was becoming a rich farm rather than a rich factory. There were many *estancieros*—owners of great estates—who resembled the business barons in the northern republic in wealth and in political and economic philosophy.

Ethnically and ecologically Argentina in this era was astonishingly similar to the United States. (The one great difference is the absence of a numerous Negro population in Argentina.) Argentina too had her frontier, long in time and long in space. The frontier closed about 1880, with General Roca's Conquest of the Desert, the final campaign against the plains Indians. Much of that "desert," as the Argentines quickly learned when they moved west and south to settle the land, was no more barren than the areas of western United States that had long been marked on maps as the "Great American Desert."

The Winchester rifle helped to close the Argentine frontier, and with the rifle came barbed wire, windmills, and railroads, as in the United States. But Argentina had no Homestead Act to provide land to settlers, nor did it have a Morrill Act to set up colleges for their education. The land generally remained in great estates, and it was nearly impossible for tenant farmers, and the peons who had replaced the gauchos, to become landowners.

The opportunities to make a living and even to become wealthy were greater in the cities than in the tightly held rural areas. In the cities, especially in Buenos Aires, the majority of the newcomers settled. As their numbers and economic strength increased, they pressed hard on the limitations placed upon them by the conservative-liberal oligarchy—conservative in politics, liberal in economic matters. The oligarchs held on to their political monopoly as long as they dared, and then wisely surrendered a good portion of it in 1912, when a distinguished member of the ruling class, President Sáenz Peña, succeeded in winning the adoption of the secret ballot.

A substantial degree of democracy came to Argentina with

the adoption of free suffrage. The Radical Party dominated the political life of the nation from 1916 to 1930, representing the interest of the growing middle class. Constitutional stability seemed to have been achieved; prosperity seemed to be its constant companion. By most gauges of material and political progress, Argentina stood at the head of the Latin American states. People in the United States who followed Argentine affairs looked with approval upon the country's gratifying advances. The world was indeed being made safe for normalcy and democracy when a Latin American country had managed to keep the same constitution since 1853. And Yankee meat packers controlled most of Argentina's meat industry.

From these pinnacles of progress in the 1920's, Argentina and the United States could look back on their matching evolution: the austere colonial eras, the wars for independence, the establishment of constitutional order, the years of pioneering, the Indian fighting, the growth of the big cities, the conquest of foreign markets. The identity of their success seemed to have much to do with the political ideas they seemed to share.

A news photograph taken in 1913 symbolizes in two representative figures the development of the two great republics of the hemisphere. The photograph shows Theodore Roosevelt, then visiting Buenos Aires, seated with Julio Argentino Roca: Roosevelt, cowboy of the Badlands, Rough Rider, ex-president; Roca, army officer, Indian fighter, and ex-president; both men corpulent, silk-hatted, gold-chained, vigorous, successful, liberal, their views on immigrants, capitalism, and public and private morals as similar as their physical appearance. Conquistador and Puritan had met after following long and often divergent trails.

The world depression that struck Argentina in 1930 was the catalyst that dissolved the apparently stable Argentine social order and revealed its flawed foundations. A troubled era began, marked by hypernationalism, increased State intervention, the near collapse of the Radical Party, and finally the fascistoid dictatorship of Juan Perón. The restlessness of the depressed and frustrated laboring class, the strains of industrialization and of

World War II, the ideological tensions set up between right, center, and left, were other characteristics of the new time of troubles.

Perón's dictatorship was based on two forces, the army and the urban proletariat. The bulk of the industrial laborers was concentrated in the metropolis of Buenos Aires, whose five million people comprise more than one-quarter of the total national population. Both the oligarchy and the Radicals had failed after 1930 to effect the reforms that were needed by the people of Argentina. It was Perón who gave Argentina a social and economic New Deal, at the cost of freedom. Aspects of the past reappeared: the destruction of the constitutional order, a reversion to autocracy, the emergence of the military, and a new generation of exiles.

The gap between the United States and Argentina seemed to be as wide at mid-twentieth century as it had been a century earlier, in the days of Rosas and Jackson. The United States had become a super-power, whereas Argentina had lost ground to Brazil and Mexico, even on the Latin American scale of power. The United States seemed to have reached workable solutions to problems of labor, religion, and partisan politics, whereas Argentina had solved none of its grave problems.

Yet, as has been the case in other periods, the United States and Argentina may be on parallel rather than divergent tracks. Certainly their people resemble each other in their manner and attitudes more than do any other two people in the hemisphere, with the exception of Canadians and Yankees. Pragmatic, energetic, materialistic, unconsciously arrogant toward foreigners, most Argentines are more "American" and European than Latin American. The ideological struggle has indeed gone badly for democracy in mid-twentieth-century Argentina, but the battle is being fought in terms and by groups that closely match issues and groups in the United States. Compare, for example, the nativist, reactionary groups in Argentina, including those who blended eventually into the dictatorship of Perón, with similar groups in the United States.

Despite the instability and conflict that have marked Argentina since 1930, it must be acknowledged that political thought and action in Argentina have broadened and matured, perhaps more than has been the case in the United States. Argentine political experience has a European quality. Politics in Argentina is a violent ideological contest ranging across the spectrum of twentieth-century thought. In addition, it is a fiercely partisan contest for power. From brushes with anarchism fifty years ago, to clashes with Communism, to fascism (complete with touches of anti-Semitism), Argentina has run a perilous, zigzag course.

There may be some hope that this striving has brought the country to a point of political maturity resembling the "take-off" point in less developed economies to which economists refer. But Argentina's tradition of democratic and republican thought is brief, extending as it does only from the end of the eighteenth century, and the period of successful practice of these political forms has been briefer still. It is doubtful, considering this background, whether Argentina will soon institute the kind of democratic system that many people in the United States regard as ideal. And if Perón's valid achievements are not taken into account, the future will be still darker.

The psychology of the Argentine people must also be considered. Their colonial era was haunted by their own version of the Spanish American El Dorado myth—the legendary, undiscovered Gilded Man, ruler over vast treasures. The creation of a mythical City of the Caesars, a golden city beyond the far horizon, was one of the reactions of the settlers of Argentina to the American land in which they found themselves. The end of three centuries of imperial rule brought another surge of optimism and self-awareness. With independence came a limitless faith in the manifest destiny of the free Argentine people. After the final organization of the country in the years from 1853 to 1880, liberalism began to produce such wealth that for a time Argentines spoke of rivaling the United States in population and goods. But immigration fell off, and other resources such as coal and iron ore turned out to be negligible compared with those of the United

States. The world's finest beef could not buy enough international power, nor did it aid greatly in solving the problems of the underprivileged. As a result, the streak of bitter self-criticism and pessimism that has always gone along with or at least alternated with the Argentine sense of individual and national superiority has come strongly to the front in recent years. The Perón revolution has been a powerful source of both optimism and pessimism, of renewed faith in the energy of the country and despair at its gross mismanagement. The Argentine people are perhaps near to entering a new era in the cycle that Professor Romero has presented.

THOMAS F. McGANN

A HISTORY OF
ARGENTINE
POLITICAL THOUGHT

To the memory of
Pedro Henríquez-Ureña,
teacher and friend,
with whose counsel many of the
pages of this book were written

FOREWORD

The author hopes that this book will provide American readers with an accurate, well-integrated, and broad view of Argentine political ideas. The hope explains the structure of the book: the absence of notes and erudite references, the abundance of quoted material, and the effort to achieve the greatest possible clarity in explaining certain phenomena that are in themselves obscure— an approach the author has taken because of the need to define the basic patterns that may help readers to understand the historic present.

The author considers it essential to state his point of view. If the history of political ideas were to be conceived exclusively as an exposition of doctrinaire thought, perhaps it would not have been worthwhile to write this book. Original and vigorous political theories have not flourished in Argentina or in the other Spanish American countries, nor would it be realistic to think that they should have flourished there. But another approach has been taken in the conception of the book. The political thought of a group always possesses the highest historical interest, not only as ideology but also, and perhaps more, as the conscience and the motivating force behind attitudes and conduct, whether or not it may be original as doctrine. If we think of some of the most intellectually significant men of Argentina, it is not strange that we note immediately the dependence of their ideas on foreign sources; but if we examine the national significance of certain ideas, whether acquired elsewhere or not, and their impact on the Argentine people, we quickly discover that the ideas are marked by a special stamp or, in other words, have assumed a halo of peculiar tones—a reflection of the conditions under which we live.

The political ideas the author has tried to define with precision and to pursue along the thread of time are not only the original thoughts that are the product of speculative genius but also those imitation ideas whose deformations constitute a profoundly significant cultural fact—those impulses that involve and presuppose certain tendencies from which clear and distinct ideas will later be nourished, although these ideas, latent, indecisive, and approximate, are seen imperfectly when they first appear. Some may object that the author overextends the meaning of the word "idea," but in the field of cultural history it is impossible to isolate the pure and perfect forms of that term from those that are rudimentary and illegitimate. Social life is the result of the *convivencia* of persons possessing varied intellectual patrimonies; it would be a dangerous historical criterion not to appreciate the importance of certain currents of opinion simply because those ideas are not expressed with complete awareness and precision. Firm in this opinion, the author has attempted to reach from the plane of sharply focused ideas into the dark depths of elemental motives and false ideas. By this road he has felt sure that he would reach the source of the life-giving sap that has nourished our fiercely held political convictions.

To give solid support to his analysis, the author has taken into account the characteristics and the evolution of the social and economic structure into which the merely political phenomena sink their roots. Based on the observation of social reality and its transformation, he has rejected the customary periodization of Argentine history and has adopted another system which in his judgment corresponds more faithfully to the course that the country has followed. Three stages of Argentine historical development are indicated in this pattern: the colonial era, the *criollo** era, and the "alluvial" era, in which we still find ourselves. Each of the three periods has merited as careful an ex-

---

* See the Glossary, pp. 265–66, for definitions of Spanish and Argentine terms.

amination as the limits of this book permitted. The development in the colonial era of two political principles destined to have long life has been studied: those principles are authoritarianism and liberalism. Attention is given at the same time to the origins and imposition upon Argentine reality of a kind of institutional structure which that reality could scarcely support. The duel between the two principles, and the other duel between reality and the institutional structure, were perpetuated, and constitute the crux of Argentina's political drama. The changing scenes of the drama are described as they appear in later eras, and the many shades of meaning they represent in each successive act are discussed.

In making this analysis the author has had to consult numerous sources and the extensive bibliography that has been accumulated through the untiring monographic labors of Argentine historians. As a result of this constant use of source materials, the author no longer knows what part of his work may be original. He prefers to suppose that his study is only a synthesis of the efforts of others, as he testifies by the Bibliography at the end of this volume. Perhaps only the particular focus on the total problem—an effort rarely before attempted—is original, and a certain caustic view of Argentine history, whose projection into the future the author has often sought to discern, sometimes with anguish, at other times with pride, but always with the anxiety of one who plays out his life mingled with the multitude which knows not who directs its steps. Some will share his opinions; others—the greater number—will succeed in discovering the numerous defects which without doubt may cloud the clarity of this study. The latter will be in the right, although the former may not be entirely disappointed. But the possession of the absolute truth need not be an indispensable condition of an intellectual exercise, and the author makes bold to offer the result of his meditations, marked by his errors—and by truth, as he sees it.

JOSÉ LUIS ROMERO

Buenos Aires

PART ONE

The Colonial Era

The colonial epoch is the first and decisive stage in shaping Argentine nationality, particularly in forming our political consciousness. For various reasons the aboriginal past lacks an enduring significance in these reaches of Spanish America, despite the fact that José Manuel Estrada was able to say without exaggeration that "the Argentine people began when our race collided with the natives." The colonial era is our most remote past; but it is our legitimate past, and the multiple contingencies of unfolding history have not been able to erase its tracks. Furthermore, the lines then marked out endure and still constrain our development.

In those years, not only was the social reality of the future Argentina formed, but our spiritual attitude toward the most serious problems of our common existence was shaped. The social reality underwent radical transformations in the second half of the nineteenth century, but until then it maintained the characteristics with which it was stamped in the colonial era, and these continued to survive in diverse and vigorous forms. It is impossible to grasp the meaning of the evolution of political ideas during the period of independence without retracing the course they followed during the long period from the conquest to our emancipation.

The colonial era is indeed Argentina, in its socio-economic structure, in its ways of daily life, in its influential moral values, and in its ideals, which permeated deeply. This epoch includes

*more than two centuries: in such a long time, many diverse char-
acteristics achieved vigorous, unified existence. It may be said of
almost all these characteristics that they maintained their representative values even when they were ceding ground in the struggle with new ideals.*

*Careful examination reveals that the colonial era in the Río
de la Plata passed through two stages, as it did in other Spanish
American regions. The colonies along the Río de la Plata sprang
up and developed slowly during the latter part of the sixteenth
century and throughout the seventeenth century. That was the
era of the Hapsburgs. During that time, certain forms of the
colonial mentality, which would continue despite the attacks of
new concepts, were asserted and hardened. But these forms did
not represent the complete colonial mind, for the Río de la Plata
did not escape the restlessness of the eighteenth century. Then,
in the time of the Bourbons, Spain attempted to reform its ways
through the inspiration of enlightened thought, and these formerly deprecated colonies began to attract the attention of progressive minds. New ideals were minted, and their lines were
etched on the men of this land; out of ancient tradition a new
shoot was put forth. Two concepts of life came face to face and
were distilled into two political attitudes: authoritarianism and
liberalism.*

*The emergence of these two beliefs was decisive for our po-
litical history. They were locked in struggle during the colonial
era, and their duel continued uninterruptedly during the period
of independence, even though they took on different appearances.
"In the end," Juan Agustín García shrewdly said half a century
ago, "one discovers that in this world the same protagonists always appear with the same passions and with the same luck; motives and events differ, it is true, in their distinct settings, but the
spirit of events is the same."*

*Today we are still living out that drama, and only by mount-
ing up the river of our history to its sources will it be possible to
grasp the secrets of the evolution of Argentine political ideas.*

I

THE HAPSBURG EPOCH

THE SHAPE OF THE AUTHORITARIAN SPIRIT

The conquest of the American land, the exploration of the vast expanses that stretched away, full of enigma and promise, from the coasts on which the conquistadors landed, the founding of cities, the first attempts at colonization, all were accomplished under the Renaissance symbol of adventure. A stern spiritual outlook characterized the conquistadors, who were backed by the grandeur and pride of imperial Spain. But the Spain of the Hapsburgs did not remain the same throughout the first two centuries of the conquest. The guiding ideas that were its spiritual skeleton lasted, but its flesh and blood, wracked by the fatigue of unstinting effort, began to weaken, until the once-vigorous body became a shadow of its former self.

Yet the growing debility did not modify these impelling convictions; on the contrary, it seemed to emphasize them. Shut within itself, Spain matured its thought and stylized the system of ideas that ruled it, converting those ideas into a rigid, dogmatic force. The Counter-Reformation and neo-scholasticism nourished its spirit; soon, in the midst of a collapse whose scope appeared to be unnoticed, Spain was pouring out its convictions into a political system whose formulas the conquerors brought to America, to root in the land with the prestige and force of the conquest. Thus the authoritarian spirit took vigorous hold in America.

The deep pessimism over the destiny of Castile, which was felt by Hernán Pérez de Guzmán around the middle of the fifteenth century, began to dissipate little by little as Isabel and Ferdinand achieved their first political triumphs. New energy seemed to vitalize the Spanish kingdoms, and the nobles abandoned their unbridled ways to join in the ventures that the Crown was planning. Triumph was complete in 1492. The Moslem kingdom of Granada disappeared, and with it went a sense of humiliation that had been gnawing at the Spanish spirit:

> . . . now I don't say
> Granada defends
> herself from Spain, but offends
> and busies her night and day,

as Pérez de Guzmán said. At the end of that year the crown of Castile won the immense and unknown lands of America, and an indeterminate but passionate desire for glory and greatness invaded the Spanish soul.

That spirit, however, had to suffer trials. The death of the prince-heir Don Juan twisted the destiny of Spain and opened the road to complicated political intrigues. Castile and Aragon halted the movement that was leading them to closer union and later had to bow to the authority of a king who, despite his legitimate rights, was, after all, a stranger. The times were hard for the haughty Spaniards, but they resisted heroically, taking dignified counsel together so that the king should recognize the worth of the Spanish people: little by little they gained their end, and at the same time they began to swell with pride at possessing the empire over which Charles V ruled. Thus a vigorous sense of Hispanic glory was created and concentrated within the frame of imperial glory, in affirmation of its own singular importance. This glory (both imperial and Spanish) motivated the conquistadors who for the first time, in Mexico, discovered the vast meaning of the conquest.

The Master of Tenochtitlán, Hernán Cortés, wrote to "The Most High and Powerful and Most Catholic Prince, Unconquered Emperor and Our Lord," these revealing words: "I write because I want Your Highness to know the things of this land, which are so many and of such quality that (as I wrote to you in another account) you may give yourself anew the title of Emperor, and with as much right and no less merit as that of Germany, which by the Grace of God your Sacred Majesty possesses." By the efforts of her sons, Spain was adding to her universal empire lands and riches that were in no way a discredit to those the Emperor already held. Pride in this feat reinforced pride in the Hapsburg empire itself, which had earlier been belittled because of the alien character of the Flemish monarch. This certainty in Spain's mission was strengthened by the new discoveries of the lands and wealth of Peru; and the kingdom of Charles V, which reached its limits in Europe with the bitter defeat at Metz, began, in the Spain of the conquistadors, a new era of dimly seen grandeur. The old, medieval tradition of a European empire having been lost to Spain, there arose before Spanish eyes a new empire of the Indies, exotic and full of promise, in whose total conquest there would be plenty of opportunities for the strong arms of the *hidalgo* and the tenacious will of the laborer, soon to become a *hidalgo* by his own efforts.

In the second half of the sixteenth century, Spanish foreign policy became more circumscribed, retreating within itself. Philip II wanted to be a Spanish and Catholic king, and he worked to achieve that aspiration. He had to destroy whatever contradicted those principles, even though he should thus erase from the vast repertory of choices some that had already begun to mature. Only what were Hispanic and Catholic satisfied his spiritual ideal and were tolerated within his vast zone of royal influence and action. Flanders, punished for its menacing heterodoxy, is the chief example of this policy, which was also shown in many other aspects of the conduct of the misanthropic Lord of the Escorial. America's wealth seemed to serve only for a relentless war against the traditional enemies of Spain—France, who was guilty of lukewarm Catholicism, and Turkey, who was the declared enemy of the Faith. The new economic strength of Europe was held in little esteem, and no effort was made to include Spain in the mercantilistic race that was then beginning among the continental powers. So the *picaresca*—the low, proletarian way of life, the reverse of the ideals of grandeur—made its appearance, because the *picaros* proliferated out of the constant misery of daily existence. And while the gold continued to arrive from the Indies, only to vanish promptly to foreign centers of production, Fernando de Herrera, true to the ideals of his king and of the nobility, sang of the defeat of the infidel, molding in his verses the heroism and the sanctity of a Spain still medieval:

> The Lord, who showed his robust hand
> for the faith of his Christian prince
> and for the holy name of his glory,
> to Spain concedes this victory.

Philip II, harsh and somber, crystallized the principles of a most rigid absolutism and committed the brave efforts of his sons and the wealth of Spain to unlimited war on behalf of his political hegemony and the threatened ideals of Catholicism. A more realistic politician would have seen that everything pointed to his failure. The flood of metal from the Indies was soon to cease, and nothing was done to retain that wealth in Spanish lands, or to stimulate the manufacture of goods that at the time seemed superfluous to produce because they could be bought abroad. Meanwhile, torrents of money were escaping from the royal treasure chests—gone to pay for incessant wars, yet without bringing victory to mitigate the disasters, which were capped by the catastrophe of the Invincible Armada. Only the immutable grandeur of his ideals stirred this dour, hard king, whose errors were glorified with the same serene confidence with which his most noble but sterile efforts were supported.

Later, these ideals became impoverished, and were converted into pallid reflections of themselves; and misery remained, menacing, wasting. The last Hapsburg kings tried to perpetuate the political designs of Philip II, but they brought to the cause only listless spirits, feeble wills, and minds enslaved by slothful fawners. Disaster began to be vaguely discerned, but nobody wished to alter the course of events, whether out of incapacity or because of self-interest. From his distant exile, Antonio Pérez, the former private secretary to Philip II, sought the attention of the chief confident of the new king with perceptive words that were, nonetheless, destined to go unheard:

Do not consent, Your Excellency, to new undertakings and feats: those are matters for princes who have an overabundance of men and money, and we speak truly when we say that both have been lacking to us because of the great costs incurred since the year 1567. Our aim should be tranquillity, to gather and concentrate within ourselves the natural energy that we possess; with time we shall easily become again what we once were, and acquire strength and accumulate money; and then we will be able to charge ahead and take the offensive as we may wish. In the present state of affairs I make bold to tell Your Excellency that no good fortune may be hoped for: no one wishes to try to haul in the heavy anchor of war, but, oh! that this might disappear, thus making all things possible. The present situation, if matters work out as planned, will only result in the assumption of new expenses, for which neither our income nor our supplies suffice. We shall only get new enemies, and of enemies we now have enough and more than enough, so that we can hardly live or breathe; and if we do not get out of our troubles, we will be left with our money lost and our reputation discredited. Look, Your Excellency, I beg of you, at how the very pinnacle of the monarchy of Austria and of Castile is being destroyed, that from which all others must take their being and receive their sustenance.

Later, Antonio Pérez went on to say in his *Norte de Príncipes (Guide for Princes)*:

Cast your eyes, My Lord, at the Indies, which is the part whence comes the money and with it also the sustenance of this monarchy, and consider that the wealth of gold and silver that is mined is only a temporal transaction that is coming to an end, and that we will have to do without those riches. But the vicious defects of which this wealth is the instrument and to which it has accustomed us will remain. If the lack of wealth would bring good, it would certainly be a condition to be desired and sought; but, I say, you should think about the conservation of this wealth and of the fruits it may give us, so that it may last and not be lacking to us, and so that it may not pass on to other nations, leaving us no more than the dust and the sadness and the harm of the vices and waste that come with such abundance.

These were prophetic words. The old Spanish glory shrank, and misery grew. Men did not learn to produce wealth, yet at the same time political absolutism, affirmed by the stubborn attitude of the Hapsburgs, remained in force, exercised by favorites for whom royal favors did not suffice, and who did not hesitate to bleed the poor in order to maintain the ostentatious brilliance of the court and to enrich themselves.

> A king is allowed to be spendthrift, to dally,
> but 'tis only just he should spend less, should tally.
> Stones not used in so many labors,
> prepare you temples of eternal honors.
> Such squanderings are never trifling crumbs
> because they are taken from the mouths of the many.
> Nor should the royal purple be lavished everywhere
> if all is tinged with the poor man's blood.
> For you gain no profit nor will find agreeable
> grandeurs mourned by so many who are miserable.

With such words Francisco de Quevedo dared to speak to Philip IV; and the poet paid with imprisonment for his boldness. Yet his was the unanimous cry aroused by the spectacle of so much misery and so many defeats. Twenty years after this *Memorial* was written, Philip IV met final defeat in the war against France, and he signed the Treaty of the Pyrenees, which sealed the loss of Spain's hegemony over Europe. A little later the kingdom itself seemed to become the booty of the victors, and foreign chancelleries debated at will the destiny of the inheritance of King Charles the Bewitched.

A defined and rigid intellectual attitude had taken shape in the two centuries that separated the two kings named Charles. Following the era of the great emperor's European predominance, Spain had begun, under his son Philip, to retreat into itself, accentuating its Spanishness and living according to the measure of its own ideals. Europe, meanwhile, shaken by the Reformation and by the development of modern thought, was beginning to elaborate other forms of life, toward which Spain sought to remain indifferent. There were those who wished to join in the new currents, but they had to conceal their intentions or escape to other lands—the latter an objective that Philip also combated by forbidding Spaniards to study at foreign universities, all of which were to a greater or lesser extent influenced by Erasmus or by the Reformation. Thus, Spanish Catholicism began to be crystallized in its typical form, stubborn in the defense of the principles it considered fundamental; closed within its own bounds, not seeking or admitting comparison with any other doctrines, all of which it condemned with impassioned intolerance, Spanish Catholicism became the first and most solid of the pillars of the Counter-Reformation. Strict vigilance over what was written and read, thought and done, assured to the Spanish State the purity of its orthodoxy and, with it, the paralysis of certain forms of thought and action that potentially existed within the Spanish spirit. The Company of Jesus, the most efficient instrument of Counter-Reformation indoctrination, emerged in Spain, and out of the Company of Jesus came a most inventive mind to re-elaborate the metaphysical doctrines of scholasticism and of absolute power. Francisco Suárez gave fresh life and renewed force to medieval thought, which had been undermined by the first blows of modernism, by reconstructing a sound and vigorous doctrine in which the Thomistic tradition was kept pure and at the same time was enlivened by the addition of new experience.

True religious feeling invigorated this doctrinaire elaboration of neo-scholasticism, which is revealed in the mystical inspiration of Fray Luis or in the theological exaltation of Calderón. But it was the vigorous imposition of these ideas by the state that assured their indisputable primacy. The State found the basis it needed for strengthening its autocracy *de jure* in the doctrines of the Counter-Reformation; joining those doctrines with the will to absolutism gave royal authority invincible power. As early as the sixteenth century, despite the lingering marks of feudalism and the aspirations of the rising bourgeoisie, the Spanish intellectual environment had hardened into a political attitude that was characterized by the primacy of the authoritarian spirit.

Charles V had already laid the foundations of an absolutist political order. He opposed the *cortes*; he opposed the *fueros*
(which were aimed at limiting his authority within his domain);
he opposed the papacy (which sought to limit his power outside
his domain). The victory of Villalar, and his strong stand against
Clement VII, whom the Emperor dared to threaten with the con-
vocation of a General Council, revealed his decision to uphold
without restriction his power as king and emperor. Charles recognized that the basis of his authority lay in his own imperial office
and in his dynastic rights, which gave him a certain independence
of the papacy. "And if you, Holy Fathers," he wrote to the car-
dinals in 1526, "should deny concession of our petitions, We, in
accordance with our imperial dignity, shall have recourse to appropriate remedies so that it may not seem that we are deficient in
Christ's glory, or in our own justice, or in seeking the health,
peace, and tranquillity of the republic."

Philip II weakened this posture by his militancy in defending
the Faith, which made him more dependent upon the papacy.
His reign was increasingly converted into a theocracy, and the
Church acquired an influence that was scarcely contained by the
king's prestige and stubbornness. Under his successors there was
a further growth of that influence, and those who studied the political scene with some detachment believed this to be a threat.
"Many will tell you," Antonio Pérez wrote from exile, "and
will have said, as I do wish to say to Your Excellency, because
this is such an important matter that no one may ignore it, that
much care must be taken in the question of the jurisdiction of His
Holiness. Rome keeps on pushing into Spain, and the priesthood
and the religious comprise such a great part of the country that
they occupy more than half of it, and, when we least imagine, we
will discover them to be masters of it all." That prediction, made
about 1602, was already being fulfilled, and it was fulfilled to a
still greater degree during the seventeenth century, both in the
motherland and in the colonies. Backed by the Church, theocratic
absolutism acquired solid, indisputable force, but its action was
conditioned on ceding to the Church the latter's fundamental ob-

jective: the defense of the Faith and of Catholic principles. This circumstance was decisive in the crown's political plans.

As a result, the policy based on rigorous Catholic principles took root so strongly that the monarchy discarded realistic policy as anti-Catholic and anti-Spanish. If the latter, carried to its extremes, might appear to be immoral, the former, equally extreme, ended by being narrow in conception and fatal in results. The wave of anti-Machiavellianism that was aroused in Spain at the end of the sixteenth century by Rivadeneyra and Márquez stemmed from a political doctrine whose intent was to ignore reality in order to submit it unconditionally to rigid moral norms and to laws that seemed to spring unequivocally from those norms. Perhaps in Spain the strength of customary law was that it averted the translation of its policies into dangerous innovations, except that of inhibiting the development of new social and economic activity; but in the American colonies, where reality was new, scarcely understood, and surprising in its exotic novelty, this policy led to the commission of innumerable errors, which wasted energy and frustrated many undertakings. A growing contempt for economic activity, which was conceived of as an inferior way of life, created a curious paradox, for it was precisely economic activity that was without any doubt the fundamental preoccupation of the conquest in the minds of the majority of the conquistadors. The result was that the State, which was so strong and active in many other directions, pretended to disdain an activity it could not control, an activity, in reality, that developed without the State's being able to guide it in any effective way. Thus a frustrated economy evolved, its lowest levels full of vicious practices that were condemned by law, but could not be avoided in fact because the government did not want to descend to the level of reality.

Out of this moral atmosphere, and nourished by this political outlook, the conquistadors came to America. They recognized the autocratic will of their master and they respected with religious fear the laws that emanated from him; but faced with natives who were at times docile and at other times hostile, and confronted by deserts and jungles, the conquistador mustered up his courage, understanding that nothing truly mattered except an iron will and a strong arm. His haughty independence, inspired by Catholic and individualistic sentiments, had to be fitted into the theoretical respect owed to the autocratic authority of the Crown. This was the first political attitude known in these lands.

THE COLONIES ALONG THE RÍO DE LA PLATA

First Mexico and then Peru were the ideals and models of colonization. The countries of the Aztecs and Quichuas, because of their organization and their wealth, seemed to be the two prizes of greatest importance, and on them the conquistadors practiced systems of political administration, social control over the natives, and economic exploitation. But when settlement of the Río de la Plata began, the condition of the country and of its inhabitants was observed to be quite distinct from that prevailing in other regions, and opportunities to be different and clearly very inferior from the point of view of the rapid enrichment of the conquistador. So it happened that the great plains deceived those who first crossed them, and that the Río de la Plata appeared to be only a port of arrival and departure for the rich metal-bearing regions lying to the north.

That was the opinion of Pedro de Mendoza and his captains in 1536, despite the preparations and the agreements they had made for conquest and colonization. As soon as Buenos Aires had been founded, the explorers wanting to locate the route to Peru left for the interior by way of the Paraná and the Paraguay rivers, turning later toward the northwest in the direction of the high plateau. While Juan de Ayolas was struggling against the tropical environment and the natives, his companions founded the city of Asunción at the junction of the rivers Paraguay and Pilcomayo. The location seemed to be more useful than Buenos Aires as a point of support, which was the role assigned to such settlements. When there was still hope of establishing a route between the Río de la Plata and Peru by means of the rivers,

Asunción grew in importance, and Governor Irala did not hesitate to remove the population of Buenos Aires to Asunción in 1541. But the overland venture was almost impossible. First Ayolas failed, and then the *adelantado*, Alvar Núñez. Irala himself made the attempt later, and although he succeeded in reaching the highland plateau, his exploration in 1547 demonstrated that the route was too dangerous because of natural obstacles and native peoples.

By this time, penetration onto the plains southward from Peru had been accomplished. In a reverse direction from the one that had brought the colonists to Asunción, and by more accessible routes, Diego Rojas and his comrades entered northwest Argentina. Through the gorge of Humahuaca and along the valleys in the land of the Calchaquí Indians they explored the region of the north and sought out the plains by following the Salado River. The road was opened, and others returned to explore it, certain now that it was the easiest route by which to reach the shores of the Atlantic. Soon cities began to spring up: Santiago del Estero, Tucumán, and Córdoba—guideposts on the road searching for the sea. At the same time that Córdoba was established, Juan de Garay was founding the town of Santa Fe on the Paraná River, and completing, almost unknowingly, a line of settlements. Later he turned toward the south to found Buenos Aires for the second time on the banks of the Río de la Plata. The year was 1580. The hope of the people of Asunción that their city would be on the road to Peru was frustrated by this new route, which terminated on the bank of the wide river. The new city became, as its founder said, "the port of the land." Buenos Aires began to grow and Asunción to decline, even though the latter kept its primacy, as an established city, for another half-century.

Asunción had begun to be a productive center. Around it Indian towns had sprung up, which were organized by encomenderos, who obtained from the Indian labor some benefits in agricultural products, livestock, and manufactured goods. But Buenos Aires was better suited for the life of the Spanish colonists.

Its climate was less rigorous for both men and livestock, and in the vicinity there was considerable wealth in wild horses, the offspring of those that had remained at liberty when the original city had been depopulated. Furthermore, its vast plains were adaptable to the easy breeding of livestock, and these Garay began to bring in, which laid the foundations of a new wealth that permitted the exportation of wool, lard, and hides by the last years of the sixteenth century. But the principal advantage of Buenos Aires lay in its greater proximity to Spain; before long the port began to be visited by ships from the motherland, until the merchants of Portobelo succeeded, in 1618, in getting that maritime traffic prohibited because it undercut their own interests. Nonetheless, as a beachhead on the plains and as an Atlantic port for Peru, Buenos Aires had sufficient importance to attract the attention of Spain, which soon recognized the possibilities of the humble *porteño* settlement.

A creole governor, Hernando Arias de Saavedra, struggled tenaciously to continue the progress of the Río de la Plata region, laboring so that the area might achieve the gains that Garay had hoped for Buenos Aires. He proposed to the Crown the division of its jurisdiction into two regions, a proposal that was accepted with the establishment in 1617 of the separate regions of Asunción and Buenos Aires. Thereafter, the Río de la Plata began to acquire greater importance, and in 1621 Buenos Aires became a bishopric. Soon after, it was said that the cultivated area extended out to a distance of some ninety miles around the city.

Thus Buenos Aires and its province continued to grow during the seventeenth century. The port was constantly harried by the privateers of Spain's enemies, while the land often saw invasions by menacing Indians. The population increased in an environment of vigilance and readiness; contraband trade provided the inhabitants with goods; the wealth of farm and pasture began to be appreciated, despite the shadow cast on them by the minerals of Peru. Suddenly, beginning in 1640, the city gained unsuspected political importance. The Portuguese, having recovered their independence from Spain, began to claim lands that had been in dispute since the earliest days of the discovery. In 1680, in an act of sovereignty over the east bank of the Río de la Plata, they founded opposite Buenos Aires the town of Colonia del Sacramento. The capital of the territory prepared to fight, defended its rights, and seized the Portuguese settlement, which, however, was returned to its founders under an agreement signed in the motherland. The situation remained unchanged until the War of the Spanish Succession at the beginning of the eighteenth century. But Colonia del Sacramento, the emblem of Portuguese aspirations and the base for a most active contraband trade, remained opposite Buenos Aires, and the motherland began to pay greater attention than before to its city and its problems. Buenos Aires at that time had somewhat more than 4,000 inhabitants, and a French traveler, Azcárate du Biscay, who visited it in 1658, described it as follows:

The town is located on land raised above the shores of the Río de la Plata. It contains four hundred houses, and it has neither rampart, nor wall, nor moat, nor anything by which to defend itself except a small earthen fort, which overlooks the river and is surrounded by a ditch and mounts ten iron cannon. There the governor resides, with a garrison composed of only one hundred and fifty men.

The houses of the town are made of mud, for one finds few stones in this area until one arrives in Peru; the houses are roofed with cane and straw and have no second story; all the habitations are on one floor and are very spacious; they have great patios, and behind the houses are large gardens full of orange, lemon, fig, apple, pear, and other fruit trees, and with vegetables in abundance.

The houses of the inhabitants of the upper class are adorned with draperies, paintings, and other ornaments and attractive furniture; those who are in more modest circumstances dine from silver service and have many servants—Negroes, mulattoes, mestizos, Indians, and those of mixed Indian and Negro blood—all these being slaves.

The slaves are employed in the houses of their masters or in cultivating their lands, since they have great farms abundantly sown to grain. All the wealth of these inhabitants consists of cattle, which multiply so prodigiously in these provinces that the plains are covered with them.

THE FORMS OF POLITICAL AND SOCIAL LIFE
ALONG THE RÍO DE LA PLATA

Unlike Mexico and Peru, the lands of the Río de la Plata did not startle the conquistadors with spectacular abundance, but, rather, with their poverty. The immense plains and their primitive inhabitants held promise of a mediocre and laborious future, in which hunger and physical fatigue could not be avoided by the *hidalgos* who had resolved upon the adventure of conquest in order to rip gold with their bare hands from the bowels of the earth. Disembarking with the men of Pedro de Mendoza on the shores of the Río de la Plata, the soldier Schmidel notes, referring to the Indians, that "they have nothing to eat but fish and meat." Even these were sometimes lacking to the conquerors of a land that jealously hoarded its riches until it had to yield to stubborn forces.

Because of the scanty cultural and natural resources, the colonists had no difficulty in occupying the land. They began to organize their rudimentary existence according to their methods, and they took it for granted that the natives must enter into the new social complex in serving them and become adjusted to the conditions they laid down. But it was natural that the active or passive resistance of the natives should cause the colonists to think about the methods concerning their treatment, and from such reflection a policy resulted. At the outset the policy was aimed at colonization: it was necessary to explore the land's possibilities, and so the colonists received in encomienda a certain number of natives with whom the task of colonization was accomplished, the colonists, in turn, having the obligation to indoctrinate the natives or, put in modern terms, to civilize them, and to try to incorporate them into the Spanish way of life. At times, brutal exploitation won out over the plan for colonization, especially in the sixteenth century when the conquest had scarcely gained firm footing and when it was still necessary to lay the foundations of the elementary organization of the colony. Frequently the colonists had unrestrained contempt for any form of control. But toward the end of the sixteenth and the beginning of the seventeenth centuries, a movement began along the Río de la Plata that was destined to give order to the position of the natives, an issue on which depended their extinction or their incorporation within the social complex. A group of men emerged who were endowed with political vision and, at the same time, with a humanitarian attitude: Governor Hernandarias, Bishop Fernando de Trejo y Sanaberia, Royal Commissioner Francisco de Alfaro, Captain-General Don Luis Quiñones de Osorio, Provincial Diego de Torres, and others, who tried to regulate the labor of the natives, pointing out to the encomenderos that their mission was not to exploit but to assimilate that population.

The difficulties—one may say the failure—of this colonization policy next led the clergy to proclaim a policy of religious instruction. The outstanding representatives of a political concept that disdained wealth as an end in itself, the priests founded *reducciones,* in which the natives worked for the good of the community, without doubt under a less inhuman regime than the encomenderos were accustomed to impose upon them. The system aimed at imposing on the Indians a plan of religious and moral instruction that would permit their genuine incorporation into the new society, but it also presupposed a political education based on the sternest authoritarianism and, above all, the separation of the natives from all contact with the Spanish colonists. Thus, the system benefited the Indians, who did not suffer the toil of the encomienda, but it failed as a plan for their social adaptation because of the contrast between the way of life followed by the Indians in the *reducciones* and how they lived later outside the missions.

By means of this dual policy of colonizing and catechizing, the Spaniards tried to build in the colony a way of life within which the two peoples might coexist. There was no problem of cultural coexistence in these regions, because the weakness of the Indian value system scarcely allowed them to indulge in anything stronger than a passive resistance or in the survival of some superstitions that resisted the arguments of the preachers. Thus His-

panic culture was imposed as the only possible form of existence.
But the colonist's culture and his catechism had to face serious
questions, particularly the ethnic problem, with all the social repercussions caused by the appearance of the mestizo and the
creole. Then came economic problems, rising from the new conditions that afforded the possibility of wealth and its exploitation,
and in turn entailed grave social problems. Finally, there was
the political problem, the product of a regime that had been
solidly structured in the homeland and now was imposed on a
reality that was being modified day by day, creating situations
dissimilar and alien to the experience of the motherland. During
the era of the Hapsburgs those problems acquired a peculiar yet
fitting character in the Río de la Plata region. Later actions
would have to reckon on these conditions.

The earth, the sole source of wealth in this land without
minerals, was taken by the conquistadors by virtue of the juridical
title awarded to the Crown by papal cession and adjudication to
the conquerors.

I, in the name of His Majesty [said Juan de Garay at the ceremony
apportioning the land in Buenos Aires], have begun to allot and I do
allot to said colonizers and conquistadors lands and sections of land
and building lots and blocks upon which they may undertake their
labors and the raising of all kinds of livestock; and the aforesaid lands
and estancias and farm-plots and blocks I give and I grant in the name
of His Majesty and that of the said governor, in order that as their
very own they may erect on them houses as well as corrals, and put
there whatever livestock and do whatever work they may wish to do
and may hold to be useful . . . as if they had inherited these in their
own patrimony.

This circumstance, joined to the legal position of the Spaniards,
gave them an absolutely privileged position over the natives, who
were not to possess any rights other than those derived from the
regulations that charitable treatment demanded in accordance
with Christian principles and natural law. This was a *de facto*
situation, fortified by an abundance of political arguments, but
rooted above all in the fact of the conquest. The inferior status
of the natives was clear and undebatable; but the needs of coloni-

zation and the Crown's policy of justice obliged the conquistadors not to content themselves merely with creating this situation; it stimulated them, on the contrary, to seek to incorporate the natives into the society so that, without threatening the privileges or security of the colonists, the Indians might contribute to the development of the settlements. There were plenty of royal decrees and ordinances, but reality was more powerful, and it went on creating a new order.

The character of the natives of the Río de la Plata contributed greatly to fixing their role. Their forceful submission caused them to withdraw within themselves. Their conquest spiritually annihilated them, and little by little they felt themselves despoiled and incapable of any real action against the conquistadors. They responded to the conquest with obedient passivity, yet full of mental reservations, which did not preclude unplanned revolts motivated by hate or desperation. But a marked indolence and a strange apathy caused them to accept their new role with a fixed determination not to offer to the conquerors any more support than was demanded of them.

Soon, however, there was added to these two ethnic groups another, which would markedly influence the economic, social, and political evolution of the colonies of the Río de la Plata: the mestizo. The mestizo had inherited as his predominant traits the native's indolence, his incapacity in economic matters, and his disinterest in work, which was a function of an alien economic system. He also added to his make-up a strong resentment against the insolent, haughty, and domineering white European whose temperament he began to understand because of his Indian mother's relation to her chance Spanish companion. A sediment of rebellion thus settled in the mestizo, to be stirred by the lingering remnants of ancient beliefs that were scarcely erased by a religious indoctrination whose content he was not able to understand but which caused him to consider himself to be a member of an inferior class in the new society. To a lesser degree, the white creole also found himself in the same position, demeaned by the commonly held belief that the Spaniards degenerated in

America, and also by the continuing influx of Spaniards from the Peninsula, who restocked the privileged caste as a matter of right. Various circumstances tended to unite the creole with the mestizo, above all because for social reasons it was easier for him to marry an Indian or mestizo woman than a Spanish woman. Thus the creole also entered onto the path of racial intermixing, creating, between the Spaniards and the Indians, an intermediate element, the mestizo-creole, to whom certain rights were granted, but who did not attain a social position equal to that of the people from the Peninsula.

Among these social nuclei, the Spaniards preserved the monopoly of the sources of production and of wealth: theirs was the land suitable for livestock; and theirs was the control over the commercial activities that could convert their products into good ounces of gold. Ranching and commerce merited the highest social esteem, whereas agricultural labors seemed to be reserved—as in fact they were—to those unfortunate ones who had not been able to obtain grants of abundant lands suited for pasturage and located near the city. Agriculture in reality provided only a mere existence; its products lacked commercial value and, since it did not make men rich, labor in the fields seemed to be worthless compared with the ideal of wealth that was the polestar of the colonist.

Ranching and commerce gave very different meanings to the countryside and to the city, and to the population of each. The country was divided into great grants of land, which were held by the Spaniards who lived together in the cities; these lands were generally worked by creoles and mestizos, although there were a good many Spaniards who chose to supervise their own properties. The plains created a peculiar psychology in those who settled them. In constant danger from ambush by wild Indian tribes, far from the city and from any protection by the government, and forced, as a result, to be self-reliant, the colonists who lived in the country, the creole-mestizo peons, and even the pacified Indians acquired a barbaric air common to those living in a state of nature. Only individual might assured right, and even the preservation of life itself. The landowner became a despot, assuming a genuinely superior status that his men respected if it seemed to them that it was honestly acquired. No one opposed his power, since the authority of the State scarcely reached him and because no one had any real desire for civilization: the boss, because he was hoping to get rich in order to return to the place from which he had come; his subordinates, because they expected nothing from fate. A rural way of life was born that witnessed few changes with the passage of time; it was nurtured by distance, by sparse population, and by the impotence of unrealistic laws.

Spanish legislation looked on the colony as a group of cities; only urban life was efficiently regulated. In the cities there were Spaniards who sometimes lived by public office and commerce; at other times they depended on the exploitation of lands that were almost unknown to them. Life was tranquil in that setting, and a narrow, rapacious outlook evolved that was appropriate to those who were awaiting only opportunities to sell more bundles of hides or to take advantage of juicy contraband-running in order to pocket doubloons and find the chance to return to the homeland. But a political attitude was also formed with the stabilization of the authoritarian system that the Crown was forcing on the colonies. There, in the overseas possessions, the cult of omnipotent royal authority was maintained; there the strict mechanism of autocratic legislation was in operation, which was never violated without denying the fact. In this manner, in two entirely different spheres and from two radically opposed points of view, the authoritarian spirit was strengthened and defined as the political attitude of colonial life.

This spirit was nourished by an unusual moral code. The country people evolved a view of life marked by their frequent adventures on the plains, by their jobs in which they constantly put to the test the courage of strong men, the sense of honor of those who know that their chances depend on their own efforts, the arrogance of those who have prevailed by their own strength, the skill of those who entrust to that skill their own prestige and salvation. From this conception of life a certain pattern of moral norms was derived, which, because it was a response to daily existence, possessed a strength that the law lacked. Rules about catechizing or colonizing were valueless. The owner was master by unquestioned right, and he acquired, beyond his attributes as landlord, the inevitable jurisdiction over the laws and their application, which he exercised without limitations. Life itself was a forfeit to obedience and fidelity. But obedience and fidelity were valid currency in an environment in which the same ideals were widely shared, since subordinates tried to demonstrate in their own spheres the same arrogance, the same skill, the same sense of honor, and the same bravery as the undisputed master. The innumerable written laws were violated constantly, but never the law of the unvanquished plains. However, no one would have dared to place absolute value on such omnipotence. Above the omnipotence of the "Spanish countryman" the all-powerful authority of the Crown was recognized and revered—without being obeyed if it opposed rural customs. Basically a Christian morality, but on the surface a most primitive one, this code was supported by a violent, unshakable will to rule, which was born of the circumstances and which no one could abandon without risking his life.

A distinctive moral code also evolved in the urban centers. The authority of the State acted more directly there, and the specter of royal authority loomed nearer; but there, too, circumstances caused royal autocracy to become transformed into an autocracy of those who exercised the royal will, often in secret accord with the oligarchy of peninsular Spaniards. A clergy armed with weapons of the Counter-Reformation gave that authority solid theological backing, but reality had its way even against them. Neither the royal will nor the laws and decrees in which it was expressed received other than the most obsequious submission; but neither royal authority nor laws availed against misery and hunger, against the appetite for riches, against the irritation that was caused by the semi-failure of those who had come to America to escape poverty and to triumph. Authoritarian in his political views and authoritarian in his personal beliefs, the Spaniard violated boldly, although with a mask of submissiveness, the laws that constrained his appetites. There is nothing more characteristic of this psychology than the continuing practice of contraband, which was engaged in by governors, by bishops, and by the most faithful vassals, without any more pretense than that counseled by prudence. Reality incited men to free themselves from the multitude of petty restrictions, while good judgment advised them that obedience be loudly proclaimed. In this manner, an authoritarian view of public power grew up that, by restraining free initiative, forced men to act on the margin of the law. This was the moral order that was created in the country and in the cities by royal authoritarianism and by the policy of principles. Doubtless the special characteristic of the colony, in accord with the concepts prevailing in the motherland, was the creation of subjects who were essentially urban and authoritarian. All the colonial institutions and their applications reflect these constituent elements; it is impossible to understand their evolution and the influence they exercised in Argentine society without insistently pointing to the conflict between the two characteristics and reality. In effect, although the colonial system was thought of as a set of institutions aimed at creating an essentially urban order, the economic life of the colony was supported in great part by the countryside, which escaped inclusion in the more rigid state structure; and although the system was thought of as authoritarian, the masses were obliged to pursue an existence that created, within the authoritarianism of the state, an individual authoritarianism that was the product of circumstances. These intrinsic contradictions hide the secret of the configuration of the Argentine political spirit.

One may say that the municipal State was imposed on Argentine reality before that reality had been shaped, and without thought of the forms it might acquire. Organized to defend the homogeneity and cohesiveness of the colonists, the municipality received a juridical structure that contradicted to a certain degree the authoritarian regime maintained by the Crown, since organizations were being created in the colony that were being restricted or even annulled in the Peninsula. However, it was imperative to predetermine the forms of colonial life given the conditions under which the colony was populated, and to ignore the fact that the opportunities for exploiting the land tended to disunite the population to some degree. Thus, the municipal regime was bound to conflict with the Crown, which, in effect, as exercised by the conquerors and by the royal officials, above all in Buenos Aires, invalidated the royal juridical organization, depriving it of its normal attributes and eventually conferring on it others that in fact lay outside its true jurisdiction. But the Crown had to struggle even more with rural reality, which not only lay outside the framework of municipal government but, in consequence, remained practically outside the law, if it were not already true by reason of accidental circumstances. In this way, individual authoritarianism was able to grow among the rural people. The will of the state was displayed in laws whose minute details usually made them impractical; if this occurred in urban centers, it occurred with greater justification in the almost deserted backlands, where the very presence of authority was occasional and inoperative.

This characteristic of Spanish legislation in general, and in particular in the Indies, is significant. Antonio Pérez had already pointed out how the number of laws and royal proclamations had grown during the sixteenth century, a phenomenon that without any doubt was accentuated in the seventeenth century. Even the authorities in the motherland came to understand that it was essential to overhaul the laws of the Indies, and they ordered the laws to be compiled into a code, which was not promulgated until 1680. Then, and later, their multiplicity, the fact that the same provisions were not applicable to all America, and the casuistry of their terminology rendered the laws useless, and they remained all too frequently as merely ideal outlines, in spite of the efforts of jurists who, like Solórzano and León Pinelo, struggled to accommodate the laws to reality.

In practice, the royal officials exercised power broadly and, at times, with absolute arbitrariness. Devoid of mineral wealth, these lands offered scant prospects to the conquerors. At the beginning of the seventeenth century, Ruy Díaz de Guzmán summarized the fortunes of the conquistadors of the Río de la Plata: "More than four thousand Spaniards came over in various fleets, and among them were many noblemen and persons of quality, all of whom ended their lives in this land in the midst of the greatest misery, hunger, and warfare that has been suffered in the Indies."

It is not strange, therefore, that little by little the idea took hold that the colonial adventure ought to be brief and profitable. First the conquistador and later the officeholder considered it a bit of bad luck to come to this colony, which was humble and held back by fear of losing its privileges and profits to the Viceroyalty of Peru. When these men did come, they aspired to stay a short time and to make the most of it. Because of that attitude, their rule was marked by a systematic forgetfulness of the abundant legislation that not only would have interfered with their own gains had it been enforced, but would have restricted their inclination to act at their own discretion, a tendency that was certainly accentuated by the demands of reality. Despite the royal laws and ordinances, the colonial officials took up local ways and thus, with rare and honorable exceptions, by protecting the ranching and mercantile oligarchy of the peninsular Spaniards, they grew rich at the price of tolerating the illegitimate enrichment of the Spaniards. Bribery and contraband were not unknown to the royal officials who, by engaging in them, recognized the relative legality of certain ways of life on the margins of the solemn provisions of the laws.

Nonetheless, this discretional use of power and this abuse of privilege were masked by a solemn acknowledgment of the monarch's absolute authority, which, when it was able to make itself felt, operated in fact with those same characteristics. The royal officials, like the conquistadors, were most faithful subjects of the king, and they did not believe that they were negating the king's authority by breaking his laws. The Crown was held in the most

absolute respect and given the most abject devotion, since there
was no other philosophy of power prevailing in Spain. But above
all, there was a lack of ideas that might negate royal authority,
because the precepts of the Faith seemed to support that political
concept. The Faith had been the theoretical foundation which
gave authority to the conquest, and the just title of the Crown
resided in a delegation of rights made by the Pope. During the
Reconquest, Spain had conceded a preponderant position to the
Church, and that position had been extended into the Indies,
where the Church appeared to be an institution as powerful as the
organs of the state itself, to such a degre that there were frequent
jurisdictional conflicts between them. As the doctrinaire support
of royal authority, the Church in the colony was the depository
of the juridical and moral principles that the Crown upheld.

The Church in this capacity, and under the influence of the
concepts of the Counter-Reformation, received dictatorship over
spiritual affairs from the Spanish State. It may be said that during
the first two centuries in the colonies there was no other system
of thought than that instilled by the Church in accordance with
the most rigorous orthodoxy. Because of the circumstances of the
conquest and colonization, it is certain that the population lived
in a state of general ignorance, to which the clergy was the only
relative exception. From this it follows that in all but rare instances there was no public education other than that provided by
the Church. Its authority, furthermore, was based on its influence
in the midst of the uninterrupted calamities that plagued the
colonists and, above all, on the fanaticism that characterized the
Spaniard, which he instilled into the natives whom he indoctri-
nated, supplanting their traditions and beliefs with those of Christian doctrine, without, however, completely erasing their deep
superstitions. Spiritual dictatorship began to be converted into a
social hegemony that was unanimously acknowledged and placed
the Church in an exceptional situation in colonial society.

The prestige of the Church supported the state insofar as the
Church proclaimed the divine bases of royal power, but on the
other hand it undermined the authority of the royal officials to

the extent that it tried to intervene for its own benefit, and that of is members, to the detriment of the civil authorities. In principle, the Church recognized the right of royal patronage, but in fact it aspired to override political authority each time it could, and it was accustomed to make use not only of the prestige it enjoyed with the people, but also of the influences it possessed at court and the threats of the Inquisition. Owing to this attitude, antagonism between the two powers was common, with evident harm to the authority of the crown officials although not to the theoretical authority of the king, which the Church defended as an article of faith despite customarily denying it in fact. This conflict was a further symptom of the dissociation between principles and reality.

Everything contributed to the assertion of the authoritarian spirit during the colony's first years; nothing developed the belief that other political forms might exist. Yet, in the shadows, the social realities of the colony were at work, setting out the seeds of dissidence that were destined to flourish later. In the time of Charles V, the Crown recognized the right of the settlers to elect their own governor when the office had become vacant and pending arrival of the royal appointment. But this concession, which was based on the principle that power derived from the people and returned to them when it was not exercised by the official to whom the Crown had delegated sovereignty, was seldom put into effect. Gradually the principle of replacement by appointment from among the constituted authorities was established. Beginning with the reign of Philip II, the increased emphasis on the principle of royal autocracy destroyed that right, and the exercise of that power came to appear to be subversive. On the juridical level, therefore, there was not the slightest suspicion of rebellion against the absolute authority of the Crown, or a hint of any ideas that might suggest the suitability of some other form of political organization. On the other hand, on the level of reality, life went on creating a *de facto* situation that gave the colonists almost complete independence from the Crown. The colonist had the feeling of being an orphan, despite the thickets of legal prescriptions around him. Here where the rule of law did not reach he did not hesitate to live in his own manner, which created beneath the *de jure* political system a *de facto* system that included extensive regions in which the colonist exercised his own authority with the same autocratic will that the royal official applied in the name of the king. Legally, nothing authorized that conduct, but no one could avoid it in the vastness of the plains and, in truth, the development was scarcely noted, unless one considers its repercussions in shaping a peculiar psychology. Furthermore, this psychology soon began to find justification: it was the jurist León Pinelo who at the beginning of the seventeenth century began to speak of the right to life, by virtue of which acts seemed to be lawful, even though they constituted violations of the law, when they did not imply the wish to deny royal authority. Symptomatically, this viewpoint was adopted especially by the country people, among whom the creoles were increasing in number and becoming more aware of their own position. Inconspicuously there developed among this underestimated element of society a way of life and of work that was different from what prevailed in the more populated urban centers, and an attitude was evolving that would mature with time until it became a definite political force.

The era of the colonizer was thus the era of the formation of the authoritarian spirit throughout society: the royal autocracy upheld by the Hapsburg States; the autocracy of the conquistadors and of the officials; the autocracy of the rural people, free to assert their own integrity and their capacity for overcoming a thousand hostile forces. Political consciousness was invariably shown to be an energetic and undisputed authority, exercised within an immobile order as the result of existing realities. To those holding this political view, any attempt at innovation was contrary to the established order and constituted a revolutionary act. Any change of the prevailing conditions seemed to be an attack on the general security and a violation of the juridical order, a mask that concealed, in truth, the actual situation. For that reason the colony became violently reactionary when it was confronted by any idea that presumed an alteration of economic, social, and political circumstances: only what existed seemed to have the right to exist. A simplistic political doctrine, these ideas were destined to be modified in some respects but in others would remain fixed, to crop out when there was an attempt to replace them by more complex and subtle systems, which were aimed at making the common will valid in the face of the indomitable autocratic will of those in power.

II

THE BOURBON EPOCH

THE SHAPE OF THE LIBERAL SPIRIT

The seventeenth and eighteenth centuries throughout Europe were marked by profound changes in attitudes. A crowned head had fallen in England, and monarchy had been replaced by an ephemeral republic that left in its wake the principle of the limitation of royal power. In 1688 the Declaration of Rights was acknowledged as the basis of the new monarchic structure, and a little later, in 1690, Locke would write categorically in his *Two Treatises on Civil Government*: "It seems clear from all we have just said that absolute monarchy, which is considered by some to be the only type of government that ought to exist in the world, is incompatible with civil society."

Louis XIV was reigning in France, Emperor Leopold I in Austria, Peter the Great in Russia, and Charles II in Spain. The rumor of the English catastrophe raced menacingly through the absolutist courts, and Locke's ideas began to germinate in restless minds. Rousseau and Montesquieu soon launched into the world the principles of a new order, accompanying them with clamorous cries against the European ruling system.

Meanwhile, Spain was bearing the cross of an imbecilic king, whose inheritance was being pursued by the chancelleries of the most important powers. At the close of the seventeenth century, Charles II died in Madrid, willing his kingdoms to the Duke of Anjou, the grandson of Louis XIV, by means of a will whose clauses injured the ambitions of the Holy Roman Emperor and brought on the War of the Spanish Succession. France poured all its power into the conflict, and succeeded, with English aid, in settling the war in its own favor. Thus the era of the Bourbons began in Spain.

Enlightened and progressive, the Bourbons had tried to assimilate some of the sound economic, administrative, and political principles that were then beginning to be developed. The Spanish kings of this house sought to introduce those ideas into their states, and the consequences were favorable both in Spain and in her colonies. The liberal spirit, still hesitant and restricted, began to spread, but not without violent opposition in Spain and in the colonies from groups representing and supporting the old, theocratic concepts. But the seed produced better fruit than had been expected—or desired—by those who had planted it, because it took firm hold in the minds of certain men who wished to carry its principles to their ultimate consequences. And the ultimate consequences were economic and political liberalism, the latter taking the form of republicanism. A radical transformation thus was engendered in the Hispanic world, out of which emerged a new political attitude: liberalism.

THE INTELLECTUAL ENVIRONMENT OF THE HISPANIC WORLD

Toward the middle of the eighteenth century, when Ferdinand VI, the third ruler of the House of Bourbon, was reigning in Spain, Voltaire wrote in his *Age of Louis XIV*:

Spain, governed by the eldest branch of the House of Austria, had aroused more fear after the death of Charles V than had the Germans. The kings of Spain were incomparably more absolute and more wealthy. The mines of Mexico and of Potosí seemed to furnish the means for buying Europe's freedom. The Spanish plan of monarchy, or rather of universal superiority over our Christian continent, was begun by Charles V and maintained by Philip II.

Under Philip III, Spain's greatness was no more than that of a body without substance, having more reputation than strength.

Philip IV, heir of his father's feebleness, lost Portugal by his negligence, Roussillon by the weakness of his armies, and Catalonia by his abusive despotism. Such kings could not long be fortunate in their wars against France. If they gained some advantages because of the dissensions and defects of their enemies, they lost their fruits because of their incapacity. Furthermore, they ruled over people whose privileges gave them the right to serve their kings badly: the Castilians had the privilege of not fighting outside their own country; the Aragonese ceaselessly disputed with the royal council over their rights; and the Catalans, who looked upon kings as enemies, would not permit the former to recruit troops in their provinces.

But Spain, united to the Empire, placed a fearful weight on the scales of Europe.

Voltaire was already able to measure the scope of Spanish decadence. Contrasting with the magnitude of Spain's international aspirations and its political schemes, its economic and administrative organization during the era of the Hapsburgs had been fatal, and had led to the loss of its position in Europe and to its serious internal debility. Furthermore, as if a stern fate were pursuing it, Spain had to support for forty years the rule of Charles II, whose physical and mental incapacity had put the throne at the mercy of courtesans and advisers, more than had been the case even in the times of Philip III and Philip IV. Political feebleness, unstable conduct, and meager plans characterized his reign, which gave Europe the impression that the ancient mistress, Spain, was now at the mercy of whoever might wish to make himself her master.

Charles III's last testament, and an armed conflict, gave the Spanish throne to a French prince, who ruled under the name of Philip V. With him began the dynasty of the Spanish Bourbons—recognized first by the treaties of Utrecht and Rastatt, and later by the treaty of Vienna—under whom Spain tried to regain its position in Europe. Progress, that ideal of the Enlightenment then attracting cultivated, lively minds, preoccupied the Bourbon kings and their ministers, and in economic, administrative, and political fields their activities were many and sustained, in an effort to bring the country out of the lethargy in which it was sunk.

The circumstance that the king was a foreigner, and the still luckier circumstance that his Italian wife Elizabeth Farnese of Parma thoroughly dominated him, opened up the kingdom to all manner of European influences that had been contained until then beyond the wall of the Pyrenees by the Hapsburgs, who were consumed with a holy fear of reform. The enlightened outlook was maintained until the reign of Charles IV; thus the eighteenth century was characterized in Spain by a vigorous ideological revival.

Perhaps most surprising was the enthusiasm for scientific thought, which had hitherto been proscribed. In educational institutions the most modern ideas of natural science began to be taught, and an excitement for knowledge of nature rapidly invaded enlightened minds. As Gaspar Melchor de Jovellanos told his disciples:

The sciences will always be in my eyes the first and most worthy object of your education: they alone can illuminate your soul; they alone can enrich it; they alone can communicate to it the precious treasures of truths that antiquity has transmitted to us; and they alone can dispose your spirit toward acquiring other new truths and further enlarging this rich depository; they alone can put an end to so many useless disputes and so many absurd opinions; finally, by dissipating the dark clouds of errors that float above the earth, they alone may some day disseminate fully the enlightenment and knowledge which ennobles the human species.

Nonetheless, this was not the dominant doctrine among the masses, who continued to be tied to the prejudices and the spiritual tutelage of the clergy, although it was accepted by the select elements who, up to the reign of Charles IV, predominated at court, and with royal approbation imposed many of these ideas.

These new ideas had a somewhat restricted influence in government administration, despite the fact that they were being accepted insofar as they involved a progressive attitude, because it was evident that if they were carried to their final results, they would lead to a political position considered extremely dangerous by the monarchy. The progressive attitude was shown primarily, as has been indicated, in education and in economic development. It was this latter aspect of national life that most profoundly disturbed and irritated sensible Spaniards who knew that impoverishment and general backwardness were corroding the nation. Father Feijoó, who was one of the most enlightened minds of the century, stated the situation in these mournful words: "Most Eminent Lord: Spain is gout-ridden. The poor feet of the kingdom are suffering great pain, and because of their misery, weakened and afflicted as they are, they can support neither themselves nor the body." Perhaps this evil condition was the result of a cause already pointed out by the same author: "When the stomach and intestines of this body politic [the administrators] drink or gulp down too much, innumerable, incurable illnesses follow, which put the entire body in danger of final ruin." In another place he writes:

What need is there to ponder the usefulness of agriculture? Who does not know it? Yet judging by the neglect that is suffered in this regard, it may be said that almost everyone is ignorant of it. I weep over the neglect of Spain, because the fate of Spain pains me. The poetic lament in which Lucan complained that the lands of Hesperia in which he dwelt—that is, Italy—were uncultivated, may be applied most literally today to that Hesperia where Lucan was born: I mean Spain.

The outcry raised by such far-sighted spirits was echoed by the statesmen who, motivated by these same ideals, gathered around the first Spanish Bourbons: Alberoni, Patiño, Carvajal y Lancaster, the Marquis de la Ensenada, the Marquis de Esquilache, the Conde de Floridablanca, Cabarrús, Gálvez, the Marquis de Campomanes, the Conde de Aranda—all of them in various ways tried to raise the economic level of Spain. It was necessary to mobilize all productive forces and involve all progressive men in the task of national improvement; thus the "Societies of the Friends of the Country," technical schools, and specialized organs of the state sprang up. But it was also essential that the wave of progress should not undermine the political foundations of the monarchy; to that end a vigilant watch was kept so that the premises of the Enlightenment were not applied to the problem of the origin and the historic forms of royal power. This attitude was naturally more energetically demonstrated after 1789.

Yet the Bourbons had modified to some extent the tenor of their political views. Absolutism maintained its vigor, but the principles supporting it underwent a transformation by comparison with the regime of the Hapsburgs. Between the medieval absolutism of the Hapsburgs and the enlightened absolutism of the Bourbons there was a marked difference, especially in the supplanting of the spiritual forces that served as the doctrinal support of the former. The theological basis of temporal power, which had so much force in the epoch of the Hapsburgs, began to weaken and give way to an increasingly secular conception of civil authority. Little by little, Spanish theocracy became attenuated under the impact of enlightened thought, and the result was a perceptible diminution of the importance of the Church as a political power. Without making a frontal attack on the Church itself—because religious feeling in that period was not much weaker than it had been earlier—royal power took a strong stand on the policy called "regalism," according to which, as an institution, the Church was not recognized as having any right to interfere with the royal will. The consequences of this attitude were considerable: in addition to its significance on the political and administrative level, it contributed to some extent toward shaking the Church's rigid spiritual dictatorship, and thus gave an opportunity for a freer diffusion of ideas of reform.

However, it is necessary to note that the predominance of theology was strongly maintained in opposition to the reforms inspired by the State. The importance of the uprising that caused the fall of the Marquis de Squillace is well known; and with no less zeal the Church tried to limit the dissemination of modern literary works, particularly those of French origin. The Church's activity bore fruit at the outbreak of the Revolution of 1789, and fear grew that the dangerous principles that had motivated it might spread. The reign of Charles IV, who came to the throne in 1788, may be considered as a backward step—a return of the most reactionary forces. The fate of Cabarrús, Jovellanos, and many other liberals is a sign of that attitude, and is corroborated by the governmental acts of Queen María Luisa and Prime Minister Godoy, whose concern with keeping his dominant position demanded the elimination of the enlightened leaders. Then it was that Manuel José Quintana recalled the peerless glory of Juan de Padilla and exclaimed in inflammatory verse:

> You were the only one
> who dared resist with stout brave chest
> the violent hurricane
> of despotism on our sad shores.
> What was the use of those
> seven centuries of zeal and our blood
> shed in torrents? Thrust out in vain
> the inclement Arab was from Spain,
> if another oppressor, more treacherous, vile,
> prepares to yoke her wretched head meanwhile.

But Godoy was not alone; in trying to oust the most enlightened figures to satisfy his own ambition, he was supported by all the reactionary forces that, following the banishment of French ideas, fought for the return of the theocratic principles formerly prevailing in the kingdom. Spanish anti-Jacobinism became a national attitude that clung to the most elemental traditions and rested on the most primitive instincts of the masses. And while the incompetent and cowardly monarchy gave way before the Napoleonic threat, the masses followed those leaders who stuck by the common beliefs and thus held back the process of enlightenment the liberal monarchy had begun. A new era was getting under way in Spain: a new duel between the spirit of reform, represented by the Cortes of Cádiz, and the spirit of the masses, blinded by a presumed tradition that incited them to acclaim Ferdinand VII with the cry of "Long live our chains!"

Meanwhile, in the colonies along the Río de la Plata, the same liberal influences had borne fruit and had succeeded in creating an atmosphere of rebelliousness among small but determined groups of creoles. They also had to suffer the reaction to the old authoritarian spirit, but conditions were favorable for carrying out their ideals, since the crisis through which Spain was passing weakened its chance of taking action. Thus the liberal preachings of the Bourbons took form in a political movement that was destined to turn against the motherland itself.

THE DEVELOPMENT OF THE
COLONIES OF THE RÍO DE LA PLATA

At the beginning of the eighteenth century, the colonies of the Río de la Plata entered a period of rapid demographic and economic development. The arrival of new Spanish settlers, added to the natural growth of the population, enlivened the cities and the countryside, increased their economic opportunities, and to a certain extent drew together the people of the region. Buenos Aires, which in 1744 had slightly more than ten thousand inhabitants, reached a population of forty thousand at the end of the century. According to Azara, Montevideo reached a population of fifteen thousand at about the same time, and there were ten towns, each of which had between four and five thousand inhabitants.

Various circumstances contributed to the expansion of the Río de la Plata colonies. Economically, the area witnessed a notable, energetic growth of farming and ranching. Ranching without doubt held first place, since it was the basic activity of the countryside and its products constituted the principal index of commerce. The aspiration of the Spaniards and the creoles in these parts was to own a piece of land suitable for ranching; only those who could not achieve this goal devoted themselves to the less productive tasks of farming. Azara wrote:

The Spaniards who live in the country are divided into farmers and ranchers, or *estancieros*. The latter say that the former are foolish, since if they were to become ranchers, they would live without labor and without needing to eat grass like horses—for so they call lettuce, vegetables, and greens. In fact, only those who cannot afford land and livestock, and thus cannot become *estancieros*, or those who find no other way of living, cultivate the soil. More than half the Spaniards of Paraguay and those who dwell near the Río de la Plata and near the cities are farmers. These may be distinguished from the ranchers because their houses are much closer to one another, and are cleaner and better furnished, and their clothes are somewhat better. Also, they know how to make their stews with meat and with vegetables and they eat bread, foods that are little known among the ranchers. In Chapter 6 I described their agricultural system, and in my study of animals I explained what pastoral activities amount to there—the care of eighteen million head of cattle, three million horses, and plenty of sheep. I estimate the numbers of livestock to be that great, one-sixth of them within the government of Paraguay and the remainder in that of Buenos Aires. Although I include in these figures the livestock of the Indians, which are cared for by them, I do not include in that number another two million head of wild cattle, or the innumerable runaway or ownerless horses.

However, as time went on, farming got a warmer welcome, especially because some of its products began to sell better, and because the State, nourished on physiocratic thought, began to stimulate it. Mariano Moreno recognized this in 1809 when he said, in defense of the rights of the farmers and the *hacendados*, who were being threatened by the monopolistic policies of the merchants: "The Crown has given repeated proofs of its conviction that we cannot be happy except by means of agriculture, and it has frequently encouraged the zeal of our officials so that they may protect and develop such an important resource."

Because of their complete influence over the public authorities, and because they were Spaniards from the Peninsula, the Spanish merchants of Buenos Aires, who were the agents of the merchants of Cádiz or connected with them, were the most important economic force. Their wealth and power had been achieved in the shadow of the protection afforded by their monopoly, thanks to which ranching received strong encouragement and agriculture did not. Trade in hides, lard, and other animal products brought fat profits to the Spanish merchants, which were increased when they invested their money in manufactured articles destined to be sold at high prices in Buenos Aires and in the other cities of the Río de la Plata. For everyone else, the monopoly was a fiction.

The products that came from Spain by the routes laid down in accordance with the monopolistic regime did not satisfy consumer needs; from the seventeenth century on, the frequent practice of open contraband was carried on, a trade that in itself provided substantial profits to those who exploited it. Despite this, the commerce along the Río de la Plata showed such vigor that it attracted the attention of the Crown, which could no longer avoid demands for better administration of the region.

In order to increase trade, piecemeal measures were decreed that were aimed at abolishing the restraints weighing upon it. In 1778, Charles III promulgated the Law of Free Commerce; other partial measures followed, thanks to which traffic between the ports of Spain and the colonies developed rapidly. At the same time, quite different events gave greater importance to the Río de la Plata. Difficulties with Portugal, which was bent on obtaining bases on the eastern shore of the Río de la Plata, stirred the Spanish government to make Buenos Aires the seat of a new Viceroyalty, established in 1776. Paraguay, Tucumán, and Cuyo were included in the new jurisdiction; thus an economic and political region was organized that tended to be oriented toward Buenos Aires. All these events contributed notably to transforming the Río de la Plata into a colony of some importance, which it had not been previously.

THE FORMS OF SOCIAL AND POLITICAL LIFE
IN THE RÍO DE LA PLATA COLONIES

This economic change involved progressive modification of the political and social arrangements in the colony. Those who began to live in a certain style, and to suffer from or enjoy their new positions, started to think about the problems of their mutual existence as a function of the new, conditioning factors. A relationship between economic problems and social and political aspirations was soon established; this relation was polarized according to special ties: for the beneficiaries of the old, monopolistic regime the attempt to modify the economic situation meant—or they pretended to believe that it meant—the inversion of the political, social, and moral content of the traditional order. They believed in the unconditional submission of the society to a system that benefited only themselves, and they considered this submission, which entailed total stagnation, to be the only attitude befitting the colonists. For their part, those who aspired to attain a regime of economic liberty within which they might better their circumstances discovered, after a little reflection, that such liberty would not be granted to the colony except to the extent that suited the motherland. It was only a step from that point to the discernment of the possibilities and the advantages of political independence—a step that events shortened day by day beginning from the moment of the outbreak of the French Revolution.

Thus the growing differences between the various social groups were emphasized. Upon the social stratum made up of Indians and African Negroes, on which the economy rested, were erected the two groups that, in spite of their differences, possessed influence in the society of the Río de la Plata: the Spaniards and the creoles.

Those groups were not cohesive. The Peninsular Spanish group was notoriously split between those who were transient and generally held public offices with the sole hope of moving on to better jobs, and those who had decided to root themselves in this land. The latter were singled out by the English traveler, Alexander Gillespie, as being disposed to "uphold revolutionary objectives," precisely because "they had said a permanent good-by to Europe and had thus identified their fortunes and their happiness with South America." He emphasized that whereas the former were indifferent to the fate of the colony, the latter were preoccupied with its future and were thinking about the conditions under which their existence might evolve more favorably. In general, the Spaniards preferred urban life, few of them settling in the country; those who did so soon abandoned themselves to a degrading indolence that, together with their isolation from urban centers, put them in an ineffectual position in the social order. At the end of the eighteenth century, Azara mentioned a singular characteristic of the Peninsular Spaniards in these lands, which everything else seems to confirm: "All men agree that they have equal rights, without any distinction being recognized between commoners and noblemen who have connections and entailed estates, or any other distinction than the personal one of the kind of work one does, which may bring with it a more or less large fortune or a reputation for probity or talent." So it was that the only aristocracy that emerged in the Río de la Plata was a new one, founded on the individual worth of the colonist.

As the gap opened between the transient and the settled Spaniards, the creoles sank their own roots deeper. There was a widespread belief in Spain that Spaniards degenerated in America. Father Feijoó believed it was important to dispel this absurd belief by the light of prudent arguments, but its mere existence shows how difficult the situation of the children of Spaniards was in the colonies in the eyes of those from the Peninsula. The creoles more than repaid this attitude: by the eighteenth century they regarded the Peninsular Spaniards as the enemies of their legitimate rights and fondest hopes, hating even those *peninsulares* who were their kin. Kept out of public office, relegated to lowly social tasks, the ambitious and capable creoles, whether they were white or, as was more frequent, mestizo, preferred a rural existence in which they did not have to bear constant witness to their inferiority. On the plains they led primitive lives, out of contact with cities and still less in touch with the current of civilization, which reached them only by reflection. The creole-mestizos developed indomitable, untamable spirits, stimulated both by their pastoral activities and by the spectacle of the open pampas. Their feelings of social inferiority, inherited by the large majority of the mestizos from their Indian mothers, created in time a special psychological attitude that united the creoles, endowing them with a sense of class that was soon to become significant in the political struggles for independence and in civil wars. Their great ally was their numbers: the creole population increased rapidly, and they came to comprise the solid nucleus of the colonial mass and even of the well-to-do class. The creoles in the cities tried to overcome the social conditions that bound them by pursuing studies at Córdoba, at Chuquisaca, or in the motherland, so that they might later engage in the liberal professions and thus open their way through the prejudices by which they were restrained. A creole core-group was formed, urban in its way of life and liberal by tradition, which added its efforts to those of the other creole elements in the strong, common desire to attain predominance within colonial society. If they had an ally in their numbers, they had another in the force of their convictions and in the interrelationship between their aspirations and the most important collective interests of the colony. In the end they triumphed, and the first stage of Argentine history may correctly be called the creole era.

The power of the creole element lay in their deep-rooted and precisely delineated ideals, which were in sharp relief to those held by the Peninsular Spaniards, especially the Spaniards who daily renewed the adventure of colonization by their hasty passage through the colony. In general, these were the men of authoritarian outlook; they were the ones who came to hold public office, which was the principal way to rule the land; they were the ones who came to manage trade, in close relationship with the merchants of Spain, which was the principal way to exploit the land. Furthermore, the Spanish clergy was in complete agreement with their ideas, and in the colony the clergy had a considerable cultural tradition and enjoyed a privileged position because of the moral and political influence that its members exercised over political affairs. The appearance of a new sort of liberal official whom the Spanish Bourbons sent to the Río de la Plata made little impression. The liberals, including some creoles, who succeeded in the eighteenth century in introducing Bourbon reform ideas into the colony, struggled to neutralize the influence of the most reactionary elements among the priests and the merchants, who clung most closely to their privileges. But the liberals did not always succeed, and frequently they were bitterly attacked by those who were injured by their policies. Yet the liberal point of view had an impact on the creole groups, and soon contributed to shaping their ideals and aspirations. If that influence did not reach the rural creoles, who also were authoritarian and untamed in their own way, it was felt decisively among the urban creole groups, who began to take a strong stand on the most important social problems in the Río de la Plata.

The creole bourgeoisie became fervently liberal because liberalism, even with the restrictions imposed on it by Spain, offered solutions to the most immediate problems and provided a system of ideas for the dim aspirations stirring in the boldest minds. The urban bourgeoisie began to sketch out a program of reform for rural life in the light of physiocratic doctrines and liberal thought, and aimed at the development of agriculture according to the latest methods. As Mariano Moreno said: "He who knows how to discern the true principles that affect the prosperity of each province cannot deny that our wealth depends principally on the bounty of our fertile fields." These urban people wanted free trade, which, by neutralizing the burdensome influence of the monopolists, would assure ready sales for the farmers' products, and they even wanted to develop small rural industries—all of which implied a profound change in the way of life that had been followed up to then by the rural creole group. Urban life, however, was the form that the bourgeoisie considered to be the ideal of civilized existence; they believed that in such an environment they could attain the degree of enlightenment that permits societies to rise from primitive conditions to the highest levels. It was in the cities along the Río de la Plata that the creoles were able to achieve the formation of a political conscience capable of facing the problem that was felt by every creole in a more or less express form: namely, the proper direction of his own destiny.

The liberal reforms of the Bourbons contributed more than any other factor to shaping, among the creoles, a revolutionary conscience for emancipation. The establishment of the Viceroyalty, which was the result of the expedition of Don Pedro de Cevallos against the Portuguese in 1776, gave political unity to an extensive region theretofore incohesive. To the areas administered from Buenos Aires and Paraguay was added all the land

that formerly fell under the jurisdiction of the *audiencia* of Charcas, together with Tucumán, Potosí, and Santa Cruz de la Sierra.
The city of Buenos Aires was made the capital of the Viceroyalty.
A new, extensive, and rich political unit was thus created, part of
which had previously been oriented toward Peru, but would
henceforth be polarized toward the Río de la Plata. The vast
region in which this bi-polarity was to endure for a long time—
with Charcas and Lima at the opposite pole from the capital—
little by little began to gain political importance. It was precisely
its diversity that identified it: the different parts, rather arbi-
trarily combined, became aware of their personality when confronted by their subordination to Buenos Aires, and they showed
their incipient political consciousness by passive resistance to the
city that was soon to attain a high destiny.

The organization of the Viceroyalty into administrative areas
called *intendencias* accentuated this activity, for each of these
quickly acquired a well-defined unity. Following the Bourbon
principles of centralization, the Crown had decided in 1782 to
divide the territory of the Viceroyalty of the Río de la Plata into
seven *intendencias* and a Supervisory Government. Buenos
Aires, Asunción, Salta, Córdoba, Santa Cruz de la Sierra, La Paz,
La Plata, and Potosí became administrative and political units in
which a local spirit quickly emerged. The old, primitive municipal organization of the colony was replaced by a territorial and
regional organization that notably weakened the preponderance
of the *cabildos,* which until then had been the most important
bodies for the transmission and execution of the royal will and
the only ones in which public opinion had some influence. Henceforth, the governor-intendent, who was the executive responsible
for war, justice, and police, became the supreme regional authority. Subordinate to the governor, the *cabildos* were limited to
strictly urban tasks, while his policies contributed to the definition
of the aspirations and desires of the population of the region.

This administrative reorganization, child of Bourbon political
beliefs, sowed the seeds of serious political problems by creating
a new situation. While the creoles in the capital were hardening

their belief that they were the nerve center of the Viceroyalty because they were cultivated men, informed in modern thought (a position indirectly recognized by the liberal policies of the Crown), the people in the several *intendencias* began to open their eyes to the actual condition being created by the accelerated process of centralization operating from Buenos Aires. The way of life and the traditional influences coming from Lima and Charcas, and that endured in Asunción, did not coincide with those prevalent in Buenos Aires after the middle of the eighteenth century. Vague unrest appeared in the last years of the colonial period: later, when the creoles of the interior joined the creoles of Buenos Aires in the desire for emancipation, the appearance of this long-matured divergence of ideas was to smash their united front.

The most transcendent fact in the political existence of the Río de la Plata in the eighteenth century is precisely the limited imposition of liberal policies by the Crown and their reception by the enlightened creoles—particularly in Buenos Aires and in Charcas—who tried to carry those ideas to their logical conclusions.

The general lines of Spanish Bourbon policy were those of enlightened despotism, but various conditions retarded their achievement, especially in the colonies. The policies were progressive and were motivated by the ambition to stimulate the development of the colonies and to benefit the American subjects of the Crown; but both in the colonies and in the motherland this desire was subjected to the necessity of not favoring the diffusion of a doctrinaire line that might end by weakening the bonds of absolute power and of Catholic thought. The result was that the greatest progress was made in the economic field, although there too with some limitations, and also in the area of social action and education.

The defense of absolute power, which implied a mistrust of the free-thinking *philosophes*, also involved an energetic policy directed against the Jesuits, whose theocratic conception of power clashed with the official view, and whose growing economic and political strength seemed to threaten the State. The Jesuits were

eliminated, and with them fell the strongest prop of authoritarianism in the colony. Perhaps this fact more than any other favored the growth of liberal views first noticeable in officials who, like the Viceroys Bucareli, Basavilbaso, or Vértiz, had responded to the tendencies prevailing at the Bourbon court and had come to impose them upon the colony. Later, these opinions began to appear among creoles of keen intelligence and deep restlessness. As examples, there were Juan Baltasar Maciel or Manuel Belgrano, who, at the end of the eighteenth century, began to study the works of the most significant modern authors, many of whom they could read only in secret because of the zealous vigilance of the reactionary clergy who upheld Jesuitical beliefs.

Maciel, a studious and reflective man, felt himself drawn to thinkers such as Descartes, Gassendi, and Newton, who stimulated him to face fundamental issues on which the University of Córdoba, where he had studied, had offered him training only in the Aristotelian and scholastic tradition. Some works of the Encyclopedists must also have been in his library. This kind of reading, however, did not begin to affect these men until a little later, particularly after the revolutionary explosion of 1789 in France. The economists and political philosophers of the eighteenth century exercised immense influence over Manuel Belgrano's generation. The future secretary of the *consulado* of Buenos Aires became aware of political economy in Spain, and he accepted the position in the *consulado* because, as he put it: "I knew that such bodies had no other object than to supplement the work of the economic societies that dealt with agriculture, industry, and commerce." While he showed in this fashion his enthusiasm for the kind of studies he had recently discovered, he was seized at the same time by "the ideas of liberty, security, and property. I saw only tyrants in those who opposed enjoyment by any man, no matter who he might be, of the rights that God and Nature had granted him and that even society itself had agreed upon directly or indirectly in its establishment." With this background, Belgrano was bound to exercise enormous influence among the *porteños*. Around him gathered questioning minds—men who secretly read Montesquieu or Rousseau, and who did not hesitate to advance in public the economic principles of free trade, and physiocratic doctrines.

The outgrowths of this restlessness were colonial periodicals, of which the first, *El Telégrafo Mercantil* (*Commercial Telegraph*) directed by Francisco Antonio Cabello, lengthened its masthead by describing itself also as "Rural, Political, Economic, and Historiographic." Manuel Belgrano wrote for it, and so did Juan José Castelli; the engineer, Pedro A. Cerviño; the naturalist, Tadeo Haenke; the poet, Manuel de Lavardén; and Canon Luis Chorroarín. As was the case with the *Semanario de Agricultura* (*Agricultural Weekly*), which Hipólito Vieytes published in 1802, and the *Correo de Comercio* (*Commercial Mail*), which Belgrano edited in 1810, the chief characteristic of this colonial journalism of the Río de la Plata is the attempt to apply to local needs and problems the doctrines learned from European writers. The colonials were just discovering and posing a great number of these questions, precisely in the light of the new doctrines. Although it was true that these problems were almost exclusively economic, this fact should be interpreted by recalling that the attribute of the Bourbon liberal movement was the limitation of reform to a field that would not injure the bases of royal power. But there could be no doubt that liberal thought constituted a unified doctrine, and that whoever was touched by its influence could not easily resist extending his inquiry into political phenomena, confronting them with the same point of view that he took toward economic data. The urban bourgeoisie of Buenos Aires and of Charcas, made up mostly of creoles who had received formal education or were self-taught, had the specific, immediate ideal of social and economic betterment and material progress; but there was also present the implicit and remote ideal of the attainment of a liberal government—for which emancipation was a prerequisite. This idea slowly evolved in the minds of the bourgeoisie.

In the closing years of the eighteenth century, events began to encourage the urban creole minority in its ideological stand.

The most important of these occurrences was the French Revolution, which from the first aroused extraordinary enthusiasm among those who understood the theoretical principles that motivated the revolutionists. There can be no doubt that this enthusiasm was evident in Argentina: first, Viceroy Arredondo and, later, Viceroy Avilés believed it was essential to take strong measures to prevent the spread of news about events in France and about the beliefs motivating them. The Marquis de Avilés explicitly stated in an edict promulgated in August 1799:

> I am informed of the introduction into this capital, and into other cities and places of the district under my command, of various foreign pamphlets from different parts of Europe and even from the settlements of our enemies in America, which not only contain odious accounts of insurrection, revolutions, and disturbances of governments that have been established and generally acknowledged, but also espouse matters that are false and injurious to the Spanish Nation and to its wise and just government. This extremism, in addition to being contrary to the fundamental laws of these kingdoms, demands special vigilance these days in order to avoid every motive or occasion for the deception or seduction of these faithful and distant vassals, so that they may not be taken by surprise by similar abominable materials. Therefore, I order and command that whichsoever inhabitant of this capital or of the other cities and places of this Viceroyalty to whom such papers are directed under the name of gazettes or under whatever other name shall immediately hand them over to me without communicating them to any other person; this under penalty of a fine of five hundred pesos for the first offense and of being dealt with, on the second offense, as nuisances and disturbers of the public peace.

By this time the course of revolutionary events, particularly the decapitation of Louis XVI, had to some degree chilled the enthusiasm of many people; but the Declaration of the Rights of Man remained as a political program that attracted men who until then had not foreseen the possibility of giving realistic form to the doctrines taught by the political philosophers.

The urban creole minority was anti-Jacobin, as in Spain, except in rare instances. The principles laid down by official Bourbon liberalism prevailed in the thinking of the creole liberals, who had a traditional respect for monarchy and a no less vigorous regard for religion. Liberalism had taken this form in Jovellanos, the guiding light of the liberal creoles, and this was the way it was generally conceived. These characteristics became still more defined as a result of the English invasion of the Río de la Plata in 1806, which, by hastening action by those who wanted independence, effectively contributed to clarifying aspects of the creole liberal movement.

The result was that in spite of the sympathy that some English ideas, particularly on economic matters, awakened among the creoles, to them the English appeared to be the criminal advocates of religious heterodoxy. An impassable chasm opened in the way of any direct and definitive understanding between the two peoples. Gillespie tirelessly refers to "this land of fanaticism and ecclesiastical domination," and it is well known how the popular masses reacted to Protestants even after independence was gained. Owing to this circumstance and to the pride and sense of revenge aroused by the English attacks, the English invasion contributed to the delimitation of creole liberal ideas: extensive in economic affairs, restricted in religious and political matters, even though in the latter area there was discrimination between reality and abstract aspirations.

It is worth pointing out that the English invasions of 1806 and 1807 had other no less significant results. The attacks caused the creoles, the group whose participation in the Reconquest and Defense was decisive, to move to the forefront of society. Social progress was achieved not only by the bourgeois minority, which partially assumed the leading role, but also by the popular mass, which linked itself to that minority, beginning to recognize it as its authentic ruling class. A notion of nationality based on the principles of birth in the colony and of adherence to its way of life thus became increasingly clear. That was the creole spirit; that was the fatherland.

No matter how sturdy the liberal movement in the colony may have appeared, authoritarianism had not abandoned all its positions. The traditional authoritarian spirit of the Hapsburgs had solidified among different social groups who adopted it because they perceived the danger of the road that had been opened by liberal Bourbon policies. The officials of the old stamp who could not conceive of any way of life for the colony other than what derived from its condition as a colony of the motherland; the monopolistic merchants who shared the profits provided by that regime; the Jesuits, and those who inherited and maintained their theocratic views—all of them agreed that if the floodgates were opened to liberal ideas, a torrent of aspirations would pour from the Spanish Americans, who were thirsting for justice and for their individual and collective development. This belief was correct, for such aspirations existed, latent and hidden beneath a resentment, already old, felt by the creoles toward those born in the Peninsula. Moreover, there is little doubt that the evolution of liberal thought unequivocally led to ideas of self-determination and independence. But the authoritarian concept, which had developed native forms, persisted with remarkable vigor in the rural environment and in the hearts of the rural creoles. Liberal political ideas could not penetrate into the back country because the people there had nothing but the primitive political experience of man abandoned to nature and to his own physical resources. The problems of crowded living conditions had never been posed in the deserted pampa. On the other hand, the rural creole, authoritarian as he might be in his daily adventure of existence, grasped the postulates of liberal political economy because those were involved with problems whose gravity he had felt personally. In this, as in his dim desire for self-determination, he was in agreement with other creole groups.

This coincidence of views created a battle front between the creoles and the Peninsular Spaniards, which was most obvious in the economic area. There, merchants and *hacendados* (the first more likely *peninsulares*, the latter generally creoles) struggled over their conflicting interests, which were scarcely reconcilable without loss for one side or the other. Whatever benefited the former, who were represented by the *consulado*, damaged the interests of the latter, represented by the Junta de Hacendados. In this silent struggle it was difficult for the creole *hacendados* to take the initiative because they were victims of their subordinate social and political role; but the Crown, motivated by liberal ideas and by the desire to stimulate the development of the colonies, took the initiative for them, and gave wing to their high hopes, not without having their rivals complain bitterly and violently and try to impede whatever measures the Crown proposed. The day came when the *hacendados* tried to carry out their economic ambitions, and they frankly solicited, through the pen of Mariano Moreno, free trade with England for their products. "Those who believe that opening trade with the English in these provinces is an evil for the nation and for the province of Buenos Aires should be covered with shame; but even should that evil be conceded, it ought to be recognized as a necessary evil, which is impossible to avoid by aiming at the general good, in an effort to benefit from it by making trade serve the security of the State." Thus Moreno wrote in 1809 in his historic *Representación de los Hacendados* (*Memorial of the Hacendados*).

But the monopolistic traders were not shamed. They persisted in their attitudes, and pointed out two types of evils in the economic policy that the others were trying to impose: one, that it injured the native Spaniards, who were proud of their rank and jealous of their privileges; the other, that they saw the dangers to which this policy was leading. Martín Alzaga, the leader of the monopolists, expressed this point of view to the *consulado* with undeniable clarity:

The trade we have had up to now is what the law has permitted as useful and beneficial for maintaining and tightening the relations between the vassals of these remote regions and the motherland by means of the reciprocal dependence of their commercial activities. This is an indisputable truth, as evident as the risk that by allowing (1) the exportation of goods and money directly from the ports of Spanish America to the Northern powers, and equally, (2) the importation of goods bought from their factories (as the author of the paper [Cerviño] implies), the relationship I have mentioned would be extremely attenuated and weakened in a short time, with irreparable damage to the monarchy.

Matters having arrived at this point, the polemic moved from the purely economic level to the political plane, where lines were not well defined.

The creole position on political issues had not yet been established: above all, because the Hispanic group possessed the enormous force of legality; next, because the subversive nature of reform ideas impeded many people from expressing their thoughts; finally, because only sentiment for the fatherland was common to all the creole groups, since liberalism had taken root only among the cultivated minority in certain cities and was probably not assimilable by the rural groups. This meant that the system of political ideas was structured cautiously, deep in individual thought or in small meetings, and this explains the inexperience that has been commented upon as being characteristic of the first acts of the independent government. From this source also stemmed the aggressiveness of the Peninsular Spaniards, who were sure of their own strength. But in each creole conscience there was silently at work a more or less obscure ideal, cast out upon the wide future. The creoles designed an objective, sketching out the golden age of the rationalist philosophers: a free and happy world in which the human being would enjoy indefinite progress and the most extensive liberty. The spirit of liberalism had taken definitive shape in this land.

PART TWO

The Creole Era

The revolutionary movement of 1810 opened a new era in Argentine history. Henceforth, the chief concern of the enlightened groups would be to give structure to the country—to organize it politically and to reform it socially and economically. This undertaking involved enormous difficulties, some of them almost insoluble without the aid of time. In the minds of the men of the revolution not even the geographic boundaries of the new-born state had been defined; their doubts were revealed in their preoccupation with the adoption of its name. Discounting the abortive attempts to include the Banda Oriental and Paraguay, the boundaries in the north were notoriously uncertain because of the influence of Upper Peru in many provinces, and because of the changing fortunes of the patriot armies; but the geographic problem was insignificant compared to the social problem brought on by emancipation.

The revolution for emancipation was to some degree a social revolution aimed at facilitating the rise of the creoles to the top level of the country's life. Enlightened creoles had been the makers of the revolution, but it was necessary for them to appeal to the provincial creoles, mainly from the rural masses, because of the strength of their convictions and the need to get solid support for the movement. The rural people responded to the call and joined the movement, but the nucleus of porteños *had already established the fundamental principles of the political-*

social order, and the masses who answered the call did not believe that they were being faithfully represented by a system that naturally gave leadership to the educated groups who had a European background. Thus began the duel: on the one side, the institutional system advocated by the enlightened minority; on the other side, the imprecise ideals of the popular masses.

The struggle between the two political-social concepts led to civil war and to the triumph of the ideas of federalism, which in turn ended in autocracy. Then a moderate tendency began to appear, seeking to conciliate the two hostile currents and to formulate a political doctrine that would permit the unification of the nation. This compromise position was worked out slowly; it triumphed with the constitution of 1853, and was permanently accepted in 1862. Beginning in 1862, the country put in play all its resources, hurling itself into a vast constructive program. But its very development, carried on with unity of opinion from 1862 to 1880, led to the formation of a new social reality. European immigration and profound economic changes struck a mortal blow to creole Argentina and obstructed the normal working of the institutional system that had been created at the cost of so much effort and so much bloodshed. Around the year 1880 the creole era ends, but in its final stages it gave birth to the second Argentina.

III

THE COURSE OF
DOCTRINAIRE DEMOCRACY

THE DIFFUSION AND CRISIS OF LIBERALISM
AND CENTRALISM

"June 20, 1789, was France's most glorious day, and would have been the beginning of the happiness of all Europe if an ambitious man, who was endowed with extraordinary talent but also with violent passions, had not forced a million men to serve the aggrandizement of his brothers by shedding their blood for their country." So Mariano Moreno wrote at the end of 1810, revealing the state of mind then dominant among the liberals. At its outset, the French Revolution had appeared to be the triumph of the ideals of fraternity and of justice for which Rousseau and Montesquieu had struggled, but the course of events compelled calm thought, since it now seemed that French genius was incapable of preserving the dignity of its principles. This circumstance moved men to look toward England, in whose political structure the doctrinaire French liberals had found their own inspiration, and who in spite of revolutionary buffeting, followed by reaction, had maintained equilibrium between liberty and authority. In Spanish America, the English example was, at different times and in different degrees, the standard of political thought for more prudent minds. This explains the swing toward monarchy, which was to be observed in trying times—a tendency that was not at all discordant with liberal and democratic sentiment—and the sympathy shown by Great Britain, which was both a protection and a hope for the newly created countries of Hispanic America.

Napoleon's conduct, on the other hand, spurred concern for the danger of Jacobinism (which was seen as the ultimate cause of the reaction), and the adoption of a moderate policy was counseled, of which the Spanish Cortes of Cádiz in 1812 and the acts of the Argentine governments between 1810 and 1814 were evidence. From that moment on a wave of absolutist and conservative reaction swept Europe and America. The restoration of Ferdinand VII in 1814 was the warning sign of the policy of both the Quadruple Alliance and the Congress of Vienna—a policy aimed at erasing the recent past by one powerful effort. War without quarter began between liberalism and absolutism. "I believe I have said enough," Bernardino Rivadavia wrote in 1817, "to explain the new kind of war that shook Europe, a war in which one-quarter or one-third of the Continent was struggling for the interests and claims of arbitrary, absolute power against the others who, armed with the advances that man has made in all fields, fought firmly and vigorously against fanaticism and against the false ideas and vices of all the old institutions." This war also contributed to strengthening England's position in the eyes of the American countries because it demonstrated her lack of enthusiasm for the cause of absolutism, which was contrary to her own political tradition. And when Spain, after the brief period during which the constitution of 1812 was in effect, received the support of the "Hundred Thousand Sons of Saint Louis" to restore absolutism, England prepared to remove herself from the absolutist coalition, and showed her position to the extent of recognizing the independence of the United Provinces of the Río de la Plata in 1824. The Quadruple Alliance virtually disappeared two years later, deprived of English support, and the cause of American emancipation, which had been sealed with the victory of Ayacucho, entered a new phase in which the impact of European politics was less severe.

EMANCIPATION AND
POLITICAL-SOCIAL PROBLEMS

The revolutionary movement leading to Argentine independence occurred within this political and ideological framework. A very brief period of elaboration, dating from the English invasions of 1806–7 to the beginning of 1810, served to clarify the ideas, invigorate the collective conscience, and define the political and social objectives of the creoles. A very short series of events imposed a revolutionary situation upon Buenos Aires that radically modified reality. Finally, the fortunes of all the people were sealed by the movement of May 25, 1810.

But this rapid progress was the work of a small group—the liberal and enlightened minority of Buenos Aires. After May 1810, on the other hand, a period of convulsions began that shook the entire community and led to the adaptation of society to the newly created situation. The fact is that if independence was the result of a state of mind that gestated surreptitiously during the colonial era and matured in the nineteenth century, emancipation, in its turn, caused radical social and political alterations in the country.

In a sense, the revolution for independence was as much a social event as a political one; and perhaps because it was, above all, social in nature, it gave birth to a complicated and difficult political problem whose solution occupied a half-century. In the closing years of the colonial period, Peninsular Spaniards and creoles were two groups separated not solely by their origins, but primarily by their social statuses. It is significant that Bishop Lué dared to say at a critical moment of the revolution that the government of the American colonies "can be taken over by the sons of this country only when not a single Spaniard remains." The opinion of Cornelio Saavedra, who three years earlier had summarized the psychological situation created by the defense of Buenos Aires against the English, is no less revealing: "I make bold to congratulate the Americans: to the proofs that they have already given of valor and loyalty, they have added this last—that by exalting the merit of those who were born in the Indies, they have given convincing evidence that their spirits are not kin to humiliation, that they are not inferior to the European Spaniards, and that they cede to no one in loyalty and valor." Creoles and *peninsulares* were two social classes who felt themselves to be enemies because of their relationship: the privileges of one determined the inferiority of the other.

The revolution was not politically significant at the beginning because of its limited scope, but it was a social upheaval that dislodged the men of the Peninsula from authority in order to give their power to the creoles. That was the idea behind Mariano Moreno's interpretation of the Spanish royalist reaction:

The great obstacle to the surrender of our rivals is their refusal to have the sons of this country enter into the government of these provinces at the highest levels. The Spaniards, surprised by such a strange and novel concept, believe that nature itself is being turned upside down, and they obstinately insist on maintaining our traditional inferior status, engaging in war against and in the extermination of the men who have aspired to command, contrary to natural laws that condemn them to perpetual obedience. Here one finds the principle that provoked the Viceroy Abascal's outburst against us as "men destined by nature to vegetate in lowly obscurity."

The sensation of having yesterday been an oppressed class and of today being triumphant conditioned the attitude of the creoles after May 1810. Now they could give free rein to old resentments and their long-accumulated, silent rancor. The rancor was soon translated into open hostility against the Spaniards, and later was extended into strong xenophobia. Spanish laws were called "monuments of our degradation," and were rejected; Spaniards were quickly excluded from public office as foreigners. Only the "sons of the fatherland" now possessed indisputable rights in the country they had just reconquered. "Since nature has created us for great things, we have begun to do them," Moreno said with angry pride. A new self-awareness—overflowing with self-esteem—henceforth motivated the creole leaders and masses.

If that common sentiment explains the attitude of the classes liberated at the outset of independence, later events may be explained by the diversity that is easy to find in the creole mass, each one of whose groups had quite different psychological, social, and economic characteristics with which they reacted to the revolution they had made. In principle, the creole mass was divided into two great nuclei: the urban *porteño* group, whose thinking was echoed in some other enlightened centers, and the groups in the back country, both urban and rural, among whom profound regional differences could be distinguished.

Europeanized and liberal, the creoles of Buenos Aires comprised a minority of considerable influence. Its members had achieved a degree of economic well-being, especially in commerce and the liberal professions, that gave them a solid foundation for their prestige, and some of them had risen to positions of importance in the colonial administration. Ideologically, this group descended directly from the liberal Spaniards of the Bourbon era. Certainly, some of the more questioning minds had been in direct touch with French or English thought, studying it at its sources. But if it is easy to prove that Mariano Moreno added Jean-Jacques to his careful reading of Jovellanos, it is not difficult to observe that he also read Rousseau with the same preconceptions as the liberal Spaniards. The result was that the enlightened *porteños* developed a liberal doctrine that was *sui generis*, but so deeply rooted that it showed itself from the outset as an unbending political and institutional system that included a conviction in the necessary hegemony of Buenos Aires, the propitious dwelling place of this constructive creed. From this fact stemmed the later clash with the creoles of the interior, with whom the *porteño* minority agreed on the ideal of emancipation and the motives for social change, but from whom they were separated in the field of political realities.

The population of the interior in general lacked both the doctrinal preparation and the political experience to assimilate the institutional system that the *porteños* wanted to impose on the new state. The predominantly rural mass was split into two groups that geographically and in other ways corresponded to the Littoral and to the land-locked interior. If the first was nearer to Buenos Aires because of common problems and even because of a common political attitude, it was separated from Buenos Aires by the old problem of controlling customs and the economically important rivers, a problem that soon provoked deep antagonism between Buenos Aires and the Littoral. The second group, in the beginning, had fewer direct motives for hostility against the former capital of the Viceroyalty but was, on the other hand, further from it ideologically. The northwest and central regions of the country, zones of Peruvian influence, repudiated the modern spirit that had taken hold in the area of European influence. Thus, both provincial groups potentially shared the same attitude toward the enlightened element of Buenos Aires.

Neither the leaders nor the back-country masses had political experience or training in ideas; theirs was a simple existence bordering on the primitive, and characteristic of rural Argentina. This condition was only slightly modified in a few populated centers and hardly affected more than their immediate surroundings. Primitivism was sharply demonstrated in politics, since both the colonial tradition and the natural organization of rural life had favored the development of an authoritarian regime, as shown by the liberties taken by officials, landowners, and ranchers. Primitivism was even more developed in the moral order. Authoritarianism was the nerve center of clerical education, the only system of education in the colony. Dogmatic and demanding spiritual authority over the secular world shaped a mentality, resistant to reality, that soon flung itself into fanaticism and superstition. Confronted by the outburst of liberal ideas, this mentality reacted with all the force and vigor of blind conviction, rejecting analysis and repudiating anything that presupposed liberty of conscience and political self-determination. For the most varied reasons disagreement between this attitude and that of the enlightened group in Buenos Aires soon broke out.

Local sentiment contributed much to the antagonism between the two sectors of the creole population. The Revolution of May aroused patriotic emotions, but while Buenos Aires advocated a national view of the fatherland, the groups of the interior showed marked indifference for what was, in their eyes, still a vague abstraction. On the other hand, they overvalued their *pequeña patria*—their "little fatherland"—which they could sense and to which they were united by daily existence. Local sentiment showed itself quickly, not only in support of parochial interests but also in defense of the local psychology and the modes of daily life. This amalgam of emotions threw the rural groups into conflict with Buenos Aires, the symbol and bulwark of hostile interests, of reform, and of a strong tendency toward economic and political hegemony. Hostility grew, silently at first, openly later, between the city that had unleashed the revolutionary movement and the rest of the country, which had to decide whether or not to join the regime favored by the city. Buenos Aires did not want to acknowledge the depth and vigor of localism, believing it was enough to proclaim the brave new world in order to have the rural masses submit to those who had summoned them. But the reply proved that the "people" conceived in the imaginations of the intellectuals of the revolution were quite different from the people of national reality. Buenos Aires wanted to dominate and to educate, but the people shut their ears to such voices, replying with their own conception of the revolutionary movement.

Gradually the panorama became clear, displaying all the difficulties. The creole mass agreed with the educated group in the belief in emancipation and in the deep desire to achieve leadership of the country, but they dissented radically from the political organization of the new State. The sons of the homeland were united, yet disjoined.

Despite the caution and prudence of the men who were to make the Revolution of May, engaged as they were in masking their wish for independence by feigning loyalty to the person of Napoleon's sovereign prisoner, the idea of independence stood forth in their words and deeds. Belgrano declared in his memoirs that the idea had appeared as early as 1808, and if, only a few days after the installation of the Junta de Gobierno, Moreno was able to say that its members "sought nothing more than to up-hold with dignity the rights of king and country," a justifiable indignation caused by the royalist reaction soon led to the unanimous opinion that Americans possessed the same rights as the Spaniards to decide upon their own destiny, once the sovereign had disappeared. The men of May defended the justice of their pretensions to a government ruled only by the "sons of the country" and by those who "care for the glory of their homeland." Soon this sentiment would tear aside the mask that hid it. At the end of the year 1810, Moreno would wrathfully challenge his enemies: "Do you believe that the sons of this country will return to the chains they have just broken?" As a profound social revolution, the movement by its very nature aimed at independence, since only emancipation could elevate the hitherto disdained and oppressed creole mass.

Independence posed the urgent problem of the organization of the new State. The entire political tradition of the colony had been impregnated with injustice toward the rebellious but finally triumphant creole class; now it was necessary to decide how to form the new nation to fit it to the new social realities. At this point, difficulties emerged, born from the conflict between the different sectors of the creole population, which were divergent and even hostile in their political experience, their ideological formation, and their conception of life. "A people that suddenly passes from servitude to liberty," Bernardo Monteagudo wrote at the beginning of 1812, "is in near danger of falling into anarchy and slipping back into slavery." The prediction of this Argentine Jacobin was based on events that were already occurring, and on tendencies among the leading elements that would shortly be fulfilled. The problem was extremely serious and the solution most difficult, despite the fact that no one could escape the consequences of failure. The problem was "to give new form to an old state; to pull up by the roots an established order and to introduce another, wholly or in great part distinct; to extinguish with a blow the ancient custom; and even to destroy certain principles that are irreconcilable with those that ought to be introduced by such a reform, despite the fact that the ideas of the men who must build the new structure are often in unhappy conflict," Friar Cayetano Rodríguez wrote in 1816 in *El redactor del congreso* (*The Congressional Reporter*): "These issues persisted for fifty years. The difficulties, which they had ambitiously hoped would be settled immediately, were, nonetheless, eliminated bit by bit, and at the end of that long time ideas and methods of conciliation appeared that were capable of unifying the creole mass, its interests, its aspirations, and its ways of living and thinking.

CURRENTS WITHIN THE "PORTEÑO" GROUP

No matter how loudly its ideas resounded in the interior of the country, the Revolution of May was a *porteño* movement created by the initiative and the decisions of an enlightened minority—that is, men who were educated in the principles of the Enlightenment. It was this group that inherited the liberal policies of the Bourbons, enriching them in many instances by reading directly from the principal authors of the movement. Manuel Belgrano, Nicolás Rodríguez Peña, Juan José Castelli, Mariano Moreno, and others composed this group at the outbreak of the revolution. But if the background of their beliefs was purely liberal, their firmest convictions were primarily and sometimes solely rooted in the forms of liberalism that the ideology and conditions of politics and society had encouraged in Spain. Liberal economic objectives, for example, were stated in that form.

Belgrano and Moreno were supporters of liberal economic policies during the closing years of the colonial period, the former as the secretary of the *consulado* of Buenos Aires, the latter as the defense attorney of the *hacendados* and farmers against the monopolists. When they gained control of the government, the men of the progressive group favored the development of free trade and the stimulation of all forms of production. In other aspects, liberal ideas were bound by certain limitations, the same ones, in fact, that were imposed in Spain by the fixity of traditional beliefs and by a respect for monarchical power (the latter precisely the source from which these innovations had come). For example, Rousseau's opinions in religious matters were deemed unacceptably extreme. Moreno, in the prologue of the edition that he ordered printed of the *Social Contract*, declared: "Since Rousseau had the misfortune to rant and rave when he dealt with religion, I suppressed that chapter and the principal passages in which he has treated these matters." The Spanish tradition of respect for authority also seemed to be perpetuated among the liberals. Both areas were made exceptions by Moreno when, in his article *Sobre la libertad de escribir* (*On the Freedom of the Press*), he asserted: "At last we perceive that the masses of the people will exist in shameful barbarism if they are not given complete liberty to speak on any matter, as long as it is not in opposition to the holy truths of our august religion and the decisions of the government, which are always worthy of our greatest respect." Also, despite the fact that the Assembly of 1813 suppressed the Inquisition, some inhibitions persisted toward religious dogma and political authority.

Considering these facts, it can be said that the *porteño* liberals adopted a moderate attitude. Moderation seemed to be one of the preoccupations of Moreno, who was the nerve center of the Junta of May, and whose opinions in this regard were frequently and categorically stated. Yet this surely was not his personal inclination, but rather the result of a planned political orientation. In essence, Moreno was a Jacobin like the other men of his group such as Chiclana and Castelli and the later heirs of his policies such as Monteagudo and Alvear. If Moreno favored moderation, at the outset taking pride in the measured calm of the revolutionists, he shortly gave way to his emotions at the signs of royalist reaction, and advised the violent imposition of revolutionary precepts. Referring to the plotters of the uprising at Córdoba, he said, "Only terror of the executioner can serve to warn their accomplices"; and in another passage: "The conspirators who agitate this land with their far-reaching plans and plots are beyond the bounds of compassion and justice. They will be the gravest threat to the State and to public safety if remedies are not efficiently applied to counter, impede, and weaken their influence."

The experience of the French revolutionists may have counseled moderation among their emulators in Buenos Aires, or the *porteños* may have taken a moderate course for fear of the reaction of lukewarm followers who would perhaps support a reactionary despotism; but most of all they feared counterrevolution and anarchy. They preferred to make arrests in Jacobin style rather than pursue the ideal of moderation, which seemed inappropriate under the circumstances. The extremist policy was followed most vigorously by Castelli in his role as delegate of the Junta in Upper Peru, and it was taken up again later by Bernardo Monteagudo, who called leniency a crime and who, in April 1812, in the pages of *Mártir o libre* (*Martyr or Freeman*), advised the establishment of a dictatorship in order to consolidate the revolution.

Events frustrated the Jacobin tendency and compelled a moderate policy, which soon became reactionary. The restoration of Ferdinand VII, the fall of Napoleon, and the establishment of the Holy Alliance contributed indirectly toward displacing the Jacobins, and they gave up leadership to the moderates and even to the reactionaries. Nonetheless, the principles and tendencies of the enlightened group remained alive below the surface, and even when they were not followed faithfully, they sufficed to contain and mitigate reaction.

Their principles were derived from the deep-seated conviction among the enlightened *porteños* that America offered optimal conditions for a republican political system. The dissolution of the Spanish monarchy had in fact set the community back to its condition prior to the founding of Spanish sovereignty; consequently it would be possible to establish on new bases a social compact like that ideally conceived by Rousseau as lying at the foundation of society.

"The world," said Moreno, "has seldom seen a setting like ours in which a constitution can be modeled that will give happiness to the people." He believed that the revolution had eliminated the colonial tradition and the psychological attitudes that the past had created in the people. On this basis, the enlightened group categorically and unanimously affirmed that sovereignty had returned to the people and that only by a new delegation of sovereignty could public authority again be constituted. Thus only a congress representing the popular will could settle the destiny of the commonwealth. The liberals struggled to convene that assembly, certain, even when lacking any basis, that the entire population shared their views and had sufficient political experience and ideological preparation to assure a republican system founded on modern and efficient representative institutions.

The republican concept rapidly took root among the people, but the principles and techniques of institutional organization presumed a tradition and preparation that the people lacked. Burdened wtih theories, the educated *porteños* and some of their followers in the interior began to spread their ideas and to reform institutions. They proclaimed the dogmas of equality, liberty, and security, ideas Belgrano had absorbed from the liberals in Spain, and they were heatedly defended by Moreno and Monteagudo with forceful arguments that they succeeded in writing into laws and decrees, chiefly in the memorable declarations made by the Assembly of 1813. Even Indians, Negroes, and slaves regained full rights under the theory of the revolutionary State— rights that were, nevertheless, grudgingly granted in practice because of pressure from established interests. To assure these public benefits and to lay the foundations of political power, the liberals asserted that "true sovereignty has always resided in the general will of the people," and, as a corollary, that "the general welfare will always be the sole object of our vigilant care." In the eyes of these exacting patriots, the public officials possessed importance and authority only insofar as they were executors of the general will, and they could exercise their offices only to serve the common good. As *El redactor de la asamblea* (*The Assembly Reporter*) put it in 1813: "All those who have been faithful to their high duties shall enter the temple of fame and receive public tributes of admiration and gratitude; but if there is anyone who, by confusing the goals of the popular will with his own self-interest, has degraded the principal offices of civil authority, he shall be delivered up to the remorse of his conscience and forever reside in the shadows where crime dwells." It was in obedience to this highest republican conception of public responsibility that Mariano Moreno resigned as secretary of the Junta, with a statement whose wording reveals the vivid actuality of democratic and republican beliefs.

For the enlightened men of Buenos Aires, in contrast to those of the interior, democratic views were indissolubly tied to institutional principles and to a particular conception of the country. Molded by visionary political theories, they firmly believed that only organic democracy, put into effect according to such norms, could express genuine democratic opinion. Confusing form with essence, they opposed as enemies those who agreed with them in fundamentals, but who differed with them superficially.

INSTITUTIONAL PRINCIPLES

An attitude clearly derived from the Enlightenment guided the political thinking of the educated class in Buenos Aires: the horror of anarchy and of unchecked, turbulent democracy. Order seemed to be the finest attribute of a rationally based society, a conviction that appeared to be certified in practice by the French political experience, in which excited popular emotions had led to an absolutist dictatorship. Only law and correct institutional arrangements seemed to offer proper solutions for preventing the social and political upheaval in the Río de la Plata from degenerating into chaos. The most informed political thinkers tried hard to point out the two dangers entailed in the lack of governing principles: anarchy and despotism.

But the solution was not attainable. Would the new regime be a mere continuation of its predecessor? If tactical reasons obliged Moreno to declare that "internally our government is the same as that prescribed by royal law," it was not long before his study of the problem of the future organization of the nation caused him to affirm openly that it was necessary to revise the bases of the social and political system. This task, urgent and inescapable in his view, ought to result in an orderly arrangement of principles and regulations, since laws were not sufficient to give structure to a new society: it was necessary to lay the foundations and to construct the crowning feature of the edifice —in other words, a constitution was needed.

As early as 1810, this decisive problem had been posed. The enlightened *porteños* maintained that a constitution was the key political objective of the revolution, and they had already thought out its general lines. In 1812 Monteagudo wrote: "Any constitution that does not bear the seal of the general will is arbitrary: no reason, no pretext, no circumstance can give it authority. The people are free, and they will never err if they are not corrupted or done violence." But this line of thought, which coincided with Moreno's, implied conviction that the people not only shared the beliefs in independence and democracy held by the enlightened minority, but also shared their opinions about its institutional framework. When Moreno contends that without a constitution "the happiness that is promised to us is a fantasy," he is saying that it is essential to elaborate a constitution on the basis of historical experience and political science, in order to know with certainty "why some institutions have given some nations a degree of prosperity that the passage of many centuries has not been able to erase from the memory of men." Those institutions, the result of theoretical elaboration, ought to be the ones imposed by a constitution that establishes "honest customs, personal security, the preservation of rights, the duties of the authorities, the obligations of the subjects, and the limits of obedience." From the beginning Moreno pointed to two fundamental ideas that must become the basis of the institutional order: the division of power and the representative system.

Rooted in liberal theory, the two principles seemed undebatable and, indeed, were never negated as doctrine. But reality put obstacles that were long insurmountable in the way of their application. The division of powers in fact clashed violently with the remnants of authoritarianism surviving among the masses—vestiges partly of colonial origin and in part born of the conditions of rural life. The representative system, in its turn, was impractical because of the dispersion of the population, the widespread ignorance, and the lack of the technical skills demanded for its correct use. Thus it happened that the constitutional principles advocated by the enlightened groups appeared to be the illusions of visionaries or the mad fixations of intellectuals.

Perhaps they were, to some extent; but from the Revolution of May to the Assembly of 1813, the enlightened leaders persevered in their legislative and educational labors, and they succeeded in establishing a political system that at times conflicted with reality but constituted an immovable position against which the forces of anarchic democracy crashed. The laws were held in low esteem, their provisions violated, and their principles criticized; but a segment of the conscience of Argentina rallied around the body of political doctrine contained in the laws. Much later that conscience would return as by right to restore the constitutional system, once the democratic masses had evolved away from turbulent forms of political power and had grasped organic law.

NATIONALISM AND CENTRALISM

The fact that those principles originated with the enlightened group in Buenos Aires no doubt contributed greatly toward arousing the resistance to them. Various reasons provoked suspicion of the former capital of the Viceroyalty: in part because of the antagonistic interests of different economic groups that disputed control of the customs and the port of Buenos Aires, and in part because of a different mentality in the landlocked interior that was shaped by the influence of Upper Peru. The government created by the May Revolution inherited the spirit of resistance that the men of the Bourbon regime had aroused at the close of the colonial era. The conservatives and those who considered all innovations to be dangerous closed ranks in opposition. And slowly another force began to organize against Buenos Aires, made up of elements in the creole mass who were in fundamental agreement with the government but dissented over its methods of achieving its objectives. These sectors reacted against the pride of Buenos Aires, against its self-assurance, against the domination, real or imaginary, which they saw in the city's attitude.

The poets who sang of the heroism of the resistance to the English invaders or who rhetorically exalted the glory of the city that was the cradle of independence were echoing the genuine emotions of people of the city of Buenos Aires:

> Let Sparta speak not of her virtues;
> nor Rome her grandeur flaunt;
> Silence: on the world's stage appears
> the mighty capital of the south!

So wrote Vicente López y Planes, the same man whose words are sung in the National Anthem:

> Buenos Aires marches at the front
> of the people of the illustrious union,

a reflection of a state of mind which, because it was justifiable, was no less irritating to the people of the interior, who saw in it an avowal of the right to supremacy. They were not mistaken. When Juan José Paso claimed in the *cabildo abierto* of May 22, 1810, that Buenos Aires was assuming the role of elder sister to the other provinces of the Viceroyalty, he was skillfully raising the thesis of political tutelage, which the men of May considered justifiable. They did not discuss its validity, but derived it from facts and existing realities; yet its projection into the interior took on marks of arrogance, which very shortly made it seem oppressive.

The revolutionary regime wanted from the outset to bring the people of the interior into the movement but, in spite of its leaders' measured words and studied generosity, it was obvious that Buenos Aires was very sure of its right to political hegemony. Moreno wrote:

It was reserved to the great capital of Buenos Aires to give a lesson in justice that the Peninsula itself had not accomplished in the days of its finest glory. This example of moderation at once confounds our enemies and ought to inspire in our brothers the most profound confidence in this city, which looks with horror on the conduct of those hypocritical capitals that declare war on tyrants only to seize the seats of power that should have remained vacant upon the extermination of the despots.

While guaranteeing the mildness and justice of its conduct, Buenos Aires left no doubt that it had secured for itself the role of capital and the right to lead the new State that was being formed.

To all appearances this attitude was motivated solely by the ambition to ensure a centralized regime that would perpetuate control of the government in the hands of the men of Buenos Aires. Although appearances were susceptible to that interpretation, the truth was quite different. Buenos Aires had conceived and initiated the revolution; therefore, in the beginning, circumstances required it to take leadership of its revolutionary phase on the assumption that only in this way would the movement not be perverted. But to Buenos Aires belonged the honor of having regarded the revolution from the outset as a national movement into which all the people should be incorporated, a principle that impelled the city to maintain its traditional position as head of the State in order to prevent its dissolution. The idea that the entire area of the Viceroyalty should be preserved as a unit, in order to make itself into a nation, was specifically voiced by Moreno when he lashed out at the conduct of Montevideo, which had rebelled against Buenos Aires: "The arrangement of the provinces and the interdependence of the people who comprise them," he said in the *Orden del día* of the Junta on August 13, 1810, "is a constitutional law of the State. Whoever tries to attack it is an opponent of the solemn pact by which we swore to guard the constitution. What would become of public order if the lesser towns were left to decide for themselves the selection of the capital, when the Sovereign has already established the center for all their affairs?" Already the idea of the continuity of the nation was seen to be inseparable from the idea of centralizing political power, and this doctrine became more strongly rooted before the threatening spectacle of the disunity of the former Viceroyalty. In 1813, the Assembly took up Moreno's idea, and its journal, *El redactor*, indignantly asked: "Can one ignore the fact that there is no salvation without strength, no power without subordination and unity, and that these do not exist among people who are at odds with each other or internally disorganized?" *El redactor* pointed out that the congress had met precisely "to establish a center of unity for the opinions and the scattered resources of the provinces, in which our true strength lies; and to lay a solid foundation for the tranquillity and the future happiness of the nation."

This concept of the State, and of centralized rule as the only sure way of guaranteeing its existence, constituted, with its liberal principles, the political platform of the enlightened leaders of Buenos Aires. But if liberal ideas aroused resistance, the belief in centralization provoked still more energetic hostility. The rural groups of the Littoral and of the interior were beginning to display their patriotism in the form of extreme localism. Regionalism, which was determined to some degree by geographic and economic conditions, grew strong, and the nation, if it had to be created at the price of centralism, appeared to many as an ideal that could be repudiated. The theory of federalism was soon raised in opposition to centralism, but it was rejected for sound reasons by the enlightened group in Buenos Aires. First Moreno and later Monteagudo studied in detail the reasons that they believed stood in the way of its adoption. But federalism was more than a theory. It represented a view of life and of political and social problems, and it grew and spread without being affected by the arguments of those most knowledgeable in political science. However, as with the principle of organic democracy, the principle of centralism remained as an unsurrendered flag, and in due course would be raised again.

BUENOS AIRES IMPOSES ITS PRINCIPLES

Secure in its role as the standard-bearer, proud of its conduct, and convinced of the universal validity of its political beliefs, Buenos Aires summoned the people of the future nation, of which the city was dreaming, to collaborate in the task of founding and defending that vision—but Buenos Aires from the beginning set up the institutional system and the main political lines which should rule that nation. When the people began to awaken from their lethargy and answer the call of Buenos Aires, they discovered that the main lines of the political structure were already drawn, and they found at the same time that the outline did not fit their own spiritual and material situation. Buenos Aires abounded in statesmen and thinkers, but it lacked prudent, realistic policies. Its ideological orientation was rigid, incapable of making concessions.

The ideas preached by the enlightened group seemed to be so universally true that none of the liberals thought that social and economic realities or the defects of the colonial mentality might work against them. "Dedicate your thoughts to understanding our needs," Moreno advised the representatives to the congress; but in his opinion there was no need, other than to educate the people, to convince them that his magic system would provide the soundest doctrines and the most just government. The progressive men of Buenos Aires believed in the people, as Rousseau had believed in them, but they did not suspect the influence exercised by new conditions or realize that the past had not been destroyed by mere political collapse, any more than the power of ideas imbedded in the populace by dogma and authority. They believed in the efficacy of words, in their own good faith, and in their personal disinterest; yet they could accomplish nothing without eliminating the stubborn opposition between the two political divisions that existed in the creole mass, which had now won control of public life: organic and doctrinaire democracy, on one side, and on the other, turbulent, inorganic democracy.

It was a fatal error on the part of Buenos Aires to act disdainfully and violently against those who did not seem able to understand its ideas. Convinced of the social nature of the revolution, the leaders of the city believed that it sufficed to "raise up the creole population and force it to take an interest in our labors," as Moreno told Chiclana—and also to support the creoles with armed force wherever they might be under pressure from their former masters. Nevertheless, experience quickly demonstrated the inefficacy of these measures. The Junta de Gobierno decided to resort to the severest violence to prevent a Spanish counterrevolution. Castelli was inflexible in fulfilling his rigid instructions, not only at Cabeza de Tigre, when he fought against Liniers, but also at Potosí, when he fought against Córdoba, Nieto, and Sanz. Soon the men of Buenos Aires became convinced that a resistance movement against them existed, and they decided to act with like energy, which only inflamed hatreds. The overthrow of the Junta Conservadora in November 1811, and of reactionary elements in the Triumvirate on October 8, 1812; the categorical opposition of Moreno to the inclusion in the Junta of the deputies from the interior; the radical policies of the Assembly of the year 1813; the campaign against Paraguay; and finally the rejection of the deputies sent by Artigas to the Assembly— all these events were bound to breed a climate of violence, which began to develop in 1814. And at this moment appeared the other specter that had been so dreaded from the first days of the revolution, unchained precisely by those who had warned of the danger: the military dictatorship attempted by Alvear, but aborted by the energetic reaction of the force of anarchic democracy.

After that, the group of enlightened leaders in Buenos Aires lost their well-defined structure. They had called the people to revolt and the people had responded, but a set of political beliefs had sprung up that conflicted with those of the optimistic followers of Rousseau. Each group responded in its own way to this phenomenon. The result was that the emergence of the people destroyed the initial plans of the revolution and began to lay out another course, one that was extremely complicated and was incomprehensible to those men of Buenos Aires who were wedded to the objectives of their original program.

THE CALL TO THE PEOPLE

On the eve of the revolution, a representative of the military leaders invited Belgrano to meet with them because (as Belgrano recalls in his *Autobiografía*), the officer said that "it was necessary to count not only on force but also on the people, for they would be the arbiters. When I heard the military leader talk thus, trying to take the people into account, my heart swelled and I had a pleasant vision of a favorable future." The ingenuousness of one of the representative men of the enlightened group shows the state of mind of the revolutionists of May. In their eyes the people were not only the source of sovereignty, but also a reality to which the intellectuals attributed ideal qualities and in whom they saw the hope of redemption. It was a Rousseau-like conception, and it was firmly rooted in the minds of the revolutionists and impenetrable to evidence.

However, facts to modify this opinion were not lacking. Moreno knew and feared the consequences of the political ignorance of the masses, but his doctrinaire convictions were stronger than experience and his optimism was immediately applied to balance the evidence. "Happily," he wrote in October 1810, "our people have ended their long slumber and are displaying a noble spirit disposed to accomplish great things and capable of any sacrifice for the general welfare." Firm in this belief, the men of Buenos Aires hoped that the people would rally to their call, full of enthusiasm for independence and democracy, and prepared to grasp the noble ideals of the enlightenment and the far-reaching ideas of freedom of thought and political self-determination.

The educated people in the capital were profoundly mistaken. The men of the interior answered their call because in fact they shared the belief in democracy and in emancipation from Spain and because they sensed their triumph in a revolution that had overthrown the old ruling class and had raised them to a position of authority. But for many reasons the provincials opposed the doctrinaire positions and the institutional principles of the enlightened group. To these ideas the people of the interior opposed a profoundly colonial mentality and local sentiments, by which they demonstrated their new-born patriotism. They were primarily opposed to the anti-religious Jacobinism of Castelli and the men of the Assembly of 1813, and in politics they were hostile to the complex institutions that inevitably placed authority in the hands of the best-educated men. Their hostility deepened as the plans of Buenos Aires became more apparent— revolutionary policies that nonetheless correctly presupposed the continuation of a centralized regime for the nation. Faced by these deep antagonisms, the people chose to obey the call of the *caudillos* of their class and of their own kind who sprang up on all sides, which gave support to a new authoritarianism that had some vaguely democratic characteristics, since, in fact, the *caudillo* exalted the ideals of his people and carried to power with him a mandate to impose and defend their wishes. The *caudillos* satisfied the basic desires of the people, who did not hesitate to deny their support to liberalism.

Faced by a population that quickly showed tendencies both discordant with and in agreement with the government of Buenos Aires, the liberals acted indecisively. Although the liberals were correct in appealing to the creole population and in awakening anti-Spanish resentment—policies that assured the full support of the people for the revolution as a movement for independence —they were mistaken in collaborating so closely with the most progressive creoles, who reminded the rural masses of their former condition and inclined them to rally around their own *caudillos*. The result was that the representatives sent from Buenos Aires frequently did not gain the people's esteem, for whereas these delegates were usually chosen from among the best educated, the *caudillos* and the people often disagreed with the logical decisions the representatives had made. By political instinct the people reacted stubbornly to any agreement.

The men of the educated class did not act any differently; they did not try to understand the aspirations of the people or attempt to discover how to reach accord, and their fault was all the graver because of their greater talents. The terms of the conflict involved such contradictions that agreement was unattainable. The men of Buenos Aires believed that only by political education and by spreading the theories of the enlightment could they attract the rural masses, ignorant but stubborn in their vague idealism. Great as he was, it was nothing less than ingenuous of Moreno to distribute the *Social Contract* among people who had scarcely any other moral training than the very slight amount—if any—provided by the rural clergy. However, Moreno had naïve faith in the doctrine of public law, not wishing that those ideas "should continue to be mysteriously reserved to ten or twelve men of letters." In his newspaper, the *Gaceta,* he taught the rudiments of liberal political theory, with the intention that the priests might read and comment upon his ideas from the pulpits.

This was the road to total misunderstanding or, better said, to proof that there was a gap between the masses of the interior and the enlightened group of Buenos Aires, which no one felt like closing. The urban groups of the interior gathered around their *caudillos* and isolated themselves; meanwhile, beginning in 1814, a vigorous antipopular reaction started among the educated people in Buenos Aires.

ANTIPOPULAR REACTION OF
THE CULTIVATED, LIBERAL MINORITY

Confronted by serious internal problems and by the certainty that it would be impossible to fit the popular mass into a pre-established system, the intellectuals of Buenos Aires began building up an increasingly hostile attitude toward the popular movement. Local conditions impelled them to that position, and they were also heavily influenced by the torrent of political reaction that poured across Europe with the restoration of Ferdinand VII to the throne of Spain, the later defeat of Napoleon, and the hegemony of the Holy Alliance. These developments brought on a dual movement in the Río de la Plata. On the one hand, they stirred the moderates to adopt a reactionary policy that perhaps was consonant with the natural inclinations they had repressed because of the prevailing revolutionary climate; on the other hand, everyone began to search for an accommodation with the new circumstances, hiding their republican sentiments in order not to excite the allied European absolutists. Thus a reactionary current was born that advocated monarchy, without denying, one should remember, democratic beliefs, since monarchy was never conceived except in its limited and constitutional form.

Locally, the growing power of Artigas over the Littoral and Córdoba deeply disturbed the *porteño* intellectuals. To them, Artigas represented the triumph of chaotic democracy, resulting in dictatorship by local bosses. This possibility horrified the men who had dreamed of maintaining the unity of the former Viceroyalty as an independent nation, and of assuring a republican and democratic government by means of the enlightened leadership of the capital. Only chaos could be expected from the rise of the *caudillos*, and the intellectuals began to resist that possibility. "Anything is better than anarchy," Alvear's envoy told the British minister in Rio de Janeiro—even the abandonment of independence.

Taking up suggestions from Europe, some of the liberals turned monarchist. Alvear, the head of the government, as Director, believed that the victories of the liberals could be ensured by putting the country under the protection of the English, in whom he saw—with reason—the sole bulwark of liberal principles against the wave of reaction that threatened the other European countries. But his plan got nowhere because he was overthrown by a coup shortly after he had taken power and had begun to initiate the necessary measures. The same tendency showed itself among several groups that sought other solutions with the aid of emissaries sent to different European courts. It was not long before there seemed to be unanimous opinion favoring monarchy, judging by the tactics prevailing in the Constituent Congress that met in Tucumán at the beginning of 1816.

However, appearances again are contrary to fact. Missing from the congress were the representatives of all of the provinces under the influence of the Uruguayan *caudillo,* José Gervasio Artigas, who despite events kept his faith in republicanism. The only delegates from the interior who were present came from the provinces that showed warmest support for colonial ideas and were markedly antiliberal, and the representatives of Buenos Aires, who also had turned away from their principles, in reaction to inorganic democracy. The congress was monarchical, unitarian, and antiliberal. General San Martín, who was in Cuyo preparing the expedition to liberate Chile, declared that the needs of war demanded a strong executive power, and he stated that he favored monarchy even at the risk of losing the gains of liberalism, which could be re-established in less difficult times. Pressed by his demands, congress declared Argentine independence on July 9, 1816—because San Martín did not want to be a mercenary but rather the leader of the army of a free nation. Beyond this, the congress did nothing to join its policy to the traditions of the *porteño* intellectuals.

In fact, the reactionary elements of the interior dominated the meeting. They hated anarchy but they hated Buenos Aires more, and their policy was guided by the two aversions. The result was that they proposed the establishment of a monarchy and considered naming as king a member of the ancient family of the Incas, and locating the capital of the State at Cuzco. But the times were too disturbed for such a grave step, and the indecision of many of the delegates prevented them from going through with an act that not only was unworkable, but would have worsened a situation that still seemed soluble. Therefore, the system of rule by the Directory was retained, and the delegates agreed to name as Director Juan Martín de Pueyrredón, a weak conservative who appeared to reconcile the interests of all parties. But the deliberations at Tucumán were evidence of the differences between the hopes of the interior and the fears of the old progressive group in Buenos Aires. A decree of the congress in August 1816 faithfully reflects the state of affairs by describing as its objectives:

an end to revolution; a beginning to order; recognition, obedience, and respect for the sovereign authority and the decisions of the provinces and of the people represented in the congress. Those who may promote insurrection or attack the powers of congress or the other authorities that have been established or may be established among the people, those who similarly provoke or work to sow discord among the people, and those who may aid or cooperate or favor such activities will be deemed enemies of the state and disturbers of public order and tranquillity, and they will be punished with all the force of the law, including death and expatriation, according to the gravity of their crime and their role or influence in it.

This was a recommendation to the future Supreme Director to save national unity because "anything is better than anarchy."

In the eyes of the different types of reactionaries—those who were so by nature and those who were becoming so out of horror at the eruption of inorganic democracy—anarchy was embodied in the people, especially in the masses of the interior who were emerging as ferocious republicans and blind democrats. Pueyrredón attacked the Federalists, and exiled Manuel Dorrego, who was the representative and head of the only liberal group that continued to be republican and to defend federalism for Buenos Aires, still hoping to find a formula for conciliation with the people. Against the Federalists of the Littoral, Pueyrredón was even more energetic, giving to the civil war an especially violent character, which daily deepened the hostility between the two bands. The result was the polarization of the antagonists. The Federalists and the Unitarians were two irreconcilable groups; their aspirations and ideologies began to emerge with increasing sharpness.

As a definitive solution, the *porteños*, who were almost all temporarily inclined toward reaction, could think only of recourse to force and the establishment of monarchy. Rivadavia advised this, from Europe, and was supported by Pueyrredón, who hurried negotiations in favor of the Prince of Lucca and at the same time urged the congress, which had been moved from Tucumán to Buenos Aires, to draft a unitary—that is, centralistic—constitution.

The task of drawing up the constitution was not easy. Its guiding principle had to be the creation of a legal order to assure the authority of a central government residing in Buenos Aires, but the condition of the country was evidence that such a constitution would be utopian and therefore would be rejected before it was written. The congress understood this, and some sensible men pointed out that these were not the times to proclaim a constitution; but the antipopular movement was growing in Buenos Aires and was welcomed by many men in the interior who were appalled by the rising power of the *caudillos*. The thesis of a centralized constitution therefore triumphed; at the end of 1819 a constitution was decreed that ignored the serious political problem that had arisen almost simultaneously with the Revolution of May. An institutional system that was technically unobjectionable hid the complete inability to deal both with the social forces unchained by independence and with the ideals, no matter how imprecise, that rejected the political formulas imposed by Buenos Aires. On the other hand, everything indicated that the constitution of 1819 was written to provide for a monarchy if the negotiations to that end should be successful. But the *caudillos* of the Littoral strongly opposed the policies behind the constitution, and it was an outright failure. The mere mention of monarchy irked the men whose republicanism had awakened the people. And just as the men of Buenos Aires had considered the demands of the people to be nonexistent, the popular mass regarded the constitution of 1819 to be nonexistent, and their chiefs, the faithful interpreters of their ideas, set off at a gallop toward Buenos Aires. Thus ended the first cycle in the history of the Buenos Aires liberals, who had abandoned their principles in inexplicable surprise at the people whom they had called to action and whom, like the sorcerer's apprentice, they could not control.

NATIONAL DISINTEGRATION

The adoption of the constitution of 1819 brought a worsening of the conflict. The troops of the *caudillos* of the Littoral arrived at the frontiers of the province of Buenos Aires and defeated the army of the Directory at the battle of Cepeda on February 1, 1820. That day put an end to the first act of the Argentine drama, for it saw the breakup of the area of the former Viceroyalty and the beginning of an era of autonomy for each province. But the drama was far from its end: the enemy-brothers could not live separately. Once the links between them were broken, the struggle to reconstruct the nation on fresh foundations was resumed. Yet civil strife continued to threaten; the future of the country darkened. San Martín, sadly contemplating the fratricidal conflict on the eve of his departure from Chile for Peru said, "An evil genius has inspired this delirium of federation—a word full of death, signifying nothing but ruin and devastation." In another place he wrote, "I fear that we may tire of anarchy and in the end long for oppression and accept the yoke of the first successful adventurer who comes along." These prophetic words were not slow in being fulfilled.

Free to follow their natural impulses, each province fitted itself to the political scheme of the *caudillos* who, with greater or less accuracy, interpreted the will of the people. Many of the provinces issued constitutions that concealed true circumstances but testified to the profound strength of republican and democratic beliefs; others did not scruple to keep their almost feudal systems, or to proclaim constitutions that did not achieve a moment of effective existence. For its part, the city and province of Buenos Aires, disjoined from the problems that had been born out of their own relationship to the other provinces, saw the reemergence of their former leadership group—now composed of new men and freed from the concerns that had inclined it to conservatism. Shortly after the battle of Cepeda there thus began what Governor Las Heras would call, four years later, "a happy experiment"—a constructive epoch which by contrast with earlier times caused Juan Cruz Varela to write:

Buenos Aires! My country! One day
   the curse of heaven
flooded your land, and shrouded
your immortal glories in darkling veil.
   In her frightful carriage
Anarchy, rolling through your streets,
drenched them in blood and tears,
and with fratricidal hand waved aloft
   the infernal torch of
impious Discord. Then it was
when not even son respected father,
   nor brother to brother
gave his due share of love.
Crime mounted triumphant
to the sovereign throne,
and the altar of the law fell in an instant
   shattered into bits,
in degradation sunk into the dust.
The tutelar gods gazed upon us
with pitiless eyes, and to her misfortune
abandoned the wretched city.

That time has flown, and in our history
the honor of your memory will not be erased,
immortal Buenos Aires: today your grandeur
rises above all other peoples',
   like the cypress, midst
small shrubs and plants that
   scarcely rise above the ground,
lifts its head to the clouds.

The administration of Governor Martín Rodríguez, which began shortly after Cepeda, depended on the inspiring work of its ministers, Bernardino Rivadavia and Manuel José García, who began a large-scale program of reform. Rivadavia was the intellect of the government. Following the inspiration of liberal thinkers such as Bentham, Benjamin Constant, and Destutt de Tracy, he inaugurated reforms that reached into all parts of public life: the problem of the allotment of public lands by means of the system of emphyteusis; the development and stimulation of agriculture, ranching, and mining; the organization of charitable works; the reform of the clergy and the army. All these merited the calm and careful attention of the tireless minister whose progressive labors were to endure, and who deserved Bartolomé Mitre's claim that Rivadavia was "the greatest civic leader of the land of the Argentines."

Eager to improve the lives of his fellow citizens, Rivadavia sketched out and began to apply a vast plan of public education at all levels; at the same time he supported every effort to develop scientific studies. But he was interested above all in political problems, and he did not hesitate to establish universal suffrage in the province, an innovation opposed to the restrictive colonial tradition. He had a wide-ranging, open mind and the talent of a farsighted statesman who grasped the great future problems of the country. Even before Sarmiento and Alberdi (to some extent his heirs) had proclaimed that the desert was Argentina's evil, Rivadavia tried to bring immigrants to the Río de la Plata, accurately pointing out the numerous benefits that could thereby be gained without harm to the economy or to the moral order.

Rivadavia's policies, continued by the government of Las Heras, quickly produced such good results that people began to cherish the illusion that the entire country was in a favorable position to be reunited under liberal auspices. Once again the differences between the social and economic conditions of Buenos Aires and those of the interior were forgotten, an error from which Rivadavia would shortly gather bitter fruit. But the problem of forming the nation tormented enlightened minds, and no one who held such attitudes could abandon the effort to find a solution.

RIVADAVIA'S STATE

One circumstance stimulated the desire to re-establish a national State: the conflict with Brazil that had originated over Brazil's annexation of the Banda Oriental, which had been approved in 1821 by an Argentine congress that met under the pressure from Brazilian arms. Atlhough it is true that the problem demanded unified efforts and diplomatic and military action, it is no less certain that Rivadavia and his group thought that they could take advantage of the affair in order to subjugate the *caudillos* and the provincial governors. Julián Segundo de Agüero, Manuel José García, and the poet, Juan Cruz Varela, were perhaps the most significant men around Rivadavia, to whom General Alvear was added after his long eclipse from the Argentine scene. The negotiations for summoning a congress in Buenos Aires, whose mission would be to create a new national State and to approve a constitution that would try to conciliate the interests and aspirations of the interior and of Buenos Aires, stemmed from the influence of this enlightened group. In 1826, the congress created a national executive authority and elected Bernardino Rivadavia as president.

Perhaps the original intention of the congress, which was in session from 1824 until 1827, was to mark out this conciliatory line, but the right time had not yet come, and the ideas presented by Rivadavia's party did not succeed in eliminating the suspicion felt by the men of the interior against Buenos Aires. Rivadavia knew well that it was not possible to force matters, and that he ought to avoid raising a political and institutional question that would again polarize interests. He told the legislators when he assumed the presidency:

The only sanction that has effect is the one that applies to actual conditions, or aims at putting an end to a deteriorating political situation, or at producing a naturally vigorous reaction; this sanction consequently will obtain the authority that gives it the effectiveness and the durability that alone can guarantee the public good. From this it ought to be evident how fatal is the illusion into which a legislator falls when he pretends that his talents and his will may alter the nature of things or improve them simply by his voting and decreeing new institutions. If you wish to satisfy yourselves with proof, turn to history, particularly that of the last thirty years.

This position was taken by his friends in congress, and when that body began to discuss the urgent need of providing the State with a constitution, every effort was made to avoid repeating the disgraceful attempt of 1819. As Valentín Gómez said: "The best constitution for the State is the one most generally accepted."

Thus committed to resolving the problem of the form of government to be established by the constitution, the congress arrived at the conclusion that it was essential to obtain a categorical declaration from the people of the interior before drafting the document, and this was done, although with slight benefit.

The intellectuals decidedly wished to compromise: the very fact of the coexistence of, first, the congress and, later, the presidency of the republic with provinces that were absolutely autonomous demonstrated a new point of view that would have been inconceivable before 1820. The so-called Fundamental Law, approved in 1825, recognized the validity of provincial institutions and provided that congress might reserve to itself only "what concerned the independence, integrity, security, defense, and prosperity of the nation." There was a basis for conciliation in this mutually admitted coexistence of two systems of government, and the men of Buenos Aires supported this point of view, as is proved by the backing they gave to the idea of consultation with the people, advocated by Julián Segundo de Agüero.

However, the tendency toward cooperation was limited by the basic question of the way in which the nation ought to be defined. The leaders of Buenos Aires maintained that the nation was pre-existent with respect to the provinces; they upheld the thesis that fundamental national institutions took precedence over provincial autonomy. This principle, rooted in the centralistic tradition of Buenos Aires and dating from the Revolution of May, was in the last analysis opposed to the creation of a state by a federal compact, which implied that the nation was a mere aggregate of varied parts, as was assumed, in general, in the federal pacts desired by many of the *caudillos*. The result was that the attitude of Buenos Aires delimited the zone of friction, which became obvious when the projected constitution was discussed.

To implement the theory of centralism, which was extremely difficult to refute, a congressional committee prepared a draft constitution which, although substantially modified, was a return to the centralized regime of 1819. Manuel Dorrego's voice was raised, vigorously but reasonably, in opposition to the approval of such a regime. Not that he was an intransigent federalist;

rather, he belonged to a group of federalists who believed in the need for conciliation. But the opinions of these men clashed with those of Rivadavia's followers over the fundamental issue of federalism versus centralism, and no solution was found. Dorrego had said at the beginning of the debate:

What reproach may not be felt toward this Congress if it should promulgate a constitution that states: "this must be the form of government," when that document does not represent the opinion of the people? The people will say: "Gentlemen, what you have shown us is good, but our customs, our beliefs, and our wishes favor another form of government, and this you have not provided. You have made a constitution against the will of all the people."

And in dealing with the seventh article of the proposed constitution, which concerned the system of government, he analyzed one by one the objections that had been raised against federalism, declaring: "It is consonant with the wishes of the majority, which not only have been formally and energetically expressed, but would be most difficult to reverse in favor of any other type of government."

The assertion was prophetic. As soon as the constitution had been approved, the *caudillos* rejected it, and Rivadavia resigned the presidency in June 1827 because of the insurmountable difficulties resulting from the continuing war with Brazil. In the proclamation he issued to the people on leaving office, Rivadavia made a final, fervent call to unity in an effort to save the country:

Sacrifice before your altars the voices of local interests, partisan differences, and above all, personal hatreds or preferences, which are as opposed to the welfare of states as they are to the establishment of public morality. Unite to face the external enemy, whose domination promises to be infinitely more disastrous for you and harsher and more shameful than these passing privations, which have been exaggerated by egoism and swelled by greed and speculation. Embrace each other like affectionate brothers and, like members of the same family, stand to the defense of your homes, of your rights, and of the monument you have raised to the glory of the nation.

His pleas could not be heard. Between the ideas of the enlightened groups and those of the rural mass, as represented by their *caudillos*, an abyss had opened which only time could fill. In the struggle between doctrinaire democracy and inorganic democracy, the latter triumphed in 1827, as it had triumphed in 1820. This time its victory was lasting. The men of Rivadavia's group comprised the Unitarian Party; their defeat created among them an aristocratic spirit, just as victory inspired their enemies with a crude arrogance that prevented them from being aware of the fatal seeds they carried within their party. Thus, with the triumph of inorganic democracy, the road was prepared for another form of unity, autocratic and all-powerful, represented by Juan Manuel de Rosas.

IV

THE COURSE OF INORGANIC DEMOCRACY

THE GROWTH AND TRIUMPH
OF AUTHORITARIANISM AND FEDERALISM

While liberalism and centralism were rising and declining between 1810 and 1827, a hostile tendency sprang up in Argentine society. It was also of colonial origin and had gathered strength in the heat of the battles between the different interests and ideologies. It was a political concept born with the independence movement and conserving some of its revolutionary vigor; it was democratic, as were the others, except that it was unique and indigenous. The duel between the two political conceptions of liberalism and centralism began soon after the Revolution of May and became most dramatic in 1820, when doctrinaire democracy succumbed with the fall of Buenos Aires, and the triumph of the *caudillos* brought disunity upon the country. Between 1820 and 1826, the different provinces adopted the regimes they preferred, or rather, those preferred by the groups or *caudillos* who represented and dominated them; but while almost all the provinces affirmed the ideals of inorganic democracy, Buenos Aires went on building a liberal and progressive government whose success made possible the hope of a new attempt to organize a unified nation. Thus, the short-lived government of Rivadavia emerged. In 1827 national unity was broken for the second time, now for a long period, and authoritarianism and federalism seemed to be definitely accepted. But within the fragmented society, the authority of the *caudillo* of Buenos Aires, Juan Manuel de Rosas, was growing. He came to power for the second time in 1835, and slowly, behind a mask of federalism, restored an authoritarian yet centralized regime by gaining control over the provincial *caudillos*. Formless, illegal, based solely on *de facto* authority, the State created by Rosas was the product of authoritarianism and federalism. Yet as the extreme form of a movement that had overthrown but had not destroyed the opposition, it succumbed to its own errors and to the efforts of those who, in the light of experience, understood and found a way to conciliate the interests and principles in dispute.

THE ROOTS OF INORGANIC DEMOCRACY

Long the victims of oppressive and humiliating domination, the people—a shapeless, indiscriminate mass in those times—greeted the *porteño* movement of May 1810 first with surprise, and then with mild enthusiasm. In every corner reached by the words of the men of Buenos Aires, the people rallied enthusiastically to the call, but friction soon developed into conflict between some of the ruling groups of the interior and the authorities of the capital. Although the ideas of independence and liberty took root promptly and began to grow and deepen, it became clear in the process that the beliefs motivating the *porteños* to doctrinaire and organic democracy were leading the people toward other political forms more in keeping with their temperament.

Despite the violence of the upheaval and the vitality of the new ideal of liberty, psychological attitudes were at work among the people, which, over the centuries, had taken shape deep in their hearts. If the Revolution of May had as its goal the winning of majority support, the manner in which its ideas were expressed was soon sharply rejected. Doctrinaire, organic democracy awakened the defective customs that were inherited from the colonial period and that survived among the rural masses and in almost all the interior of the country; they were reasserted in the guise of vigorous antiliberalism. One cause of this persistent

attitude was the unusual rural way of life, which led to the evolution of authoritarian regimes, on a small scale, perhaps, but
with an effectiveness that was bound to influence the political
temperament of the masses. The colonial past had a still greater
role in shaping religious feeling, which was reinforced by a super-
stitious tendency that was of Indian and Negro origin, as well as
being the result of the powerful influence of the clergy.

Despite their precautions, the liberalism of the men of May
appeared to be an attack on the beliefs of the common people.
Some of the liberals had indeed exhibited their Jacobinism in a
highly impolitic fashion. Belgrano wrote to San Martín in 1814:

The concerns of the people are worthy of much respect, and many
of their beliefs, limited though they may be, have a basis in religion.
I certainly hope that you will keep this in mind, and that you will
see to it that liberal opinions are not spread too widely, especially among
the towns of the interior. You will be obliged to wage war there,
not only with weapons but also with ideas. You should always appeal
to the natural virtues, Christian and religious, since our enemies have
made themselves our enemies by dint of calling us heretics. By proclaiming that we have attacked religion, they have been able to sum-
mon their barbarian followers to arms. Perhaps some people will
laugh at these ideas, but you must not let yourself be swayed by
foreign opinions, or by men who do not know the land in which they
walk.

Belgrano's observation was penetrating: it was the liberalism
of the Revolution of May that isolated it from the people, who
were in agreement with its fundamental objectives. The division
had led to the appearance of a wide spectrum of political beliefs
and, despite the unity of ideals, to the establishment of two hostile fronts among the patriots.

In opposition to the liberal ideas of organic, doctrinaire democracy advocated by the men of Buenos Aires, another set of
ideals began to emerge. Since the ideals were not derived from
any systematic thought or doctrine, they were characterized by
imprecision and resistance to any strict organization. On the
other hand, they had the force of practical conviction and the
energy of a primitive reaction. All this amounted to a system,

because in its various manifestations there was profound internal unity—a moral attitude that furnished the stubborn vigor behind the beliefs. The error of the liberals of Buenos Aires lay in believing that the growing conflict stemmed from opposition between two doctrines, when in fact the situation was much more serious: it was a struggle between a doctrine and an emotion, and time alone could reconcile them. The ideals of the masses, vaguely formulated and somewhat confused in substance, were clearly shown in three main areas: independence, the creole revolution, and democracy. The three objectives coincided with those of the liberal and centralist movement of Buenos Aires, but they were given quite a distinct meaning because of the deep-seated attitudes from which they derived.

To the intuitive mass mind, the crisis of 1810 was a decisive step toward emancipation. The movement quickly became patriotic and anti-Spanish, but since the rising against the Spaniards swept away with it the idea of the unity of the Viceroyalty, the movement took the shape of a narrow, parochial patriotism focused on each locality or, at best, on each province. The people's only real interest was in local affairs; the idea of the nation, which weighed so heavily on the men of Buenos Aires, did not move the masses, despite insistent demands from the capital. As the antagonism between the localities and Buenos Aires developed into a crisis, the people began to regard the nation as a mere superstructure created by Buenos Aires in an effort to maintain its own privileges. This narrow conception of patriotism was the origin of the regional, separatist tendency skillfully used to advantage by the *caudillos* to ensure their own rule, which they did by waving the flag of local autonomy in opposition to the might of Buenos Aires.

To the extent that it was an anti-Spanish insurrection, the popular movement quickly revealed a desire to consolidate the gains of the creole revolution. Oppressed and held in contempt, the creole masses saw in emancipation the chance to shake off their old bondage and to change their position in society from one of submission to one of power. This idea was energetically seized upon by the people and translated into a violent xenophobia, which displayed itself not only against persons—Spaniards or any foreigners—but also against foreign ideas and customs. The attainment of creole domination seemed to depend on the total exclusion of foreign influences; therefore, every effort to organize the revolutionary movement into institutions based on foreign theories necessarily appeared to be an attack on the rights of the creoles.

But no matter how obstinate the majority of the creoles were toward organizing institutions, the basis of their political attitude was truly democratic. The creoles were accustomed to the enjoyment of immense personal liberty. The desert assured them that freedom, although at the cost of their total exclusion from public life, which was run by the cities. When the revolutionary movement triumphed, the creoles wanted to transfer their feeling of indomitable liberty to political life, since mere obedience to laws appeared to them to be oppression. The envoy of the government of the United States, Henry Brackenridge, observing the customs of the gauchos in the Banda Oriental, wrote in 1817: "Their ideas, beyond what relates to their immediate wants and occupations, are few; and these are a passion for liberty, as it is understood by them—that is, an unbounded licentiousness—together with the most absolute submission to their chiefs, which, contradictory as it may seem, depend on popularity." Indeed, given this view of liberty, hammered out by a life on the plains and the labors of ranching, any subordination to laws and institutions was taken to be coercion of a man's conscience. The acts of the boss who imposed his authoritarian will were matters of fact, resulting from the collaboration the men gave to their boss in recognition of his superiority in the very virtues they admired and were trying to attain. From this unlimited sense of freedom was born a democratic desire to have their own chiefs rule; but there was also born, because of the elementary nature of the political techniques brought into play, the constant danger of the tyranny of the man who might establish his authority illegally and allege that he had the support of the people. Thus inorganic democracy was born, pure in origin, but full of perils and imperfections.

The people cast their ideas along these lines. Antiliberalism, independence, the creole revolution, and elemental democracy were evidences of a collective conscience whose roots lay deep in the temperament of the common people, but one that lacked clear perceptions of the contradictions and risks that were involved. Hatreds and special interests, prejudices and aspirations, erroneous or superficial beliefs were all bound together in the popular mind, which was, nonetheless, guided by certain positive impulses and instincts. Slowly they all blended into a word that took on an enigmatic significance, a word whose strict meaning was quite different from the content given to it: federation. In this word were a multitude of vague ideals, emotions, and hopes. José María Paz, a declared enemy of federalism, but a tolerant, intelligent person, put the matter well when he said:

It may be useful to note that the large faction within the republic which comprises the Federal Party was not fighting only for a mere form of government, since other interests and other beliefs were united in its victory. First, there was the struggle of the most enlightened part of the population against the most ignorant. Second, the country people opposed the city people. Third, the common people wanted to gain superiority over the upper class. Fourth, the provinces, jealous of the domination of the capital, wanted to bring the city down to their level. Fifth, democratic attitudes were opposed to the aristocratic and even monarchical views that were made apparent by the ruling groups at the time of the unfortunate negotiations concerning the Prince of Lucca. All these passions, all these elements of dissolution and of anarchy, were ignited by terrible violence and prepared the way for the conflagration that soon broke out.

The ideal of federation was an alloy of these elements. To the common people it was much more than a political formula; it was the symbol of a way of life, of a temperament, of a historical view of existence. This attitude took shape as a political movement and, step by step, adopted a set of principles that at times shifted with events, but in general maintained a steady course that was based on a firm, vital attitude: federalism, the doctrine of the union of free states into a loose national state.

THE PROFILE OF FEDERALISM

Some of the conditions that have been mentioned doubtless favored the spread of federalist ideals. The localism in which patriotic sentiment was manifest after 1810 was a function not only of a primitive concept of political life, but also of reality: the undeniable differences between the various regions that comprised the former Viceroyalty. While Paraguay kept the characteristics imposed upon it by the nature of its indigenous population and by the faithful administration of the Jesuits, and was slowly developing within the constraints of its geographic position, Tucumán maintained the unmistakable stamp of the influence of Upper Peru. In both cases, marked differences could be noticed compared with the Littoral, which, in turn, showed considerable variations, particularly because of the dominant role of Buenos Aires. The Banda Oriental, on the other hand, was subject to many external influences, while the provinces along the Paraná and Uruguay rivers, blocked in their growth by the capital, comprised subregions that showed, like the two areas cited, an increasing diversity in their local interests, their political tendencies, and their patterns of existence.

It was not only localism that favored the spread of federalism. The paucity of urban centers, their small populations and their limited influence, together with the primitivism of rural life, were contributing factors. If Spanish rule had prevented the growth of political skills among the people of the Río de la Plata, the isolation of the immense majority of the population prevented them from understanding the profound changes that had taken place in the true situation in which, no matter how separated from each other they might be, these regions existed. The political naïveté that lies at the root of authoritarian attitudes was retained by the people, and was later stimulated by the unskilled conduct of the enlightened groups of Buenos Aires. Indeed, if there was ingenuousness and inexperience in the people of the interior, there was an excess of doctrinaire orthodoxy and inexperience in practical matters among the men of the capital. At the beginning of 1812, Monteagudo put his finger on the error of the Revolutionary Junta, when he said: "Its plans would have had happier results if maturity had balanced the fiery temper of one of its principal leaders [Moreno], and if, in place of a plan of conquest, a political system had been adopted for mollifying the provinces." But this was not to be: centralism and the primacy of liberal principles appeared to be unavoidable conditions of independence; slowly, the two seemingly immutable concepts became polarized. There now emerged a new force, the *caudillos*— the spokesmen of the people—to challenge the overruling authority of Buenos Aires, and although the *caudillos'* claim to power might be debatable, at least it had a practical foundation in their closeness to the people.

Nevertheless, conditions were not entirely favorable to the spread of federalist sentiment. In addition to the fact that the geographical nature of Argentina imposed a degree of unity— since the economy was oriented toward the Río de la Plata—that unity was the country's only political tradition, whereas federalism had no tradition. Furthermore, the exercise of local authority forced local attempts not only to define institutional problems (to which, apparently, solutions were sought by imitating Buenos Aires), but also to solve problems at a high economic and international level, which frequently exceeded the abilities of the isolated provinces and, at times, the capacity of the men who bossed them. The federalist movement was therefore checked in its development, and even though it originated in a basic emotion that did not recognize the pre-existence of the nation, it was continually molded by reality and was unable to establish itself as a successor to the nation. Thus, the way was prepared for an understanding as soon as the two conflicting points of view were clarified and adjusted to actual conditions.

Of the various factors, both positive and negative, that contributed to the spread of federalism, the positive ones predominated at the outset. At the end of 1810, the provinces succeeded in having their representatives included in the Junta de Gobierno; a little later they were able to have local juntas established in the several *intendencias*, which to some extent followed the bound-

aries of the geographic regions. But this first offshoot of autonomist sentiment brought quick reaction from the cities; within each
intendencia, they were subordinate to it, yet they sought their own
autonomy. Following instructions from the *cabildo* of Jujuy, its
representative, Juan Ignacio Gorriti, upheld the principle of the
equality of all the towns and their right to govern themselves in
local matters. To the Junta Central he said: "I see no obstacle
to direct relations between each city and the Supreme Government. Santa Fe, Corrientes, Luján, and the whole Banda Oriental are in direct communication with this Junta, without the need
of an intermediary; thus their affairs move rapidly, and they
benefit from that arrangement. Why should not all the other
cities have equal good fortune, if all of them have equal rights?"

The hope of the smaller cities to achieve autonomy did not
imply contempt for central authority; some regions, however,
refused to collaborate with the new government established in
Buenos Aires, and they laid down the principle of regional autonomy, limited only by a pact of federation. Paraguay, led by José
Gaspar de Francia, first posed the problem in these terms.

A lawyer of penetrating intelligence, Francia gave these vague
aims a clear formulation that would serve in the future as a basis
for those who would again take up his banner. In order to incite
Paraguay to rise and join the revolutionary movement, the Junta
of Buenos Aires sent into the region an armed expedition; although it failed militarily, it contributed indirectly to the accomplishment of its objectives, since Paraguay deposed the Spanish authorities and installed a provisional government that soon
after came completely under Francia's influence. A question that
soon came up was that of relations with Buenos Aires, and in the
face of the centralistic tendencies of the *porteño* Junta, Francia
categorically stated his federalist views in a note to the Buenos
Aires government:

There can be no doubt that the structure of the supreme political
authority has been abolished or dismantled, and that power should
fall back naturally upon and be recast by the entire nation. Therefore, each town may consider itself to some extent to have attributes

of sovereignty, and even public officials should obtain the free consent of the people in order to hold office. . . . The confederation of this province with others of our America, and especially with those in the area of the former Viceroyalty, ought to be a most immediate, attainable, and also a most natural objective for people who are not only of the same origin, but who also are linked by specific mutual interests and appear destined by nature itself to live and endure united. Whoever might have imagined that the intention of this province was to deliver itself up to any external control or to attach itself to any other authority was deceiving himself. Nothing would have been gained by such sacrifices other than the exchange of old chains and masters for new ones.

Firm in those beliefs, Francia succeeded in imposing his point of view, and soon the government of Buenos Aires implicitly authorized the final separation of Paraguay from the Argentine provinces.

Francia was motivated chiefly by the urgent need to make Paraguay independent of economic domination by the port of Buenos Aires. To this end he had to obtain the cooperation of the Littoral and the Banda Oriental. In the latter region, José Gervasio Artigas, whose relations with Buenos Aires had already become difficult at the end of 1811, was taking the same position. Artigas aspired to follow Francia's policy, and he made this known in an official communication in 1811 in which he pointed to the identity of their points of view:

When a political revolution has reanimated spirits formerly oppressed by arbitrary power, and has torn away the veil of error, the people look with such horror and hatred on the slavery and humiliation they once suffered that no action seems too extreme if it will save them from straying from the lovely path of liberty. The citizens, as though fearful that evil intrigue will again subject them to tyranny, generally aspire to unite their efforts and thoughts in a government that promises most swiftly and easily to preserve their rights and reconcile security with progress. Commonly, an amorphous state that has been tyrannized under an iron scepter splits into smaller states. But wise nature seems to have marked out for the present the limits and relations of societies; and the links that completely bind the Banda Oriental of the Río de la Plata to that province [Paraguay] are obvious. I believe that as a result of the prudence and maturity with which the people of Paraguay have declared their freedom and won the admiration of all lovers of liberty with their wise system of government, one must acknowledge the reciprocal convenience and benefit of tightening our communications and links in the way demanded by the relations of states.

Artigas was simply following the lead of Francia in his doctrinaire definition of regional autonomy.

However, the movements in Paraguay and the Banda Oriental soon differed. While Paraguay turned within itself in an effort to shut its economy and its life behind its own frontiers, Artigas showed that he shared the liberal principles of the *porteños*, perhaps because he had been subjected to the same influences. This was obvious in his instructions to the deputies from the Banda Oriental who were elected to the Assembly of 1813. The document was a true definition of a type of political thought; it agreed with the ideas of the men of Buenos Aires on emancipation and the installation of a republic, which would be representative and based on the division of powers, but it differed greatly on the organization of the nation with respect to the provinces, demanding total autonomy for them in local matters and a federal relationship in everything else, and, above all, freedom of trade and reorganization of the revenue system for the Provincia Oriental. Symbolic of this point of view is article 19, which stated categorically: "it is indispensable that the seat of the government of the United Provinces be outside of Buenos Aires"—a government that would have authority to resolve only matters of general concern.

The federalism of Artigas, so unlike that of Francia, spread through the Argentine Littoral and was echoed in the provinces. But these two were not the only forms of federalism. The North adopted its own ways, concealing behind a political mask other beliefs that were as strongly antiliberal as those hidden in Francia's thoughts. Thus the complex structure of federalism was revealed, with points of agreement that still did not include all the variations among the social sectors composing the popular masses of the interior. Despite all, before the first five years of the revolution had ended, federalism had been defined as a political attitude and was battling the centralism and liberalism of Buenos Aires.

THE LIQUIDATION OF THE COLONIAL ORDER

The outbreak of the Federalist movement and its later definition as a political attitude were met by varying responses in Buenos Aires. Sometimes its principles were received with a certain tolerance by the liberal groups; at other times they were violently rejected—reactions derived from circumstantial political interests. But among the liberals, and primarily among the conservatives, a faction appeared that violently opposed federalism, seeing in it only savagery and anarchy. This attitude was motivated to some extent by disdain for the provinces, and in turn was derived from the hesitation with which they had replied to the call to unity sent out by the *porteños*. In 1812, the *cabildo* of Santa Fe protested against the conduct of the governor who had been appointed in that province by the administration in Buenos Aires, stating:

At the time when Your Excellency is proclaiming popular liberty on all sides and directing affairs in a spirit of generosity and freedom, striving to teach us the sacred rights that nature has granted us from the cradle, . . . it seems that despotism and the old tyranny have been reborn and enthroned in Santa Fe, revealing with still greater force all their fury and hatred in order to oppress our deserving people and to deprive them of the liberty and the rights that Your Excellency wishes to bestow on them.

The attitude of Buenos Aires—one of conquest and not of conciliation, Monteagudo had said—produced the results that might have been expected; five years later the deputy from Buenos Aires to the Congress of Tucumán was telling his colleagues that "mistrust, ill-will, and rivalry have been publicly displayed toward Buenos Aires."

The Federalists' hostility toward Buenos Aires and its leaders became more open after 1814, when the antipopular reaction spread in the capital. Owing to its protean nature, federalism now showed itself as republicanism, and the monarchical leanings of the men of Buenos Aires seemed treasonable because, as General Paz sensibly pointed out, "they have used their doctrines and their example to thrust the masses toward democracy, making them despise monarchy and consecrate republicanism as a dogma." The same reaction occurred among some of the liberals of Buenos Aires, and the uprising of Fontezuelas in 1815 showed that there were men who were considering the need to reach an agreement with the *caudillos* in order to defend republican principles against Alvear's schemes.

This situation became delicate. Moved by varied hopes and aims, all regions of the country united in marked hostility toward the capital, whose resources were not sufficient for a conflict of that magnitude. The Federalists of the Littoral and the similar movements that were springing up in the interior were bitter against Buenos Aires, some because of rivalry over the control of the rivers, others because of hatred for alien liberalism. At the Congress of Tucumán there were those who, like Artigas, claimed that it was necessary to seize from Buenos Aires its rank as "the Great Capital of the South." Beset on all sides, Buenos Aires resorted to violence. The provinces of the Littoral and the Banda Oriental felt the weight of the punitive expeditions sent out from the capital, but this method was self-defeating, and on all sides the *caudillos* rushed to strengthen their authority by embracing the banner of local autonomy. The situation came to a head as a result of the confused policies followed by Buenos Aires against the Portuguese invasion of the Banda Oriental, and more particularly because of the Directory's negotiations to crown the Prince of Lucca. Congress was then in session in Buenos Aires and was working on a draft of a unitary constitution, despite the fact that it was well informed about the state of mind of the men of the Littoral and in the interior. The constitution was approved in April 1819 and promptly disowned, which precipitated a crisis in the Littoral. In the interior, only the presence of the army commanded by Belgrano acted as a brake on dissolution but, even so, collapse came at the end of the year. In November, General Bernabé Aráoz rebelled in Tucumán and declared the independence of that province; at the same time Córdoba was giving unmistakable indications that it was about to take the same course. "Following the events that have occurred in Tucumán," Governor Castro wrote, a few days later, "the partisans of federalism have tried all kinds of intrigues and measures to undermine the government. Even the most zealous vigilance cannot keep down the plots that await only the right moment to be put into effect." The climax came quickly. In January 1820 the Army of the North, the last hope of Buenos Aires, revolted at Arequito, and Colonel Bustos, the leader of the movement, marched on Córdoba, proclaiming himself governor of the province. Defenseless, her prestige gone, Buenos Aires was poised on the brink of disaster, unable even to reorient her policies.

San Martín had refused to aid the Directory, which demanded that he come to the defense of the government of Buenos Aires with the army he was training for the march on Lima. "San Martín," the General replied a little later, "will never shed the blood of his fellow patriots; he will unsheathe his sword only against the enemies of the independence of South America." His refusal was the final blow. Artigas had incited the *caudillos* of the Littoral to put an end once and for all to the pretensions of Buenos Aires. On February 1, 1820, the troops of Francisco Ramírez and Estanislao López, the *caudillos* of Entre Ríos and Santa Fe, defeated the army of Director Rondeau at the battle of Cepeda. A few days later, following the abolition of the Directory and the dissolution of Congress, the central government was liquidated.

Federalism won complete victory at the battle of Cepeda. The nation having been dissolved, each province had to take the course it judged most suited to its own interests and aims. But economic questions linked the provinces of the Littoral, and they combined formally in an alliance—the Treaty of Pilar—in which they agreed upon provincial autonomies, a federal alliance, and freedom of river trade, the latter having been the cause of the entire conflict.

The other provinces, for their part, obeyed the military chiefs who either by luck or by popular support seized power, and each followed its own course according to its capacities and inclinations. Soon nothing remained of the former national State. In the several regions the local peace that had momentarily been interrupted by the revolutionary drive of Buenos Aires was restored.

Yet reality and the dynamism of the Revolution of May continued to nourish the desire to rebuild the nation. The representatives to the Congress of 1819 believed so, and one of them, Gregorio Funes, declared that "since the year 1820, when the provinces went their separate ways, far from wishing to destroy the federal pact that unites them, they have shown much concern about their division." But until the return of conditions suitable for a fresh effort at creating a national State, the *caudillos* flourished in the provinces, maintaining by force a type of authority that for a long time shaped the political life of the country.

THE "CAUDILLOS"

The *caudillos* were the leaders of the popular masses in the provinces. Generally unaware of the subtleties that to the enlightened groups were implicit in the exercise of power, the *caudillos* undoubtedly had qualities that magnetized emotions and aroused admiration. That is why they were popular chieftains; they had come to power by violence and held no juridical title to its exercise, but they had the tacit support of certain key elements that backed and sustained them.

The secret of this support lay in the close relationship between the *caudillo* and the masses. The *caudillo* almost always came from the same social level as the people; he shared the same life and rejected with the same aversion the higher forms of social organization that others wished to impose. In the midst of his people, the *caudillo* generally stood out because of the excellence with which he practiced the virtues they admired: he was the bravest, the most daring, the most skillful. These qualities alone had little importance, but when added to a natural gift for command, they became valuable assets. The *caudillo* received his mandate as leader not from any specific legal enactment, but indirectly, by drawing on the support of elections and plebiscites to legalize his *de facto* authority. Essentially, it was the people's obedience he had won, given to him in recognition of his innate gift for command.

Yet his authority was not solely based on his personal qualities as a fighting man and plainsman: it also rested on the well-established belief among the rural masses that their *caudillos* were endowed with exceptional gifts. As General Paz put it:

Quiroga was held to be a man inspired—one who had attendant spirits who could go any place and who obeyed his commands. He had a famous horse that, like the doe of Sertorius, revealed the most hidden things to him and gave him highly beneficial advice, and he had squadrons of men who, when he gave the order, changed themselves into wild beasts, and so on with a thousand other such absurdities.

To a greater or lesser extent almost all the *caudillos* carefully guarded their prestige and made use of their psychological insights to show their superiority. In this fashion, resourceful and wily, the *caudillos* tightened their grip on the people, only secondarily needing legal confirmation of their right to rule. "They would have gone straight to their deaths in order to prove their unwavering loyalty to him," Paz says, referring to the fidelity of the gauchos of Salta toward Güemes.

The origin of this loyalty was the conviction, well-founded or not, that the *caudillo* was the defender of common regional interests. The *caudillos* upheld autonomy against the preponderance of Buenos Aires, and upheld popular traditions against the new ideas of the educated group. Despite this, they probably would not have obtained such personal authority if they had not been so skillful in influencing the emotions and opinions of the people. In short, the *caudillos* depended on the masses and gained popular support by exacerbating class feeling. Brackenridge pointed out that the "people of the so-called gaucho class" kept Artigas in power, adding that "the respectable part of the community is far from unanimous in his support." These mass attitudes could be observed later as applying to all the other *caudillos,* assuring them a solid basis for their authority, which the cultured minorities of the cities attempted in vain to smash.

This support did not take merely the form of moral backing and tacit approbation of the *caudillos'* policies. The popular masses gave their leaders material force—the irregular troops called "Montoneras"—thanks to which the power of the *caudillos* was consolidated, quickly acquiring the characteristics of a military dictatorship. In 1826, Lucio Mansilla, the representative from Entre Ríos to the Congress, said in reference to the settlements of the Littoral, to one of which he belonged: "Those settlements are not ruled by any system of government, but only by the military sword." Thus, what was in the beginning a defense of regional interests and popular aspirations soon turned out to be in almost every case personal autocracy. In the hands of the *caudillo,* government was converted into the exercise of paternalistic authority within which there co-existed fellowship and cruelty, generous protection for humble folk and rapacious defense of the leader's own interests, and, in the end, recognition of popular sovereignty together with effective usurpation of command.

Doubtless the *caudillos* in their way perpetuated republican sentiments. But in almost every case they represented antiliberal reaction, which was especially obvious in their contempt for any rational delegation of power. The *caudillo* felt that he was "the representative man," and so too in many cases did the people who supported him. But nothing except direct intuition could justify the grant of popular sovereignty to these men, since they belittled the very institutional mechanisms that might have served the people. For that reason, although in some instances the *caudillos* were effectively backed by popular support, their authority was always *de facto,* and their policies always authoritarian and "realistic," in the technical sense of the term. At the bottom of this attitude of the people and their leaders there was unquestionably a profound love for the basic liberties and a certain radical democratic sentiment; nevertheless, inorganic democracy and unbridled freedom did not guarantee the establishment of a permanent political system. And the *caudillos,* who led the effort to regain the rights of the people, very quickly became the illegitimate beneficiaries of power, zealously defending their privileges. Estrada was correct when he wrote: "The Argentine masses have exalted barbarism by exalting democracy, and out of love of liberty they have supported tyrannies."

With marked local variations, the *caudillos* were the ones who organized the provinces after the dissolution of the national State in 1820. Some of them, like Estanislao López in Santa Fe, deigned to grant constitutional liberties to their provinces, but the majority maintained their power on a *de facto* basis and, if they organized their states constitutionally, exceeded in practice their legal restrictions because of their all-inclusive authority. No one, however, explicitly denied that national disunity was anything but transitory; at the root of political activity in the provinces lay an enduring awareness of nationhood. This awareness saved the country and, with the passage of time, allowed a new attempt at organizing the nation as a unit.

DOCTRINAIRE FEDERALISM AND
DEMOCRATIC AUTONOMY

The *caudillos* who overthrew the national State created by Rivadavia were also of this type. The conciliatory attitude of Rivadavia and his followers might have overcome the obstacles to national unification; but besides the basic questions alienating both parties, there was also the new fact of the personal position of the *caudillos,* who were now firmly in power and determined not to give up their positions. For an Heredia or an Ibarra, the problem was no longer one of finding a formula for establishing relations between the government of the province and that of the nation, but one of not tolerating any authority that might be imposed on their own power in any area. In such a state of affairs, all attempts at agreement were useless, and the national government could not continue to function, no matter how moderately it might exercise its authority.

The separatist movement of 1827—more serious and more profound than that of 1820—carried with it Buenos Aires, until then the bulwark of the ideal of nationalism. Rivadavia had sacrificed the prosperity of the richest people of the provinces to the national interest, and this policy brought down on him the hostility of fellow citizens of the province who, headed by Manuel Dorrego and urged on by Juan Manuel de Rosas, favored the secession of Buenos Aires in order to free it from its heavy burdens. The customs revenues and the wealth of each province, the secessionists maintained, ought to be kept for it alone, and every sacrifice that did not involve a strengthening of the leading position of the province began to look like treason to local interests. The problem became most serious when the city of Buenos Aires was made the capital of the nation; this not only had the result of diminishing the territory of the province of Buenos Aires, but also meant the loss of its most important source of income. Reaction to this was not long delayed; with the fall of Rivadavia, the Federalists of Buenos Aires showed themselves decidedly in favor of secession, for they were disposed neither to sacrifice the economy of Buenos Aires to the other provinces nor to burden themselves again with the expenses involved in having the national government located in their capital.

Manuel Dorrego, who was elected governor of Buenos Aires province when the national State disappeared, and Manuel Moreno, his minister of government, were the most distinguished representatives of this secessionist tendency. The other provinces warmly welcomed the new policy because, although it entailed an economic loss to them, it was a guarantee to the *caudillos* that Buenos Aires would not attempt again to meddle in their local affairs. But Dorrego was not in complete agreement with the *caudillos* of the interior. He was a convinced Federalist and he had energetically opposed the constitution of 1826, but his federalism differed from that of the *caudillos*; if they were in agreement on fundamentals, they varied notably on the form that this political idea had assumed at the hands of the omnipotent masters of the provinces. For the *caudillos*, federalism was a password, a magic term that embraced the desire for autonomy and, even more clearly, implied an autocracy that they could exercise by force to their own benefit. For Dorrego, on the other hand, federalism was a political doctrine set on solid juridical foundations. He had studied it during his exile in the United States, and his careful examination of local circumstances revealed to him opportunities for applying it in Argentina, to the exclusion, in his opinion, of the self-interest of the *caudillos*. Federalism for Dorrego was a guarantee of a republican regime. He told Congress in 1826:

There is only a single source of power in the unitary system; in the name of government it arranges all the machinery and makes it run. But under the federal system, all the wheels run at the same time as the main wheel. I do not know if there is any case of a country that has had a well-established federal system and has ever turned into a despotism; but it certainly seems clear to me that the next step for a unitary system is absolutism or monarchy.

Furthermore, in his eyes, federalism was the best way to stimulate the country's culture, population, and wealth. Above all, it was the best guarantee for freedom. "Let us not deceive ourselves," he added, "and this is a practical matter: under the federal system the public officials adopt a Spartan attitude, which is of primary importance to new-born governments such as ours, and which not only advances the economy but also encourages the love of liberty."

Dorrego tried to use suitable means for solving all the institutional problems confronting him. It is significant that he proposed the formation of blocs, to include various existing provinces, in order to eliminate the economic difficulties caused by the shortage of resources in each one of the members of the federation. Although his political views appear to have been refined and perfected by experience, he avoided making concessions to the prevailing conditions the way the *caudillos* and those who aspired to be *caudillos* did. When he became governor of Buenos Aires, he tried to realize his goals by means of an agreement with the people; this was the aim of the Convention of Santa Fe, whose accomplishments were frustrated by the sudden change in the political panorama of the country brought about by the *golpe de estado* of Lavalle, who took over power in Buenos Aires on December 1, 1828.

The military officers who had fought in the war against Brazil attempted to halt national disintegration by force of arms, and generals Lavalle and Paz sought to destroy the *caudillos* once and for all. But the result did not work out according to plan. The political struggle quickly became a civil war because the military state conceived by Lavalle and Paz was different from the one the *caudillos* wanted to establish. The Convention of Santa Fe asserted that the cause of the federalist provinces was "the cause of reason, law, and popular rights against military force," but the cause of the provinces had also long rested on military force and now two armies faced each other, both disposed to renew a civil war that was bound to be prolonged and bloody.

In no time it was clear that behind the ideologies lay a bitter struggle for the domination by some groups over others or, more exactly, by some *caudillos* over others, since those who proclaimed the necessity of organizing and unifying the country showed the same characteristics as the *caudillos* who wanted to secede. Pacts of alliance followed one another rapidly, and in a short time two great leagues were established: one, under the authority of General Paz, included the provinces of the interior and was organized in August 1830; the other, which hid the ambitions of López and Rosas, grouped together the provinces of the Littoral and was established in January 1831. It would be difficult to distinguish between them in spite of the fact that the first raised the flag of the constitution and of the centralistic organization of the country, and the second carried the banner of federalism. Both comprised political, economic, and military blocs that supported the authority of their leaders and demonstrated that civil discord had dragged all the political parties toward military anarchy.

The civil war produced its first bitter fruit when Dorrego was shot down at Navarro. Hatred and violence were unleashed on all sides; the hope of bringing the country under the rule of law became increasingly remote. The struggle between the federalist leagues implied a balance of power that only military force could disrupt; on the other hand, their creation involved a principle of coalition and organization that was based on ideals which, although in conflict, promised the remote possibility of reconciliation. Even that possibility soon disappeared. On May 10, 1831, a crucial date in this struggle, General Paz fell prisoner to the forces of Estanislao López, and the League of the Interior was dissolved, leaving the provinces at the mercy of Juan Facundo Quiroga. From then on, the whole country lay in the hands of secessionist *caudillos*, and the triumph of inorganic democracy was secure for many years. Three men—Quiroga, López, and Rosas—divided political control of the country and gained the submission of the lesser *caudillos* who had taken power in the various provinces. Despotism, many times prophesied as the inevitable sequel to uncontrolled liberty, was the political system that triumphed in this quarrel—a despotism exercised for a time by the three autocrats, but only for a time. What Quiroga and López did to the lesser *caudillos* was done to them and to other leaders on a larger scale from Buenos Aires by Juan Manuel de Rosas. A little later, after Quiroga and López died, Rosas' all-encompassing authority spread across a land that lacked a constitution and laws and that was now subjected to a more absolutist and centralized authority than any it had previously known. Thus, despite the lack of legal forms, it is possible to speak of "Rosas' State," the antithesis of "Rivadavia's State."

ROSAS' STATE

Juan Manuel de Rosas was a powerful *hacendado* in the province of Buenos Aires, whose political prestige grew unchecked after 1820. As an *estanciero*, he was able to count on great resources to gain control of the countryside; as the chief of a military force organized at his own expense—the "Colorados del Monte," or "Red Rangers"—he was able to influence decisively the events in the capital during the crisis brought on by Lavalle's seizure of power and the later execution of Dorrego. Rosas saw clearly that this was his chance to impose his authority, and he declared himself in favor of federalism. Henceforth his importance in the capital was unequaled, his power grew to near omnipotence, and at the end of 1829 he was made governor of the province.

His first government lasted until the end of 1832. In that period, Paz, who might have been his worthy rival, fell prisoner, and the League of the Interior, which Paz had organized, collapsed. At about the same time, the League of the Littoral was organized. With the disappearance of Paz, other provinces joined the new League, and they, like the original signatories of the pact, delegated to Rosas the conduct of the foreign relations of the country. Thus Rosas, on leaving power, had contributed to the establishment of a loose national regime—the Confederation—which merited the cooperation of the *caudillos* and permitted Buenos Aires to exercise a certain hegemony that did not weigh greatly on the economy of the other provinces.

From 1832 to 1834, the provincial government of Buenos Aires was in the hands of men on whom Rosas could rely, yet who were zealously watched by his followers. His authority was by now unchallengeable, and it increased—as did his wealth—thanks to the campaign he led against the Indians of the desert. The popular masses and the most reactionary anti-Rivadavian groups supported him, especially the *estancieros*, whose interests Rosas rigidly defended, since they were also his interests. This coalition of forces propelled him to power for a second time, despite his tactics of pretended reticence by which he succeeded in obtaining the grant of "Extraordinary Powers," which was contrary to all republican tradition.

Events favored him, but he had the cunning to create favorable conditions for his own plans. Although he sought only to exercise exceptional powers as governor of Buenos Aires, he counted on obtaining *de facto* authority over the entire country. To that end, he conceived the plan to leave control of the provinces in the hands of *caudillos* who were all-powerful in local affairs, and later to bring those leaders under his own influence. The only obstacle to this plan of action was the presence of two *caudillos* who exercised notorious control over vast regions: Estanislao López and Juan Facunda Quiroga. But Rosas knew how to dominate them, and with a lucid mind, marked sagacity, and, above all, long patience and invincible tenacity, he accomplished his plans.

His views on the problems of the political organization of the country were expressed in two notable documents in 1834, shortly before his second ascent to power. As a result of a conflict between the governors of Salta and Tucumán, Quiroga was given the responsibility of mediating between the two men, and from the governor of Buenos Aires he received instructions that doubtlessly had been inspired by Rosas:

Señor Quiroga should take advantage of every opportunity to make all the people whom he will meet during his trip understand that a congress ought to be convened as soon as possible, but that at present it is useless to demand a congress and a federal constitution, since each state has not arranged its internal affairs and does not give, within a stable, permanent order, practical and positive proofs of its ability to organize a federation with the other provinces. For in this system, the general government is not united, but rather is sustained by union, and the State represents the people who comprise the republic in their relations with other nations; neither does the State resolve the disputes between the people of one province and those of another, but rather limits their activities in compliance with the general pacts of the federation—to watch over the defenses of the entire republic, and to direct their negotiations and general interests in relation to those of other States, since in cases of discord between two provinces, the constitution usually has an agreed way of deciding them, when the contenders do not arbitrate the dispute.

So expressed, this statement shows a sound and justifiable grasp of the situation. But these ideas have real significance only if one takes into account the fact that at last some of the *caudillos* —even Quiroga himself—were beginning to recognize the need to establish a national government, although under a federal system. Rosas' plan, therefore, was both the result of his interpretation of existing conditions and the disclosure of a scheme. His plan had been sketched out in the instructions that the mediator officially carried with him. But Rosas assumed that Quiroga was not convinced of the advantages of the plan, and tried to rein-force his arguments at a meeting; afterward he summarized his ideas in a letter he wrote to Quiroga in December 1834, at the Hacienda de Figueroa, before the two leaders separated:

> After all that experience and evidence have taught and counseled, is there anyone who believes that the remedy is to hasten the consti-tutional organization of the State? Permit me to make some observa-tions in this regard, since, although we have always been in agreement on such important matters, I wish to entrust to you with bold antici-pation, and for whatever service it may be to you, a small part of the many thoughts that occur to me, and about which I must speak.
>
> No one is more persuaded than you and I of the necessity to organ-ize a general government as being the only means of giving responsible existence to our republic.
>
> But who can doubt that this ought to be the happy result of em-ploying all the means suited to its accomplishment? Who may hope to reach an objective by marching in the opposite direction? Who, in order to form an organized, compact entity, does not first seek out and arrange, by thorough, permanent reforms, the elements that ought to compose it? Who organizes a disciplined army from groups of men without leaders, without officers, without obedience, without rank—an army in which not a moment passes without internal spying and fighting, and thus involves others in its disorders? How may a living, robust being be created out of members that are dead, torn, and diseased by corrupting gangrene, since the life and strength of this new, complex being can be no greater than what it receives from the elements of which it must be composed? Please observe how costly and painful experience has made us see in a practical way that the federal system is absolutely necessary for us because, among other powerful reasons, we totally lack the elements required for a unified government. Furthermore, because our country was dominated by a party that was deaf to this need, the means and resources available to sustain the State were destroyed and annulled. That party incited the people, perverted their beliefs, set private interests against each other, propagated immorality and intrigue, and split society into so many factions that they have not left even the remnants of its common bonds. They extended their fury to the point of breaking the most sacred of those bonds, the only one that could serve to re-establish the others—religion. With the country in this pitiful condition, it is neces-sary to create everything anew, first laboring on a small scale and

piecemeal, and thereby prepare a general system that may embrace everything. You will observe that a federal republic is the most chimerical and disastrous that can be imagined in all cases when it is not composed of internally well-organized States. Since each part preserves its sovereignty and independence, the central government's authority over the interior of the republic is almost nonexistent; its principal, almost its only role, is purely representative—to be the voice of the people of the confederated states in their relations with foreign governments. Consequently, if within each individual state there are no elements of power capable of maintaining order, the creation of a general, representative government serves only to agitate the entire republic over each small disorder that may occur and to see to it that an outbreak in one state spreads to all the others. It is for this reason that the Republic of North America has not admitted to its new confederation the new people and provinces that have been formed since independence, but rather has admitted them when they have put themselves in a condition for self-rule; meanwhile, they have been left without representation as States, and have been considered as adjuncts of the Republic.

Considering the disturbed condition of our people, contaminated as they all are by Unitarians, lawmakers, seekers after political power, the secret agents of other nations, and the great secret Lodges that spread their nets over all of Europe, what hope can we have of tranquillity and calm for making a federal compact, the first step a congress of federation must take? And in the impoverished state to which political agitation has driven our people, with what funds can they pay for a permanent congress and a general administration?

Steadfast in his ideas, Rosas set out to maintain the *status quo* of the country, and he put off every attempt to organize the State. But if that was his intent in its legal aspect, his practical plans were quite different. What he sought was that the *de facto* power of the *caudillos* be brought under his own *de facto* power, on which there were no legal restrictions and for which there were no predetermined forms. Quiroga's death, which occurred on his return from his mission to the North, eliminated Rosas' most important rival, one whose goal seems to have been the prompt constitutional organization of the country. A few years later, in 1838, Estanislao López also died, in Santa Fe; henceforth, there was no one in the interior who could rival the governor of Buenos Aires, who exercised his authority over the whole country and progressively brought the *caudillos* under his control with threats, promises, or gifts. As Domingo F. Sarmiento wrote in 1845, in *Facundo*:

At last we have our centralized republic—and all of it bent under the arbitrary rule of Rosas. The old issues debated by the political parties of Buenos Aires have been stripped of all significance; the meaning of words has been changed; the laws of the cattle ranch have been introduced into the government of the republic, which was once the most war-like and the most enthusiastic for liberty, and sacrificed most to achieve it. The death of López delivered Santa Fe to Rosas; the death of the Reinafé brothers gave him Córdoba; Facundo's death gave him the eight provinces on the slopes of the Andes. To take possession of all these, a few personal gifts, some friendly letters, and some hand-outs from the treasury sufficed.

On this basis a national State with unusual characteristics took form, founded on a system of alliances and on the authority of an all-powerful chief—principally the latter, because, since Rosas' State lacked legal form, it was merely an extension of his personal power.

An analysis of the characteristics of this situation, and of the idea of power it involved, is highly suggestive. Intelligent—more than that, supremely astute and profoundly knowledgeable in the psychology of the creoles—Rosas had succeeded in creating among the people the deep-rooted conviction of his natural right to exercise authority. Only he appeared to be capable of restoring the traditional way of life and of putting an end to civil strife; this belief, which was held by his most devoted adherents, was corroborated by the plebiscite that he had demanded be taken before he accepted the grant of total authority. In effect, this belief was generally held, and his prestige quickly turned it into idolatry, and not without magical overtones pointing to the mysterious origin of his power:

> He, with his talent and his science
> keeps the country secure,
> and that is why he gets his help
> from Divine Providence.

So the people sang, and Rosas himself tried to make them believe it, allowing his image to appear in the churches, where it received popular homage. The vague awareness of the force behind his authority facilitated the shift to autocracy, and no person or thing altered his will or succeeded in decisively influencing his resolution. "During the time I presided over the government of Buenos Aires, charged with the foreign relations of the Argentine Confederation and holding total authority, as granted to me by law"—he wrote in 1870—"I governed according to my conscience. I am solely responsible for all my acts, good or bad, and for my errors as well as for my successes." Rosas became so powerful that years later, his nephew, Lucio V. Mansilla, could say: "There was no discussion during the time of Rosas; no criticism; no opinion." His was a personal power, independent of that granted to him by law, and he was so sure that his authority sprang from himself alone that he once hinted at the possibility of transmitting his power to his daughter, Manuelita.

Despite the broad popular basis of his support, Rosas had many influential enemies. From the outset, he was opposed by the followers of Rivadavia, against whom he had fought as a federalist; later, he had enemies among all the groups that had any sense of honor, which was an obstacle to the submission that he demanded. Rosas was implacable with all his opponents: many fled to foreign lands, and many suffered violent persecution. As Paz said: "The historian who undertakes the job of narrating these events will be hard put not to give the appearance of exaggerating what happened, and posterity will have to work as hard to persuade itself that the events we have witnessed were possible." Thanks to the use of violence, thanks to the skill with which he managed the instincts and inclinations of the creole masses, Rosas obtained apparently unanimous support. He who was not unconditionally with Rosas was his enemy—"a savage, filthy Unitarian." The fact is that Rosas succeeded in planting in the minds of the people the conviction that all their enemies—among whom were doctrinaire Federalists and many old Unitarians who had later become convinced of the advantages of federation—made up a single group, characterized by unswerving centralist beliefs and by alien, anti-creole attitudes. And these qualities were precisely the most hateful ones to the masses.

Rosas' ideology stemmed directly from a colonial inheritance that is noticeable as early as the May Revolution. As Sarmiento wrote: "Where, then, did this man learn about the innovations that he introduced into his government, in contempt of common sense, tradition, and the conscience and immemorial practices of civilized peoples? God forgive me if I am wrong, but this idea has long possessed me: he learned them from the cattle ranch, where he has spent his whole life, and from the Inquisition, in whose tradition he has been educated." The author of *Facundo* was correct: not only was Rosas the culmination of the secessionist movement that had appeared after 1810 and that was, in a strict sense, more than mere federalism; also he was the distillation of the antiliberal movement that was part of the authoritarian tradition of the colony and that retained its vigor among the rural masses.

These trends may be clearly seen if one analyzes the symbols he employed with such marked success. Defense of the Catholic faith had been the order of the day of Quiroga, whose motto was "Religion or Death," and it was seemingly one of the basic objectives of the Rosas dictatorship. The ultramontane party, represented by men like Francisco Tagle and Father Gregorio Castañeda, had struggled hard to enthrone Rosas; their faithful followers were known as the "Apostolic Party," and when the people wanted to describe their enemies, they said that they were

> mocking religion; the result:
> heretics who had blasphemed
> what is most holy, what most sacred
> of our divine cult.

Ultramontane reaction was but one aspect of the antiliberalism that followed the revolution of 1830 in France. Anything that recalled the ideas of the men of the Enlightenment, of whom the followers of Rivadavia were the direct heirs, was violently condemned by the partisans of Rosas, as is conclusively shown by

General Mansilla's comment to his son, Lucio, on the day he found him reading Rousseau: "My friend, when one is the nephew of Rosas, he does not read the *Social Contract* if he intends to remain in the country, or he gets out of the country if he wishes to read the book with profit." This antiliberalism, seen clearly in the political and economic views that Rosas put into effect during his long period of rule, was intermingled with creole reaction. If he was called the "Restorer of the Laws," it was not so much because the people regarded him particularly as the defender of legal norms, but because they felt he was the guardian of the traditions of the common folk and the zealous defender of a way of life that seemed to be condemned to extinction. This explains his political xenophobia, which was, nonetheless, compatible with his alliances with the governments of countries that traded with the *estancieros* and with the producers of hides and salted meats. It explains the devoted support given him by the masses, who were proud of their "Americanism," and who were by tradition and by inertia opposed to progress, and infatuated with the superiority of their virtues as a pastoral people—courage and manual dexterity.

Along these lines Rosas built the indisputable popular basis for his policies, and this support allowed the all-powerful governor of Buenos Aires and proprietor of its port to impose his authority on the Confederation, which was the elementary form in which he conceived the national State. No doubt he unified the country, as Sarmiento said, but he exhausted the Confederation's possibilities during his long rule, and gradually he awakened the desire to attain unity through a solidly founded constitutional system. It cannot be denied that he fulfilled a mission, despite the overtones of barbarism that darkened his labors as governor, although it is certain that he would have been able to achieve this result by other means if such violent prejudices and rancor had not been at work within him.

The fear felt by Moreno and Monteagudo at the beginning of the federalist movement was borne out: federation, insofar as it embraced the native ideal of untamed liberty, led to despotism. Rosas was the triumph of the authoritarianism that was hidden in the recesses of the creole soul; but federalist ideas emerged victorious because fear of a new Rosas taught the old, intransigent Unitarians to give full weight to the authentic sentiment of localism felt by the masses. From the time of Rosas' ascent to power in 1835, everything pointed to the advantages of a policy that would reconcile old antagonisms. And when Rosas' autocracy had been erected on the ruins of Rivadavia's State, the doctrine of conciliation began to be elaborated by the most clear-minded men of the country, almost all of whom were under proscription and living in foreign lands.

V

THE CONCEPT OF CONCILIATION
AND THE ORGANIZATION
OF THE NATION

From the very moment when war without quarter began between the Unitarians and the Federalists—two philosophies of life rather than two political beliefs—there began to germinate in the minds of a few wise men who resisted dogmatism and prejudice the conviction that it was necessary to restate the political and social problems that burdened the country. Although it is true that they had predecessors, the merit of having discovered the road to salvation went to the youths of the Generation of 1837. Thanks to their initial approach, which was to scrutinize carefully both reality and experience, they were able to find data for a more just and dispassionate interpretation of Argentine problems; from those facts they were to gather the inspiration needed to postulate a program of reform and revival.

The new interpretation of reality, and the new policy proposed for the future, triumphed at last, for they were views hard held by the men who overthrew Rosas in 1852. These ideas were crystallized in the national constitution promulgated in the following year. Later, when the province of Buenos Aires seceded from the Confederation, it seemed that the abyss was about to open again, but a communality of principles overcame the opposition of transient interests, and in the end the country found the lasting formula of reconciliation that allowed national unity to be consolidated under the presidency of Bartolomé Mitre.

The accomplishments of the first three constitutional presidents of the united nation, from 1862 to 1880, were no more than the realization of the ideas advanced by the movement that had begun in 1837. A cycle in the life of Argentina was completed, by way of the slow, difficult adjustment of institutions to reality.

THE CALL TO REALITY

The attainment of power by Rosas in 1835 was a hard blow to the men of the educated element of society. They had struggled obstinately and sincerely for the rights of the people, wishing to lead their fellow citizens by a shortcut to a dignified, responsible life; but the people had advanced their own stubborn claims, preferring unhesitatingly the man whom they considered to be the genuine interpreter of their view of life. The plebiscite by which they ratified the grant of total public power to Rosas left no doubt regarding this decisive fact of Argentine society.

The first reaction of the educated minority was unrestrained contempt for the people who were forging their own chains. But that was not the only reaction. These uncontestable events startled the most acute minds in Argentina from their dreams and led them to reflect on the significance of what had happened. In the light of the sociological doctrines spreading from France at the time, these thinkers discovered an enigma that had precedence over any political question: the enigma of social reality.

The old Unitarians, unbending and blind, believed that the effort which some men were making to understand reality must be treasonable. Events later demonstrated that this was not the case. When Juan Bautista Alberdi, in 1837, declared in his *Fragmento preliminar al estudio del derecho* (*Preliminary View of the Study of Law*) that Rosas was "a representative of the people and that he depended on their good faith and on their love," he was only expressing the result of a careful analysis which, far from being a compromise of principle, led him to propose a long-range policy directed against the tyrant and his tyranny, and against the conditions that had made his existence possible.

"We have asked philosophy for an explanation of the enor-

mous vitality of the present regime," Alberdi said, referring to
the rule of Rosas, "and we have found the answer in its eminently
representative nature." To Alberdi, and to all the young men of
his generation, political events had value merely as symptoms.
The important thing was to understand the profound forces that
motivated such occurrences. The majority had triumphed, and
the chief preoccupation henceforth ought to be to learn with scientific certainty the sociological characteristics of that majority.
Then Alberdi went on to show his essential principles and his
real intention: "A new era is opening for the people of South
America, modeled on the beginning we have made, and it has a
double character: the abdication of what is alien for what is national; of plagiarism for originality; of the extemporaneous for
what is suited to conditions; of enthusiasm for reflection; and, in
the end, of the triumph of the majority over the popular minority." With exemplary intellectual heroism the youthful Generation of 1837 prepared to reject the tradition in which they had
been reared, in order to forge a set of beliefs that would avoid
the disorders of which they must now purge themselves, since
all signs seemed to point to the failure of the noble generation
that had preceded them.

The collapse of the champions of doctrinaire democracy was
no less resounding and unfortunate because it was explicable. As
Sarmiento wrote in *Facundo*: "What else could happen when the
fundamentals of government and the political beliefs that Europe
had given us were riddled with errors and full of absurd, mis-
leading theories and evil principles? Why should our politicians
have been under obligation to know more than the great men of
Europe, who up to that time had achieved no definitive knowledge of political organization?" The fact is that the events that
were occurring were a result of the faithful imitation of European
political thought of the eighteenth century. Alberdi pointed out
the excesses to which we were heirs: "They may be found in having included pure and primitive Christian ideas and religious sentiment in the attacks on the forms of Catholicism; in having proclaimed the untrammeled will of the people, without restriction

or bound; and in having spread the doctrine of the unlimited materialism of human nature." These were among the facts that our reality demanded to be recognized, and that the defenders of doctrinaire democracy had not been able to see; and so the people —the beloved people of Moreno and Rivadavia—abandoned their teachers to bow before their masters, with whom they felt close bonds.

For the rising generation, the gravest charge that could be made against the men of the Revolution of May and the unitarian movement was that of blindness to the country's economic and social problems. Those leaders had believed that the imposition of institutional formulas sufficed to give direction to national life, but harsh reality had overflowed the channels that they had traced out with their exuberant vitality, ambition, and quick idealism. Now there was nothing to do but to accept the consequences of their errors and to prepare slowly what was called the "regeneration" of the country. The new generation had to submerge itself in Argentine reality and drink from it the lesson that would make its efforts fruitful. From his exile in Chile, Sarmiento wrote in *Facundo*: "To untie this knot, which the sword has not been able to cut, one must study in detail the twists and turns of the threads that form it, and seek in our national antecedents, in the character of our land, and in the customs and traditions of the people the decisive points from which these changes stem." Almost at the same time, Esteban Echeverría, in exile in Montevideo, was writing in his book, *Dogma socialista (Social Dogma)*:

The take-off point, we may say, for the clarification of these questions must be our laws, our customs, and our social condition—first to determine what we are, and then by the application of principles to seek what we ought to be and toward what point we must gradually direct ourselves. . . . We must not depart from practical grounds nor lose ourselves in abstractions; we must always have our eyes intelligently fixed on the inner workings of our society.

This was the great and enduring lesson that had been bequeathed to reflective minds by the triumph of inorganic democracy, which had finally led to Rosas' dictatorship. It was a hard and beneficial lesson. Those who learned it and forged their thoughts in its heat would be the victors of Caseros, the builders of a united nation, and the artisans of its institutional structure, which would be sound to the degree that it was legitimate.

THE NEW INTERPRETATION OF REALITY

The certainty that Rosas' complex ideas corresponded exactly to the sentiments of the majority had already begun to take hold of the first generation of *proscriptos*, the old Unitarians who had begun to emigrate in 1829. Their hatred of Rosas was extreme and uncontained, but from experience they knew their acts would be useless if they did not satisfy the natural political ideas of the masses. This attitude caused the *emigrados* to orient their activities in two directions: on the one hand, by accepting federalism, they tried to regain the popular sympathy they had lost; on the other, they concentrated their fire on the person of Rosas, whom they accused of dominating and corrupting the people. Juan Cruz Varela, one of the most prominent men of the first group of exiles, wrote in 1838:

> Like a cowardly, treacherous assassin,
> he waited for the moment when the Argentine
> people, prostrate, would abandon their civil
> discord; and seeing them conquered by their
> own forces, assaults and oppresses them, mocks
> them and forces them to drag along slaves in
> chain and cord.

But if the tyrant deserved eternal hatred, the masses, who followed him because they regarded him as the genuine defender of their ideals, appeared to the Unitarians as worthy of being taken into account. From the moment in 1839 when preparations were getting under way for the invasion of Argentina from Montevideo, the official creed of the federalist leader General Juan Lavalle recognized the fact that federalism was a universal desire. In spite of his own hidden convictions, he declared in his proclamation of September 2: "I bear with me no memories of the past; I have cast away my traditions; I do not want to have opinions that are not those of the entire nation. Federalist or Unitarian, I will be what the people make me." This attitude was expressed even more categorically when Lavalle spoke to the Congress of Paraná a few days later:

Ten years of exile and suffering have taught me many lessons about the true interests of the Republic, Honorable Representatives. I swear before God and the Fatherland that I shelter no personal ambition and that I aspire after victory only to lay my sword on the altar of Liberty and to obey blindly the national will of the people, the only sovereign, and to labor with all my influence for the organization of the Republic under a representative, federalist system, which is that sanctioned by the vote of the Nation.

Some of the exiles had certain objections to this thesis, but it was accepted, and the old unitarianism never again raised its head as a dogma. As the sequel to its failure, it left a secret and profound contempt for the ignorant masses, whom the Unitarians had not known how to understand or to lead—a contempt for the people, "the idol they apotheosized and deprecated at the same time," as Echeverría would say in 1846. As a result of the long struggle, there also remained a somewhat simplistic view of Argentine political problems, which were reduced, in the eyes of the leaders of the first wave of exiles, to two fundamental points: the elimination of Rosas and, in order to gain popular support, a change of slogans.

Quite different was the attitude of the second generation of *proscriptos*, who are known in the history of Argentine thought as the "Generation of 1837." Its members also learned the harsh lesson of the tyrant's triumph, but they knew how to draw from it rich and promising conclusions. For them, the problem did not stem from the person of Rosas. "Governments," Alberdi said, "are nothing more than the work and the fruit of societies: they reflect the character of the people who create them. . . . For this reason there is nothing more stupid and brutal than the doctrine of political assassination." Nor did the solution of Argentina's political problems lie in the creation of a new *de facto* situation by means of a military victory. "If Rosas should fall tomorrow," Echeverría wrote, "and we were called to power . . . what program for the future would we present that would satisfy the needs of the country, without complete knowledge of the way of life of the people?" There lay the true problem—to disentangle the secret of this society, which the Unitarians had ignored, and which Rosas seemed to interpret faithfully, if only to exploit it to his own advantage.

That was the task that the Generation of 1837 set itself. The Literary Salon, organized in that year in the bookstore of Marcos Sastre, brought together the most restless minds in tranquilized Buenos Aires; there they discussed the most controversial literary and social questions. In the group were Esteban Echeverría, Juan Bautista Alberdi, Juan María Gutiérrez, Vicente Fidel López, Miguel Cané, and many others. There they read Echeverría's *La cautiva,* and discussed Alberdi's *Fragmento preliminar al estudio del derecho;* most importantly, they began to reflect, in terms of French Saint-Simonian ideas, on the problems facing the country. It was this political direction that the youthful group took that provoked Rosas to order the Salon to be closed. Nevertheless, the young men persisted in their desire to spread the new thought. In various periodicals—*La Moda, El Seminario de Buenos Aires, El Iniciador,* and later in other journals—romantic literature was discussed, and consideration was given to European social movements, pre-eminently those led by Saint-Simon and Mazzini. This was not enough for the youths of the new generation: their militant spirit eventually found an outlet in a secret society, the Association of the Young Generation of Argentines, which was organized in 1838 from among the members of the former Literary Salon. Out of the Association came a fundamental document, the *Creencia* or *Credo,* drawn up by Echeverría and Alberdi and incorporated by the former in 1846 into his essay entitled *Dogma socialista.* In it was laid out a broad system of ideas, the nucleus of the doctrine of reconciliation and compromise that was to lead to the final organization of the nation. Closely linked to the ideas of the Association, Domingo Faustino Sarmiento wrote in Chile in 1845 his book *Facundo, o Civilización y barbarie*, which rounded out this extraordinary intellectual flourishing caused by the Rosas tyranny.

The thoughts of this Generation were quite clear concerning a constructive policy for the future, and they were no less clear as an interpretation of national reality. If their policy turned out to be efficacious, it was because their comprehension of reality was profound and just. Nothing, or almost nothing, that was decisive and basic in that reality escaped analysis, and their rigorous examination of the diverse elements of the situation afforded a clear image of the national essence—a schematic image, perhaps, but faithful to what was primary and significant. Creole Argentina was throbbingly alive in the work of the men of 1837, with all its virtues and defects, with its implicit grandeur crudely contrasted with its present misery. And when the hour for action arrived, this mighty effort in the pursuit of Argentina's enigma gave them a profound understanding of the nature of the clay that had to be modeled.

Surely the great merit of the Generation was its discrimination between political and social reality. Influenced by French thought—Saint-Simon, Fourier, Leroux, Lamennais, Lerminier—and, in part, by German thought—Hegel and Savigny—which reached them by way of the French, the Men of 1837 observed that political solutions lacked foundation if social reality were not intensively analyzed. Alberdi followed Savigny (by way of Lerminier) in his *Fragmento preliminar* when he affirmed that every attempt to transplant laws from one society to another was doomed; and Echeverría showed himself to be a faithful disciple of Leroux when he analyzed the phenomena of reality and advocated solutions suited to the environment. Perhaps their practical suggestions had little influence on political platforms, but what, without any doubt, did weigh heavily and decisively was the discovery that beneath political questions pulsated social and economic problems that usually determined political events.

Motivated by this conviction, the Men of 1837 threw themselves into an investigation of the nature of our social reality. Very soon they noted that there were two conceptions of life, and not two political doctrines, hidden in the duel between federalism and centralism. "One may say," Echeverría wrote, "that a social war began in 1829, a war between two opposed principles: the principle of progress, free association, and liberty, and the antisocial, anarchic principle of the *status quo*, ignorance, and tyranny. Both principles aspired to power, to seize the initiative in society; thus was born the struggle that still splits Argentina." This dialectical concept was developed by Sarmiento in *Facundo*. Each of these two principles, in his opinion, was incarnated in a way of life: the first, by urban existence, the second, by rural life. As he put it: "The nineteenth century and the twelfth century coexist, the one, in the cities; the other, in the countryside." He expressed this contradiction in his perceptive formula "Civilization versus Barbarism" because he saw in rural Argentina only the vices of a primitive past, which he abhorred, while he believed that he saw in the populous centers, above all in Buenos Aires, the seedbed of civilized life.

This thesis was for a time shared, but later rejected, by Alberdi. In 1839 he advised General Lavalle to lead his forces directly against Buenos Aires:

The objectives are the liberty, dignity, and regeneration of the country. Nowhere else is the importance of these things so well understood and the need for them so felt and, in consequence, so desired, as it is in the capital. . . . The back country has already twice subjugated the city people; if today it is employed to conquer them a third time, the rural folk will be convinced that they are the lords of all the people —the most fateful belief that they could acquire. It is imperative never to lose sight of the fact that the city best represents the principle of progress, and the country that of stagnation. Therefore, every time it is necessary to gain a victory for progress, the initiative ought to be given to the city people.

In the heat of his polemic with Sarmiento, Alberdi later maintained—in his third letter from Quillota—that the distinction he had made was arbitrary. But the entire political program of his book *Bases* coincided with his early opinions, which were, furthermore, those of all the men of his Generation.

The social structure of the cities, and especially of Buenos Aires, was no enigma, but the very nature of rural life was a mystery, and Sarmiento devoted his *Facundo* to disentangling its secrets. He discovered that the vast plains had an "Asiatic aspect," and he believed that he had found surprising analogies between the life that was lived there and the life of the Bedouins. The racial composition, the habits, and the peculiarities of those who dwelled on the plains all attracted his attention because he saw in them the explanation of the decisive phenomena of our history. But nothing stirred him as much as the spectacle of the forms of social organization that he found on the great Argentine prairies. It was there that the spirit of the *montonera*, the armed band that followed a *caudillo* and raised him to power, was spontaneously and naturally formed: "This is the way, through such strange practices, that brute force came to predominate and the rule of the strongest, and authority without limits and without responsibility among those in command, and justice administered without system or discussion, came to be established in Argentine life."

The plains conditioned the destiny of Argentina. "Space is the evil that afflicts the Argentine Republic," Sarmiento said. "The desert surrounds us on all sides and insinuates itself into our very bowels." Space was the lasting impediment to the triumph of civilization, since the influence of the cities, scattered here and there, could not affect the immense, underdeveloped, and underpopulated pampa. Cities, for Sarmiento and for the educated men of his generation, were the only hope. "In the cities are the studios of the arts, the houses of commerce, the schools and colleges, the courts—everything, in short, that characterizes civilized people." The city, to these men, meant European civilization, the antithesis of *criollismo*. Cities were viewed as the bulwark of progress, and as the means of annihilating native American folkways.

Sarmiento pointed out the contrast between the two forms

of life—the conscious opposition between the city man and the country man:

Leaving the precincts of the city, everything changes appearances: the country man wears different clothing, which I shall call American, since it is common to all the people; his habits are different; his needs are peculiar and limited. These seem to be two distinct societies, two peoples, one foreign to the other. And that is not all: the country man, far from aspiring to be like the city dweller, disdainfully rejects the latter's luxuries and courteous manners. No European symbol can appear with impunity in the countryside, not even the saddle, or the dress of the citizens of the cities—the formal coat, and the cape.

In such terms Sarmiento viewed the antagonism between civilization and barbarism.

Yet perhaps, as Alberdi later commented, there was a somewhat schematic quality to the formula. When Alberdi asserted in his *Cartas quillotanas* (*Letters from Quillota*) that "to locate civilization in the cities and barbarism in the country is an error of historical judgment and of observation," he was trying to defend the significance of the rural people. At the same time, he showed that in his opinion the cities also had certain colonial inheritances that were serious obstacles to progress. Esteban Echeverría made a shrewd observation on this point. In *El matadero* (*The Slaughterhouse*) he described with vivid realism the life on the outskirts of Buenos Aires, where society had a mixed character, both urban and rural. Echeverría notes among this suburban element the perpetuation of some forms and habits mixed with belligerent hostility toward urban ways of life, with which, nonetheless, it shared certain formal aspects. It was this mixed social group that most categorically resisted the concept of progress and civilization because it exerted direct influence on the city, whereas the rural element did so only incidentally. "The throat-cutting butchers of the slaughterhouse were the apostles who preached with verge and dagger the Rosas federation," Echeverría wrote, showing how the suburb introduced the belief in inorganic democracy into the Europeanized city.

With the contributions gained from diverse insights, the Generation of 1837 uncovered the crude social reality that had displayed its secrets with the triumph of Rosas. No less shrewd was their intention to determine the nature of the political process that had evolved since the Revolution of May. Although their observation of reality and their eagerness to establish useful policies led the educated youths of 1837 to recognize the important role played by the masses, nothing could prevent them from having an aristocratic disdain for the people, which was demonstrated by the widely held opinion that it would be necessary in the future to reduce the influence of the masses on political life. Referring to the men who had led the Revolution of May, Echeverría wrote:

They needed the people in order to clear their enemies from the field in which the seed of liberty was to germinate, and they declared the populace to be limitlessly sovereign. . . . But the people, being in *de facto* possession of sovereignty after having destroyed the tyrants, were hard to restrain. Sovereignty was a right they had acquired at the cost of their blood and their heroism. To attain power, ambitious and evil men often fanned the flames of the primitive instincts of the people, and led them to trample on the laws which, as the sovereign power, they had decreed, and to overthrow constituted governments, in order to bring anarchy and disturbances into the social order, and in order to surrender themselves without restraint to their whims and to the violent aberrations of their illogical dislikes. The principle of the omnipotence of the masses was bound to produce all the disasters it did produce, and to end in sanctioning and establishing despotism.

The grant of universal suffrage to the ignorant masses had been, in the eyes of this new generation, the cause of the predominance of inferior groups over the enlightened minorities. "In what respect did the Unitarian Party err?" Echeverría inquired in one of his polemical letters to De Angelis; and he answered himself: "In giving the ballot and the lance to the proletariat, which put the destiny of the country at the mercy of the mob." Alberdi arrived at the same conclusion. When he wrote to Juan María Gutiérrez, referring to the law of 1821, which established universal suffrage in the province of Buenos Aires, he said: "This system bore the fruits it will always bear: as long as the mob is called on to vote, the mob will elect children who mouth pretty phrases." Yet universal suffrage, which the Men of 1837 condemned, was the finest political creation of the Unitarians, who had fallen in disgrace because of their utopianism and their insensitivity toward the secrets of immediate reality.

This image of the people as a political entity was projected into the interpretation of the traditional parties made by the new generation. The Federalist Party meant to these educated youths not only the essence of localism but also the persistence of colonial ways of life. It was Echeverría who defined the Rosas regime as "counterrevolution," because he saw in it a rebirth of the system that had been abolished by the Revolution of 1810, whose ideals the Unitarians had embraced. As he pointed out in *El matadero*: "Perhaps the day may come when a person will be prohibited to breathe the free air, to take a stroll, or even to chat with a friend, without permission from the proper authorities. So it was, very nearly, in the happy times of our grandfathers, which unfortunately were disturbed by the Revolution of May."

The Generation of 1837 considered itself to be the heir of the ideals of the May Revolution, but it repudiated the means by which the Unitarians had gained victory for their views. The Men of 1837 looked on unitarianism as having been sterilized by its blind adherence to principles, and by its inability to adapt to real needs. They viewed it as having been incapable of confronting the transformation of Argentine society. Alberdi harshly criticized the constitution of 1826 because "it neglected the economic demands of the Republic, on whose satisfaction the entire future depends"; and he criticized Rivadavia because "he organized the disintegration of the Argentine government." Thus, although they differed in orientation and substance, the traditional parties, in the opinion of the Men of 1837, represented only partial aspects of social reality: the Federalists were the party of the masses, and were opposed to progress; the Unitarians represented the utopian minorities. Only by complementing both positions, only by reconciling national reality with doctrinaire ideals, would it be possible to escape from the stalemate to which the triumph of either of the two parties was leading. But reconciliation was now impossible for them because their long duel had filled their partisans with resentment, and bitter intolerance had been unleashed in both factions.

Despite these factors, the youths of 1837 showed greater sympathy for the Unitarian Party. Obstinate defenders of the ideal of nationhood, this generation compromised with the localistic tendencies of federalism as long as federalism fitted itself to an institutional system that would not endanger the unity of the country—a point of view upheld by some Unitarians, including Rivadavia himself. For this reason the Men of 1837 were closer to the Unitarians, who, furthermore, had been their guides and predecessors in the field of theory. With complete objectivity these men unhesitatingly recognized that Rosas, in his own fashion, had achieved the unification of the country, as Sarmiento explicitly declared. To their minds, the policies of the traditional parties had been total failures. If there were numerous lessons to be learned from the activities of the parties, they were to be derived precisely from the errors that had been committed. The two principles in dispute, which Echeverría, Alberdi, and Sarmiento had identified, had become embodied in two antagonistic groups, although no one realized that each was a vital element of reality and would be impossible to eliminate without fatal results for the nation itself. Another policy was needed.

This policy, which the Generation of 1837 defined with precision, could not be laid out without understanding the social structure of the country as well as the psychology of the masses. It was the people who had given life to the principles of federalism and centralism and to the political parties in which those ideals had been militantly displayed.

Two traditions seemed to have been locked in conflict since the Revolution: (1) the Hispanic-creole tradition, inherited and maintained vigorously by the rural masses and the conservative groups, and (2) the European tradition (especially the French), adopted with blind loyalty by the educated minority. "We are no longer oppressed by the arms of Spain," Echeverría wrote, "but her traditions cast dark shadows among us." Fortified within the conscience of the masses, which was a rich source of native values opposed to the pressure of foreign ideas, the followers of the Hispanic-creole tradition became refractory and violent. The enlightened group had believed that this tradition would be demolished by emancipation, but they were surprised to find that it withstood the blows of their doctrinaire sermons, and they could find no other way to deal with it except by a face-to-face fight, which they carried on ingenuously. Religious beliefs were the core of the resistance; confronted by liberalism, which showed itself in some people as irreligiosity, the masses and the clergy who were their spiritual governors reacted violently. As early as the War for Independence, the people of the North turned away from the revolution because they saw in it nothing more than atheism, and this hatred—later made obvious in the preaching of Father Castañeda against Rivadavia—became embodied in the Unitarians, "whose impieties, according to the federalist preachers," Echeverría wrote, "had brought the flood of divine wrath upon the country." The Generation of 1837 observed the error of the men who had led the revolution and of the Unitarians. "Do you believe, you who have been in power," wrote Echeverría, "that if religious beliefs had been duly cultivated in our country—since there was no popular education—Rosas could have depraved the people so easily or found them to be such docile instruments for that cannibalistic barbarism that has brought such infamy to the name of Argentina?" The analysis was correct, because fanatical religiosity was as firmly rooted as the sentiment of localism and the rural customs that the liberals, too, had ignored.

Thus, in all its aspects, the analysis of reality made by the Men of 1837 was wise and subtle. The result was the development of a policy of reconciliation based on reality. With the passage of time, that policy triumphed because it tried to include all the elements of the social complex.

THE DEVELOPMENT OF A REALISTIC POLICY

The fundamental ideas of this policy are expressed in books that were decisive to the evolution of Argentine thought. Domingo Faustino Sarmiento elaborated them in *Facundo*, in *Argirópolis*, in *Educación popular,* in *Las ciento y una;* Juan Bautista Alberdi did so in *Bases* and in *Cartas quillotanas;* Esteban Echeverría, in *Dogma socialista;* and one could cite numerous lesser studies and published articles in which there was a constant preoccupation for defining the ideas that should guide action after the fall of the tyrant.

As Echeverría wrote: "Theories are everything; facts alone matter little. What is a defective political fact? It is the result of an erroneous idea. What is its opposite, an act rich in good results? It is the product of mature, precise ideas." This conviction, held by the exiles, gave them the courage to develop a system of ideas which, translated into deeds, was destined to orient the future of their distant fatherland. But the experiences of the theoreticians of liberalism and unitarianism taught those men that their doctrinaire baggage would serve them little if it were not adjusted to reality. Alberdi had written: "the form a government takes is a normal thing, the inevitable result of the moral and intellectual situation of a people; it has nothing about it that is arbitrary or casual." And Echeverría pointed to the method to be followed: "to examine all our institutions from the democratic point of view; to study everything that has been done toward the organization of power during the revolution, and to deduce from that critical examination the dogmatic and complete plans for the future. It is the greatest work that can be undertaken now."

This interpenetration of doctrinaire thought and realistic historical analysis was profitable. It provided a means of grasping the direction of Argentina's social and political evolution, and it fixed on the significant components among the various currents that were disputing for authority. Soon a solid point of departure for future political planning was established: the body of thought that had motivated the Revolution of May. "Take away the Revolution of May," Echeverría wrote, "and leave the counterrevolution that today grips the Argentine Republic, and you will have no Argentine people or any free association destined to make progress; you will have not democracy, but only despotism." The tyranny of Rosas was, in effect, an act of treason against the spirit

of the Revolution of May. José Mármol translated this truth
into verse:

> Ah, Rosas! You did nothing for the holy oath
> sublime, eternal, pronounced in May;
> that's why you scorn and hate it so,
> and even on its tender sons your curse did fall.

Surely those youths who erupted in 1837 onto the political
stage of Buenos Aires considered themselves to be the children of
the Revolution of May: "That generation of young men," Sarmiento said, "who hid themselves in their European books to
study in secret with their Sismondi, their Lerminier, their Toc-
queville, their journals—*Británica, Ambos Mundos, Enciclopé-
dica*—their Jouffroy, their Cousin and their Guizot," discovered
one day that their literary and philosophical pursuits were being
nourished by a tradition that was then only a forgotten joke.
Without disregarding their European readings, the youths of
1837 turned back to the Revolution of May in order to track
Argentina's spiritual course. They found the trail almost covered
by the dust of time, but firm and deep. Inspired by the example
of their elders, they prepared in exile for the struggle, and they
fulfilled their duty by putting their intellects at the service of
what they called "the regeneration" of the country.

To regenerate the country was, above all, not to fall into the
old errors. For the exiles, the point of departure was clear: the
task was not merely to restore bankrupt schemes or to make exaggerated concessions to unorganized realities; the task must be
to obtain victory for progressive ideas on the basis of the prior
transformation of reality. This belief guided the political and
social thought of the Generation of 1837 and set it on the road to
success.

A careful examination of reality had established a basic principle of this policy of regeneration: the evil in Argentina was
the desert. The first watchword must be to destroy that evil at
its roots by developing communications, by populating the vast
expanses of land, and by multiplying urban centers. The old
political problem was retraced to its origins, and, as Sarmiento

would say in his *Carta de Yungay*: "the idiotic dispute between Federalists and savage Unitarians was transformed into the economic issue of the navigation of our rivers and the building of arteries of communication."

Solutions were easy to find. In *Facundo*, the chief task of the new government that would emerge after the fall of the tyrant was shown to be the transformation of the desert by immigration. "The new government," Sarmiento wrote, "will establish great associations to bring in settlers and distribute them on the fertile lands along the banks of our immense rivers, and in twenty years the same thing that happened in North America will occur here in the same span of time: as though by magic, cities, provinces, and states will have been created in deserts that a short time before knew only the tread of herds of wild bison." Thus one of the fundamental dogmas of the regeneration of the country began to take concrete form, which Alberdi would express in his famous phrase, "To govern is to populate." And in his *Bases y puntos de partida para la organización política de la República Argentina*, Alberdi categorically asserted: "Which constitution is best suited to the desert? It is the one that serves to make the desert disappear; the one that serves to make the desert cease to be a desert in the shortest time possible, and converts it into a populous land. This, and no other, ought to be the political objective of the Argentine constitution."

The colonization policy was aimed not only at populating the land; to the exiles to populate also meant to stimulate the social transformation of the back country by means of the mingling of races. There was a strong, long-standing prejudice in the minds of the exiles against the Hispanic race; as a result, the exiles assumed that the addition of Anglo-Saxons would have a powerful influence in modifying traditional habits and customs.

The Republic will never become a fact with three million Christian and Catholic inhabitants. Nor will it be achieved with four million Spaniards from the Peninsula, because the Spaniard is incapable of establishing a republic, either there or here. If we must construct our population to fit our system of government; if it is going to be more feasible for us to fit the population to the political system that we have proclaimed than to fit the system to the population, we must increase the Anglo-Saxon population in our land. They are the ones who are identified with the steamship, with commerce, and with liberty, and it will be impossible to establish these things among us without the active cooperation of that progressive and cultivated race.

So spoke Alberdi, eager to see the old prophecy of Argentine grandeur fulfilled, and disposed, like all the men of his Generation, to complete the gigantic task of creating a new country by the use of rational and far-sighted policies. This fervent wish was realized, and by this and by other means creole Argentina was successfully transformed.

The fall of Rosas was the first and indispensable condition of the triumph of this policy. His fall would come, without any doubt, and Sarmiento hastened to evaluate the merits of the tyrant in historical terms, pointing out that in his own way Rosas had accomplished the country's unification: "The idea of the Unitarians has been carried out; now only the tyrant remains," he wrote in 1845. Indeed, only one final effort was required, and so the Generation of 1837 argued for the benefits and the propriety of resorting to the civilized nations of Europe for assistance in putting an end to the tyranny. In the eyes of the Rosas' enemies this plan did not seem to be disloyal to Argentina; it was an alliance of civilization with civilization, and to put an end to barbarism at any price lay well within their political perspective. Above all, the young generation felt certain of its political plans and saw no danger in the future; for the exiles, there would be no wavering advance but rather a sure movement toward their ideals of civilization and progress.

Once the nation had become the master of its destinies, once the tyrant who was oppressing it had been eliminated, the country ought to march rapidly toward its constitutional organization. That was the most urgent task to accomplish; the men who had been proscribed considered and discussed at great length the principles that should be fixed in that constitution.

The destruction of Rosas was, in their opinion, essential, but it was no less urgent to eliminate any chance that a similar despotism might rise again. This danger would continue to exist if the principle of the total sovereignty of the people were to be maintained, because the majority, given the social and moral situation of the country, was incapable of the thoughtful practice of representative democracy. This interpretation of events led some of the Men of 1837 to a conservative position—a sort of enlightened despotism. Echeverría wrote in his *Dogma socialista*:

Collective reason alone is sovereign, not the collective will. The will is blind, capricious, irrational: the will desires; reason examines, weighs, and decides. Thus it happens that the sovereignty of the people can reside only in the reason of the people, and that only the prudent and rational part of the social community is called to exercise that sovereignty. Those who are ignorant remain under the tutelage and safeguard of the laws decreed by the common consent of the men of reason. Democracy, then, is not the absolute despotism of the masses or of the majority; it is the rule of reason.

Alberdi agreed with Echeverría, as for example when the author of *Bases* tried to imagine a mechanism that would avoid the dangers of universal suffrage, affirming that "without a profound change in the electoral system it will be necessary to abandon the hope of obtaining good governments through the ballot box." This was, in general, the position of Sarmiento, López, Gutiérrez, and the other capable leaders among the exiles, although later, in Buenos Aires, there were some who returned to Rivadavia's old liberal principles.

Sarmiento himself believed in the possibility of salvaging the noble qualities lying in the depths of the human soul, and of returning to society as useful members even those who had been on the side of the tyrant. In *Facundo* he states:

It shows little knowledge of human nature to believe that an entire people can turn criminal, and that men who have fallen into bad ways and who go so far as to commit assassinations when there is a tyrant who impels them to such acts are at bottom evil. Everything depends on the ideas that obsess and dominate people at certain moments: the man who today feeds fanatically on blood was yesterday devout and innocent and tomorrow will be a good citizen, once the stimulus that induced him to commit crimes has disappeared.

Out of this moral stand, taken by a few perceptive men, came a humane policy: to erase the opposition between the Federalists and the Unitarians, and to channel their ambitions in another direction; to create new goals that would lift public interest above self-serving, factional hatreds; finally, to found a "new entity," a new party that would know nothing of yesterday's struggles.

It was not difficult to find the path along which to direct the nation. To the extent that they represented defined policies, unitarianism as well as federalism had failed, but it seemed evident that there were valuable elements in both doctrines and that it was necessary to combine them in various ways in order to get the country out of its plight. Alberdi foresaw as early as 1857 the new golden age of his country: "Dawn is breaking in the Argentine Confederation, in the guise of the idea of a national sovereignty that reunites the sovereign provinces without absorbing them in an all-encompassing organism, the idea of which has been rejected by Argentine opinion and by Argentine bayonets." This point of view was held by the Association of the Young Generation, which declared that it recognized in each of the conflicting parties legitimate antecedents and justifiable objectives; but at the same time it denied that it would be possible for either party to gain complete control, and it particularly denied that either had the right to impose on the people the heavy burden of hatred that had accumulated during the lengthy dispute. Echeverría wrote:

The logic of our history demands that a new party come into existence, one whose mission it will be to adopt all that is valid in both the other parties and to dedicate itself to finding peaceful solutions for all our social problems, the key being a higher, more national, and more complete synthesis than those offered by the other parties—one that will satisfy all legitimate demands by embracing and fusing them in unity.

The new party was the party of reconciliation based on the analysis of reality. The young Generation weighed the contributions of the traditional parties, elaborated on their principles, argued for "renunciation of any emotional ties that might link us to the two great factions," and laid the foundations for the organization of the country along the lines of what Alberdi called "*la república posible.*"

To achieve this goal, and not fall again into utopian errors, Alberdi resorted to solutions derived from compromise and inspired by the ideas of the Association. His book *Bases* is nothing more than an enormous effort to find the juridical formulas for reconciliation, formulas that would derive straight from the interpretation of reality. He was convinced that "if a constitution is not original, it is bad, because, since it ought to be the expression of a special combination of events, men, and things, it should manifest the essential originality which that combination produces in the nation to be founded." And in testimony to that belief he searched for a mixed regime combining federalist and unitarian elements—the way out of the contradictions that had devoured the republic. This was little more than the legal consecration of a *de facto* situation, because the State that Rosas had created had already achieved this fusion of principles, as even his enemies recognized. All that was needed was to substitute the rule of law for his despotic will. And this desire—an old one among the enlightened minority—came to be a general aim of all sectors in the country, which were fed up by their experiences with bloodshed and oppression. Hence, the call of Urquiza was echoed, and the doctrine of reconciliation, which had been evolved during the bitter hours of exile, triumphed.

However, reflective minds well knew that the constitution was not everything. The constitution presupposed the existence of a nation conscious of itself, and Argentina at that time seemed to have only a vague image of its nature—not much more than an ancient, irrational instinct. For the men who had been proscribed, it seemed imperative to labor to strengthen the national conscience as the only means of giving life and vigor to the constitution. "A nation," Alberdi had said, "is not a nation except in the deeply thoughtful conscience of the elements that compose it." And he added: "It is necessary, therefore, to conquer a political philosophy in order to attain nationhood." But this was not an easy job. The nation, which had been created by the efforts of its finest sons, had to try (according to the men of the Generation of 1837) to counteract the influence of the Hispano-creole tradition. Echeverría was thinking along those lines when he wrote: "American social emancipation can only be accomplished by repudiating the heritage left to us by Spain and by concentrating all our acts and all our faculties on establishing an American social system." And since that society should comprise "all the elements of civilization —political, philosophical, religious, scientific, artistic, and industrial"—it was necessary to conceive it in new forms, and thus give a new character to the nationality being constituted—traits that would distinguish it from the tradition which had been repudiated. His judgment was categorical with respect to politics: "It is utopian, it is a dream and pure false reasoning to think that our Hispano-American race, in the condition in which it emerged from its dark colonial past, can today found a representative republic." And the Men of 1837 were no less critical of religious practices, which seemed to them to assure the most hateful forms of fanaticism and intolerance. Other matters were more complex, but the decision to adopt radical solutions appeared to provide an answer to every question. It was imperative to achieve, through immigration, a mixture of the Hispano-creole tradition with that of other people of different political aptitudes. It was imperative to restore the former purity and spiritual outlook of religious life. Finally, it was imperative to draw upon French and Anglo-Saxon culture which would develop creative abilities that would apply to other aspects of life distinct from those that had been inherited from the Hispanic tradition. Alberdi phrased his thoughts on the subject in an unusual way: "The War for Independence endowed us with a ridiculous and disgraceful mania for the heroic." That kind of idealism seemed to him to be the cause of all the evils of the nation; therefore it was necessary to create another human type, the economic and progressive man, the producer, the creator of wealth. When the basic accusations against the Hispanic tradition are examined, one notes that in the last analysis they can be traced back to the absence of an understanding of economics, a defect willed by Spain to Argentina.

For the Men of 1837, the transformation of society had to be at least as profound as these plans implied. Practical and realistic, weary of the burden of metaphysics, and oriented toward the light of materialistic civilization, they attempted to reach their objectives by any and all means. To achieve political stability they made whatever concessions to reality that were unavoidable, but they proposed to modify reality immediately by a systematic policy laid on a firm empirical foundation and by holding to clear objectives. They did not waver in undertaking to transform the moral character of the Argentine people, and in fact they succeeded in this to some extent. They labored sincerely, and they triumphed because they knew how to adjust to reality. Theirs seemed to be the only possible program, and Urquiza himself, the victor of Caseros and the former lieutenant of the tyrant, Rosas, was already imbued with the same hard-won ideals. The writer, the thinker, the "forerunner," as Alberdi said, gained the victory by moving the *caudillo*'s arm and by nourishing his spirit.

THE TRIUMPH OF REALISM AND CONCILIATION

Armed opposition to Rosas began in 1839, but it was sterile for many years. Yet the reaction provoked by the tyrant continued to mount, especially along the Littoral, and the day came when it stirred General Justo José de Urquiza, the governor of the province of Entre Ríos, who formerly had been a faithful follower of the somber *caudillo* of Palermo. What Lavalle had represented to the exiles in 1839, Urquiza embodied in 1851, when he issued his pronunciamento against the governor of the province of Buenos Aires. From then on, the most eminent men of the opposition joined Urquiza's ranks, along with old Federalists who believed that the hour had come to put an end to the autocrat's domination. All of them joined the Grand Army, and those who did not join accompanied it with their sympathy and their hopes. At the battle of Caseros on February 3, 1852, Rosas was defeated, and then fled the country. Urquiza's triumph was the triumph of new policies that encountered momentary difficul-

ties, but they succeeded later because of their value as an orderly
and workable system.

Despite his background, Urquiza had already absorbed the
ideals of the "regeneration," which had been hammered out by
the men whom Rosas had proscribed. On many occasions Urquiza
had called the exiles "savage, filthy Unitarians"; he had fought
against Rosas' enemies, and had struck them down ferociously at
Pago Largo and at India Muerta, but now he was convinced that
there was no other road to the salvation of the country than a
political program "based on the principles of order, fraternity,
and forgetfulness of the entire past," as he said when he took the
oath of office at San Nicolás de los Arroyos. His motto from the
very day on which he had proclaimed his revolution was that there
were to be neither conquerors nor conquered, and he defined his
views at the inauguration of the Constituent Congress of Santa Fe,
opposing them to Rosas' doctrines in the following words: "As
an antagonist of his policies, I took this opposite track in order to
unify the views and interests arrayed against him. Intolerance,
persecution, and extermination were the foundations of his policy;
I adopted as my emblem forgetfulness of the entire past and the
fusion of all political parties." It was no longer enough to advo-
cate extreme and incompatible doctrines, but it was time to insist
on conciliatory solutions, structured into a constitution that, as
Urquiza concluded, "would henceforth make anarchy and despotism impossible. These two monsters have devoured us. One
has filled our lives with bloodshed; the other with bloodshed and
shame."

Nonetheless, it was most difficult to accomplish this program.
Despite the noble intentions, old hatreds and mutual mistrusts
persisted, as well as material interests that were extremely difficult
to unite. Urquiza had to maintain national authority, and the
Agreement of San Nicolás, which was entered into by the provincial governors, conferred upon him the title of Provisional
Director, with extensive authority. Conflict broke out immediately between those who believed that solutions should be reached
step by step, and those who mistrusted the conqueror's intentions.

Buenos Aires rose against Urquiza and separated itself from the other provinces which, meanwhile, succeeded in meeting at the end of 1852 in the Congress of Santa Fe, where the constitution was drawn up. No doubt this secession was based on the *porteños'* fear that their interests were being neglected in an assembly in which the most populous province of the country had only two representatives, which placed Buenos Aires on a par with provinces that were nearly deserts, and in which preponderant influence would be exercised by the former governor of Entre Ríos, who had the country in his power and who was now invested with the highest authority. But if one analyzes the viewpoints of the men who debated the Agreement of San Nicolás in the legislature of Buenos Aires—Mitre and Vélez Sársfield in opposition to the accord, Vicente Fidel López and Juan María Gutiérrez in favor of it—one notes that only secondary problems were discussed, and that their general political attitude was the same as that of the rest of the country. Thus the split between Buenos Aires and the other provinces did not compromise the ultimate unity of the country, and neither the national constitution of 1853 nor the Buenos Aires provincial constitution of 1854 closed the doors to a future understanding.

After Buenos Aires had broken with the Argentine Confederation as a result of the revolution in the province on September 11, 1852, the other provinces sent their representatives to Santa Fe, where the General Constituent Congress opened its sessions on November 20 of that year. There the Minister of Foreign Relations of Urquiza's government read that measured and conciliatory speech in which he proclaimed the Director's constructive desires for his country—hopes that were doubly memorable if one recalls that Urquiza was then at the head of the troops that were attempting to obtain the submission of the rebellious province of Buenos Aires, which was for the time-being in the power of his personal enemies. The influence of the conqueror of Caseros was negligible or null in the drafting of the text of the constitution; debate in the convention was also minimal because the main ideas had already been accepted in the minds of all the delegates, and only on specific points was there any dissension or conflicting opinion.

In general, the preamble of the constitution, largely drawn up by Representative Gorostiaga, followed the outline prepared by Alberdi in *Bases*. The previous constitutions of 1819 and 1826 were not without influence in shaping general attitudes, and the Constitution of the United States was also in the thoughts of many of the representatives, but the principal clauses showed the great weight on the representatives of the political system advocated by the Generation of Exiles, some of whom were members of the assembly.

The first part of the constitution was made up of Declarations, Rights, and Guarantees, a body of prescriptions that set the general orientation of the political structure. Here the fundamental ideas developed by the Generation of 1837 appeared categorically formulated in the republican, representative, and federal form of government, the revenue system, the relations between federal and provincial authorities, the civil and political rights of the citizens and inhabitants, the laws regulating persons and property, the immigration policy, the regulations for the free navigation of the interior rivers, and the other questions that had been extensively discussed in books and articles. The characteristics and attributes of the various national, provincial, and municipal authorities were specified in the second part of the document, and these also were organized according to the traditional ideas of the revolution and adapted to the lessons that had been taught by Argentine history. The idea of "a strong executive power," which was one of Alberdi's mottoes, in general governed the political thinking of the convention, while the principle of indirect elections brought with it memories of the desire to provide against the dictatorship of the masses, which had so preoccupied the Men of 1837.

The constitution was approved on May 1, 1853, and promulgated on May 25 by Urquiza, the Provisional Director of the Argentine Confederation, who with these warning words sent the document to be sworn to by all the provincial governors: "Peace, toleration for all parties, and the religious observance of public duties are the principles that will give stability to the institutions that Congress has sanctioned, which it has turned over to the care of all good Argentines." He promised, for himself, to employ all his energy and strength to make sure that the constitution was respected and obeyed.

The constitution had enemies. Buenos Aires was separated from the rest of the country, and had not joined in approving the document, so that it was not obliged to obey it; therefore it was a delicate task to incorporate the views of Buenos Aires into the life of the Confederation, and much time would pass before that would occur. The most zealous Catholics protested against the religious freedom proclaimed in the constitution, but the Bishop of Catamarca, Friar Mamerto Esquiú, induced them to give it their respect and obedience: "Obey it, *señores*: without submission, there is no law; without law, there is no fatherland and no true freedom; only passions will exist, and the anarchy, dissolution, wars, and evils from which may God forever liberate the Argentine Republic." And there were provinces in which, from time to time, *caudillos* continued to appear, seeking to return to the past and to substitute their own authority for the rule of law, but they did not last in the face of the unanimous decision not to abandon the path of constitutional organization.

The problem of Buenos Aires was the most difficult to settle. Sure of its own resources, jealous of its privileges and its political convictions, it resisted confederation from the outset and took up arms to assure its own autonomy. Urquiza acted with noble prudence and without forcing events, and ways to mutual understanding were slowly opened. After a period of friction, the governments of Buenos Aires and of the Confederation found a formula for reconciling their views. Buenos Aires stated its legitimate objections to the text of the constitution, and another convention which met in Santa Fe in 1860 deemed them to be acceptable. Soon after, Bartolomé Mitre, the governor of Buenos Aires, took the oath to the constitution, saying in an impassioned speech:

After a half-century of anxious hope and struggle, of tears and bloodshed, we are to fulfill the testament of our forefathers and effect their last wishes by founding the Argentine Nation under the rule of law.

After so many days of trial and conflict we may say with joy in our souls and with our hearts full of hope: this is the Constitution of the United Provinces of the Río de la Plata, whose independence was proclaimed at Tucumán forty-four years ago, on July 9, 1816; this is the Constitution of the Argentine Republic, which was voted into existence thirty-four years ago by the Unitarian Congress of 1825; this is also the Constitution of the Federal Congress of Santa Fe, complemented and perfected by the September Revolution in which Buenos Aires vindicated its rights. As such, this is our definitive constitution —the true symbol of the perpetual union of the children of the great Argentine family who have been dispersed by storms but who at last have returned to find one another in this place in more serene times and to embrace each other as brothers under the shelter of their common laws.

But the end had not been reached. Still another battle was fought at Pavón because Buenos Aires continued to distrust the Confederate government, in which factional interests and the appeal of old alliances remained strong. A bloody incident in the province of San Juan precipitated the final conflict, but the battle of Pavón in September 1861 put a permanent end to these difficulties. Urquiza was conquered, and a little later the first constitutional president was elected for the whole nation—a man who had won his spurs at the siege of Montevideo and had matured his ideals during a harsh exile. On October 12, 1862, Bartolomé Mitre became president of the nation and began a new era in Argentine political history.

APPLICATION OF REALISM AND CONCILIATION

The leadership of the country was in the hands of liberals between 1862 and 1880—men who were unaffected by foreign influences. Mitre, Sarmiento, and Avellaneda set about carrying out the extensive program that had been prepared in the long years of the dictatorship and during the interlude caused by the conflict between the Confederation and Buenos Aires. While in power they carried to triumph two ideals that were close to their hearts: the assertion of national unity, and the affirmation of a "policy of principle."

Without any doubt it was Mitre who had struggled hardest to defend national ideals. If he had embodied the resistance of Buenos Aires against the Confederation, it was only because he feared that personalism would re-emerge with Urquiza; Mitre's policies for the State of Buenos Aires were categorically opposed to any step that might compromise the early reunion of the province with the rest of the country. This is shown by his statements during the debate in 1854 over the constitution of the province of Buenos Aires when he said, "The nation is pre-existent," thus asserting his opposition to any attempt at secession. This motto guided him while he directed *porteño* policies, and he followed it later when he was president of the republic.

It was not easy to carry out this policy. The organization of a national administration necessarily created frequent friction and difficulties, since almost every step meant injury to provincial privileges. But Mitre brought exquisite tact and incorruptible decision to the service of the nation; he was also able to count on the support of eminent men who seconded his labors, not the least of whom was Urquiza, who, with generous understanding, attempted, without giving up his personal ambitions, not to assert his own strength and thus disturb the process of the organization of the country. The war with Paraguay, which broke out in 1865, also contributed effectively to the establishment of national unity. The entire country made a gigantic effort to meet the crisis; at the end of five years, a more dynamic idea of the Argentine commonwealth had arisen out of the ashes of mutual sacrifices.

National unity was also defended vigorously and with utter conviction by Sarmiento. He had maintained from the start of the conflicts between the Confederation and Buenos Aires that he was a *porteño* in the provinces and a provincial in Buenos Aires, and he showed the political and patriotic validity of this claim during his term as president. A domineering, energetic man, Sarmiento defended presidential authority to the limit, implicitly affirming the jurisdiction of national authority over any sort of regionalism. Since he was less involved in political compromises than anyone else, he was assured of Urquiza's complete favor, and thus was able to neutralize the threat that the conqueror of Caseros represented to national unity because of his position of strength in the Littoral. Thus the idea of a common destiny for all Argentines took on life and strength, an idea to which the historic labors of Bartolomé Mitre and Vicente Fidel López gave vigorous backing.

A political movement that was destined to have profound influence on the future of the nation began during Sarmiento's presidency (1868–74). Until then Buenos Aires seemed to dominate the country, and Urquiza by his example had shown the men of the interior that they had to restrain their aspirations to avoid compromising national stability by arousing mistrust of their supposed personalism. But after the assassination of Urquiza in 1870, the political groups of the interior began to line up in a struggle to assert their power. Little by little nuclei of men of influence in the provinces began to establish contact among themselves, and they grouped around the men who, because they shared the principles and ideals of the liberal *porteños*, would not awaken justifiable suspicions. Sarmiento, who had fallen out with Mitre and was opposed in congress by the followers of the ex-president, began to seek support among those groups, and he did not hesitate to favor Nicolás Avellaneda, a well-known leader from Tucumán whom the governors of the interior provinces looked to as their leader. For reasons similar to those of Sarmiento, the leader of the Autonomist Party of Buenos Aires, Adolfo Alsina, also gave his support to Avellaneda. In 1874 Avellaneda became president, after an election in which he was opposed by Mitre.

Avellaneda's victory was an event of surpassing importance. Buenos Aires had suffered a defeat, and the victors were the politicians who controlled the provinces. Some of them had been followers of Rosas and many of them had later been partisans of Urquiza. Now all of them were shifting toward liberalism in order to keep themselves in power, but even if they may be accused of hypocritical maneuvering, it was clear that the election was to some extent a triumph of principles, as Avellaneda, an upright and broad-minded person, confidently acknowledged. But Mitre was intransigent, and took up arms, having decided to oppose Avellaneda in the election only because he was convinced, as were many before him, that it was necessary for Buenos Aires to retain control of the republic in order to strengthen constitutional and liberal principles. On accepting his nomination to the presidency, Mitre had said:

So it is that on seeing the threat to popular sovereignty and to honest elections (which are the legal means of demonstrating sovereignty), and considering them threatened by bastard leagues of political bosses who may attempt to impose themselves on the will of the majority, I have not hesitated to accept the candidacy, which has been so spontaneously offered to me by truly popular elements. I think that this noble attitude of the people of Buenos Aires, which gives civic tone to public opinion and enlivens the free suffrage, will contribute powerfully toward making the will of the Argentine people prevail. My ambitions will be satisfied on this occasion if my name may serve to gain victory for a principle that is the only source and the only reason for political power, even though my candidacy may not achieve the honors of a triumph.

The belief that sound liberal convictions could be found only among the people of Buenos Aires isolated Mitre from the provincial groups who supported Avellaneda and contributed to the suffocation of Mitre's post-election revolution in 1874.

Still the conflict was not ended. Avellaneda governed with the support of Alsina, the leader of autonomist sentiment in Buenos Aires, and with the backing of General Julio Argentino Roca, who was linked to the ruling groups of Córdoba and Tucumán. However, despite the fact that he seemed to embody the viewpoint of the interior, Avellaneda had already been spiritually absorbed by the city of Buenos Aires, and he wanted the port metropolis to be the patrimony of the entire nation—a demand that international commerce was already making—and not the economic and political bulwark of a single province. Events came to a head at the start of the presidential campaign of 1880. Carlos Tejedor, then governor of Buenos Aires, and a representative of the liberal *porteño* tradition of Mitre and his followers, aspired to the presidency. In opposition to Tejedor was Roca who, with the support of Avellaneda, was preparing his own climb to power. Roca represented the aims of the interior. Out of this dispute grew a conflict between the two governmental powers that resided in Buenos Aires, the provincial and the national, and civil war broke out again.

Nevertheless, the time had passed for a repetition of the episode of Pavón. The national government could now count on powerful resources, and the situation of the country had changed considerably. Tejedor was conquered, and in 1880 the nation consummated the plan to take the national capital from the province of Buenos Aires and deliver it to the country with the status of Federal Capital. Thus the long dispute between *porteños* and *provincianos* seemed to come to an end, with the triumph of the latter; but the truth is that in the long run the victory belonged to the province of Buenos Aires and to its city and its port. From Buenos Aires the government of the nation would raise itself above the provinces, because of its abundant resources, and extinguish the last vestiges of federalist localism. Leandro N. Alem, a representative in the legislature of the province of Buenos Aires, clearly warned of this event when the draft law to federalize the city of Buenos Aires was being considered:

By approving this project, the province of Buenos Aires will be left in an impoverished political and economic situation. If these principles were not going to redound to the detriment of the nation, but on the contrary were to bring it the benefits that have been so loudly proclaimed, then all *porteños*—each one of us—ought to choke back our feelings for our homes, for the general good of the country. But I am thoroughly convinced that the damage that the province of Buenos Aires will suffer is not required to unify the nation or to conjure away imaginary perils. On the contrary, the *porteños* are perhaps compromising their own future because by this act they are striking the hardest blow against the democratic institutions and the federal system in which they also are involved. By this action we are obscuring the horizon with dark clouds, and even if we have been saved until now from the authoritarian governments that some people wish to establish, it is quite possible that once this solution—which has been brought into this debate in such an ill-prepared way—has been given to this historic political problem, we may get a government so powerful that it will end by absorbing all the strength of the citizens of the republic.

The federalization of the city of Buenos Aires ended the process of national unification. Deprived of the resources provided by the customs of the port city, and stripped of the prestige of its historical capital, the province of Buenos Aires lost a great part of the advantage it had possessed over the provinces of the interior. It was possible now to establish an equilibrium between the several parts of the country, with a substantial chance that the balance might last. However, the spirit of Buenos Aires did not reside in the province but in the capital, and the surrender of the city to the nation meant in fact only the hard-fought conquest of the country by the metropolis. Alem's predictions were in part fulfilled, and the republic's march toward a centralized government backed by a strong executive power was soon to begin in the administration of General Roca.

The policy of principles advocated by the men who had organized the nation also triumphed during the three first constitutional presidencies. Mitre's victory at Pavón and his later rise to the presidency of the republic were in truth triumphs of principle over personalism. Mitre labored tirelessly to guarantee this triumph. In the so-called *Carta de Tuyú-Cue*, in which he stated his views on the presidential election of 1868, he struck a hard blow at the political aspirations of Urquiza, in whom he saw as always the menace of antirepublican extragovernmental power. Sarmiento won the election against the wishes of President Mitre. The new president's administration, opposed by all the other parties and challenged in the congress, proved that the provisions of the constitution allowed authority to be used without there being need for the personal rule of an autocratic chief. Once in power, Sarmiento fought against all the outbreaks of the old *caudillismo* in the interior, while supporting the evolution of political groups that favored liberalism. He did not waver in supporting the candidacy of Avellaneda who, to Sarmiento, embodied that evolution. And, indeed, even though supported by what Mitre called the "bastard alliance of bosses," Avellaneda kept faith with the tradition of principles and continued to develop the program of liberal and progressive action initiated by his predecessors.

This program had been designed in the era of the exiles; now it was necessary only to put it into practice. Urquiza, as governor of the Confederation, had already taken the first step by attracting foreign capital and groups of immigrants, and by planning railroads and stimulating commerce, agriculture and livestock production. Meanwhile, the government of the State of Buenos Aires had accomplished similar work. But beginning with the presidency of Mitre, these plans were executed with feverish intensity. Reality had to be transformed, and the order of the day was to create the structure of a civilized country in order to force society to accommodate itself quickly to that mold.

Four great problems preoccupied Argentine statesmen: the increase of immigration, economic progress, the legal organization of the State, and the expansion of public education. In order to solve the problems presented by the desert, they considered it indispensable to attract European immigrants and to distribute them over the agricultural regions of the country that needed laborers. This was the main policy among the men running the government, who believed that they could measure the efficacy of their administration by the number of immigrants who entered the country. The statistics were eloquent. In 1862, a total of 6,716 immigrants entered Argentina; during 1870, more than 41,000 came in; by 1874 the figure had risen to 70,000. Out of preference, these people settled in the Littoral. As a result, agricultural centers of some importance sprang up in a very short time. Everything seemed to indicate that the number would continue to grow, but to the extent that it grew, it became more important to develop a well-conceived colonization policy for settling these forerunners of the flood of immigrants and for uniting them with the community.

At the moment, immigration seemed to be only an instrument of economic progress; soon it would be seen that it was a factor of enormous importance which raised serious new problems. Thanks to immigration, agricultural production grew to such an extent that by the time Avellaneda had become president, Argentina had succeeded in exporting wheat, thus inaugurating an era of economic prosperity that was to bring increased benefits to the country. In 1865, total imports had surpassed exports by 4 million gold pesos at a time when the total foreign trade scarcely exceeded 56 million pesos. Fifteen years later, exports reached 58 million pesos; imports amounted to 45 million pesos; and the total volume of foreign commerce exceeded 100 million pesos. The increase of wealth could be noted in the proliferation of credit institutions and in the quick development of mercantile activities, whose growth was related to the transformation that occurred in the style of living, especially in Buenos Aires. Further, the railroads, of which more than 1,250 miles were laid in twenty years, began to awaken various regions of the country, drawing them nearer to the ports and stimulating the establishment of groups of immigrants in the interior. Yet the tendency to make Buenos Aires the focus of the entire economic life of the nation was already noticeable. The city grew; around 1880 it had more than 300,000 inhabitants. The railroads contributed to the centralization of activity, and the construction of a modern harbor, authorized by law in 1875, was to assure the position of Buenos Aires as the unchallenged national port.

Institutional development paralleled this economic growth. The organization of a judiciary, the writing of various codes, the organization of the administration of immigration, the establishment of an electoral system and of monetary, revenue, and accounting systems—all were objects of careful study by public officials who decreed more than one thousand laws during the first three constitutional presidencies (1862–80). On all sides there was a fervent will to organize the country, and there was constant activity in the branches of the government, whose officials fulfilled faithfully and resolutely the republican duty of serving the highest interests of the nation.

Education was one of the basic concerns of the times. As Mitre said in a speech to the Senate:

What is urgent and vital—since it is absolutely incumbent upon us to educate the ignorant—is to expand our activities against the ignorance that invades us. We must be on guard day and night, not losing a moment, not misspending a single peso from the treasury whose use has been entrusted to us, applying our revenues to the greater progress and the greater happiness of society, before the brute masses gain the upper hand and become ungovernable, and before we lose the vigor necessary to guide them onto the road of salvation.

This conviction was firmly held by the men who interpreted the tyranny of Rosas as the product of collective ignorance, and who put all their zeal into bringing to the most remote corners of the country teachers and schools to spread the catechism of civilization. Sarmiento, in his book *La educación popular* and in many articles, had advocated numerous ideas for the expansion and improvement of elementary education, and the whole country seemed to share his concern for this critical matter. The result was a rapid increase in the number of schools. These were not only elementary schools: Mitre was preoccupied with the establishment of secondary schools, which were then called "colegios nacionales," and Sarmiento created by law the first normal schools for training teachers. Avellaneda, who certainly did not neglect the expansion of these two branches of education, also interested himself in the organization of the university. As rector of the University of Buenos Aires, shortly after leaving the presidency of the nation, he presented, as a senator, the draft of the university law, which was approved in 1885. Through his initiative, institutions of higher education were developed, and some of the most capable minds in the nation, who honored our culture, received support. All this formed part of the vast educational plan aimed at the extirpation of the "barbarism" against which Sarmiento had declaimed.

So culminated the labors of the liberals who, in a spirit of eager reform, had imposed upon themselves the fulfillment of a policy of realism and reconciliation. They were an elite, but they were republicans and austere men who lived in honorable poverty and who stepped down from their governmental positions to con-

tinue as citizens the daily struggle for their ideals. They firmly
believed that they were closely linked to the mass of the people
and they dreamed, as Sarmiento said, "of making the poor gaucho
into a useful man." Yet, in the final analysis, they did comprise
an elite that kept power in its own hands and whose disputes never
amounted to more than mere squabbles among persons or groups.
Below them were the popular masses, the "gauchaje," which felt
itself oppressed by the new ways of life and voiced its complaint,
comparing the past with the present, in the poetry of José Hernández in the gaucho epic, *Martín Fierro*:

> The gaucho was there in his stomping grounds
> feeling quite safe and at ease;
> but now . . . damn it all!
> things are so messed up
> that the poor guy spends all his time
> running from the authorities.

And Martín Fierro ended by expressing this hope:

> And I let the ball of fate roll on
> for it has to stop some day.
> The gaucho just has to grin and bear it
> until death comes to swallow him up
> or we get a criollo chap to rule
> this land in the gaucho's way.

The members of the liberal elite were in agreement among
themselves on broad principles, and they comprised a party that
acknowledged the opposition only of those who under the name
of "Federalists" continued to follow Urquiza and to perpetuate
the dictatorial tradition to some extent. After national unity had
been secured, the Liberal Party achieved marked political superiority, but it split into two groups during the presidency of Mitre.
The Autonomists and the Nationalists were, in truth, nothing
more than Alsinistas and Mitristas—followers of Alsina and
Mitre—but the Alsinistas quickly learned how to gain popularity
by enrolling former followers of Rosas, which won them the
support of the old Federalists, who were disunited after the assassination of Urquiza in 1870. The Nationalist followers of Mitre,

jealous in defense of their policy of principles, opposed what shortly became the National Autonomist Party, out of which emerged not only Avellaneda in 1874, but also Roca and his successors. In the time of Avellaneda this was not yet a true party, but only a variant of the old liberalism of the exiles. Later the party came to be a very different thing, when it was converted into the mainspring of a political machine that was directed from the Executive Mansion and was intended to ensure to an aristocracy (which had transformed itself into an oligarchy) the enjoyment of the privileges that the flood of wealth brought to those who held the monopoly of power.

PART THREE

The Alluvial Era

Although the beginning of the creole era can be precisely dated at the revolutionary outbreak of 1810, it is not as easy to determine the moment at which the alluvial era—the era of the flood of immigrants—began. It was a period that unfolded slowly and whose characteristics were defined only at the end of a long process. The alluvial era was the result of the social transformations that accompanied the fulfillment of liberal policies, especially the immigration policy; its beginnings, in other words, lay in the program of national organization, and its first stage, uncertain and obscure, coincides with the last period of the creole era. But around 1880 the country underwent a profound mutation: it is then that the alluvial era begins, looming up with its ever-changing faces and posing a multitude of new problems that cannot hide or dissimulate their novelty and their diversity, although they are diffused throughout the society.

The first sign of this era in the political-social field is the new divorce of the masses from the elite. The masses changed their structure and appearance, and as a reflection of that shift the minority changed its position and attitudes toward the masses and toward the country's problems. The results of these changes were immense, and they persist even today on the Argentine scene. The institutional system established and put into effect by the liberals little by little ceased to be adequate, being more advanced than actual conditions in some ways but deficient in many others. The system had been adapted to the regulation of the conventional interplay between parties of the same social class, and it had assured the political functioning of a society in which the masses admitted the legitimate monopoly of power by a minority and acknowledged the elite's authentic republican virtues. But the system turned out to be inadequate with regard to the struggle between classes that were fighting for their own privileges and ambitions, without giving quarter or recognizing pre-established rights. Thus two antagonistic political lines were drawn, and their conflict had repercussions on the stability of the institutional system.

In response to the confused opinions of the new masses—in part backward and in part progressive—that were forming below the ruling minority, the liberals became increasingly aristocratic and conservative. The masses in turn adopted popular, democratic attitudes that in part coincided with the ideals of liberalism and in part opposed them. Diverse groups successfully took up each of these banners and threw themselves into the struggle in defense of either the entire set of partisan principles or, at times, the particular idea that might be attracting the widest support.

The struggle between these different elements (the popular democratic group soon split into various factions) extends down to our own day. We are still involved in the combat, although it is not given to us to foresee how it will work out in its final stages. The cycle of alluvial Argentina is still unfinished. It offers us only questions and enigmas; yet in diagnosing an era, one finds a great deal of value in identifying objectively the hostile elements that struggle in its depths. On the result of this contest depends the historic course that the republic will follow—its near future and its distant destiny, at once promising and menacing.

VI

ARGENTINA IN THE ALLUVIAL ERA

Because of the stability of its elements—the result of the inter-play of clearly defined social forces—creole Argentina followed an orderly social evolution during the first half-century after in-dependence had been achieved. The profile of political life be-gan to alter after 1853 because a profound change had occurred in the composition of society—a change that was the product of the liberal policies then beginning to be resolutely and energeti-cally put into effect.

Even at the risk of describing this change with a precision it lacks (as do almost all social processes), one can point to the transition from Avellaneda's presidency to Roca's as the start of a new era in Argentina's social evolution. In that period the deep-seated disturbances taking place among the various strata of society become obvious, and one notes that the social structure blurs, alters, and assumes different forms. Agustín Alvarez ob-served in 1894 that Argentina was "a new country, rapidly emerg-ing from barbarism, a land that is changing every five years be-cause of immigration, schools, and railroads, so that, as with children, one who does not see them grow does not recognize them." Indeed, the changes stemmed from an uninterrupted process that started soon after the fall of Rosas, developed slowly during the twenty years following the organization of the unified nation, and manifested itself on the surface of national life be-ginning in 1880. Henceforth, the disequilibrium among the social and economic elements, which comprised Argentine reality, was to be increasingly accentuated and marked by foreign characteristics.

There is nothing more difficult than to define the nature of a social complex that is being formed and altered at the same time in a continuing process of readjustment. But there is nothing more necessary to an understanding of the panorama of the political ideas of this period—a cycle in which the country still finds itself—than to analyze the factors that have contributed to shaping that era, especially its economic and social elements. Without first understanding the transformation of reality that then occurred, one cannot appreciate the significance and the transcendent importance of the political phenomena of the alluvial era.

THE ECONOMIC TRANSFORMATION

In the process of transforming reality, undertaken by the liberal statesmen to modify the rudimentary forms of social life, a preferential position was given to demographic policy. Alberdi had categorically asserted that to populate the land was the chief mission of the State in a country whose ills came almost entirely from the dominant fact of its "deserts." Sarmiento had dreamed of quickly multiplying the population, auguring a happy destiny for the country if his ideas should be carried out. These objectives, if they were not in fact achieved to the extent hoped for, were fulfilled to some degree.

In the half-century between 1810 and 1859—the approximate period that may be called the creole era—the population of the country had grown from 405,000 inhabitants to 1,300,000 inhabitants. This growth, which was almost exclusively by natural increase, amounted to slightly less than 900,000 persons in a half-century, that is, a rate of 18,000 people per year. No doubt this was an insignificant figure of natural growth for a territory of almost 1,000,000 square miles, and it could not be assumed that the country would emerge from its desert-like condition by following only this course. This conclusion counseled the development of a positive immigration policy, and the Argentine State put that policy into effect beginning with the first days of the organization of the republic.

The results were visible and significant. With a rising rhythm the waves of immigrants kept on arriving in the country, thanks to both an active propaganda campaign and the financial guarantees offered by the State. The numbers of immigrants reached very high levels. During the first presidency of General Roca (1880–86), a total of 483,000 immigrants entered the country, and this average of more than 80,000 persons per year was exceeded on several occasions, reaching 261,000 people in 1889, and an even larger figure in 1906. Italians and Spaniards predominated, and to them were added lesser contingents of people of diverse origins. This river of immigrants, which also stimulated the natural increase of the population, resulted in a rapid demographic change.

The first national census, taken in 1869, had shown a population of 1,830,214 inhabitants. Twenty-six years later, in 1895, this number had reached 3,956,060 inhabitants, an increase of more than two million people, and an average of 81,700 persons per year. Of that total, more than one million were foreigners, almost all of them immigrants, which gives an idea of the rapid transformation of Argentine society, especially if one realizes that in 1869 there had been scarcely 300,000 foreigners in the country. The percentage of foreigners had climbed from 16.6 per cent to 25.4 per cent, and the effects of this circumstance were to become even more accentuated. The census of 1914 gave a population of 7,885,237; the increase of almost four million people in a period of nineteen years is an average growth of 207,000 inhabitants per year, and the proportion of foreigners rose to more than 30 per cent of the total population. And in the sixteen years that elapsed up to 1930, the population kept on growing at an annual average of 223,000 inhabitants, until it reached the figure of 11,452,374 people. (In 1960 the population was estimated to be 21 million.)

This growing population tended to accumulate in the Littoral, and preferentially in the urban centers. The relative size of the rural population, which, if a sound colonization policy had been followed, ought to have increased, diminished markedly: in 1869 it represented 65.8 per cent of the total population, but in 1895 it amounted to no more than 57.2 per cent, and in 1914 to only 42.6 per cent—a declining curve that became even more pronounced until by 1960 the rural population was only about 25 per cent of the total.

The tendency to urban concentration may be noted particularly in the city of Buenos Aires, which had only 85,400 inhabitants in 1852, but which began a disproportionate and dizzying growth in 1870. By 1889, Buenos Aires had more than 500,000 inhabitants, and it doubled its population in less than twenty years, reaching a figure of 1,244,000 in 1909. In the next twenty years the population again doubled. Although the city did not keep up this pace, it continued to grow out of proportion to the rest of the country. The majority of the foreigners settled in the city, which developed the largest share of the nation's economic activity. As a corollary, the interior regions of the country, particularly the Northwest, showed a stagnation of their population, indicating their economic stagnation. The immigrants settled there only on a very small scale, and the creole element retained all its traditional characteristics. Thus a considerable contrast began to appear between the interior and the Littoral, a difference that became one of the social peculiarities of the country.

The growth of population, together with other causes, set off an intensive development of national resources. Ranching long continued to be the basic activity, but its character changed, thanks to improved stockbreeding. Soon a livestock industry emerged, which opened new horizons for national commerce, especially when the exportation of meat in refrigerated ships became possible. However, the activity which most benefited from the new population of immigrant origin was agriculture. Starting with the founding of the colony of Esperanza—Hope—in 1856 in the province of Santa Fe, important agricultural settlements sprang up in the Littoral. Not without difficulties the fencing of the fields with wire in order to protect them from livestock was undertaken, and the cultivated areas were expanded and improved. In 1880 the extent of cultivated land amounted to 4,940,000 acres; in 1895 the area had grown to 15,350,000 acres; in 1905, to 30,640,000; in 1923, to 50,820,000; and in 1960 it reached approximately 74,000,000 acres. The expansion of agriculture, which had notable effects on the enrichment of the nation, followed an appreciable subdivision of landholdings. Nevertheless, over vast regions there continued to exist—and still exist—extensive *latifundios*, which, no doubt, were required for cattle raising, but which were maintained principally by the stubborn, defensive policies of the *terrateniente*, or landlord, class. Growing activity could also be observed in the exploitation of mineral wealth, notably petroleum, beginning in 1907, but that activity could not compare with the wealth in agriculture and livestock, particularly if one takes account of the export of surpluses.

Industrial activity began to grow after 1880. By 1895, the number of industrial establishments in the nation had reached 24,114, employing 175,000 workers; the number of factories had doubled by 1913, and they employed 410,000 workers. The amount of capital invested in industry had quintupled. But this expansion was far from reaching the proportions acquired by foreign trade. From the time when the exportation of grain had begun during the presidency of Avellaneda, international trade had shown a rapid increase of exports and a proportionate and no less rapid increase of imports. The figures for the total value of trade indicate the intensity of this economic activity and the growing volume of invested capital. The total value of international trade had been 104,000,000 pesos in 1880. It climbed to 254,000,000 pesos in 1889; after the financial and political crisis in the early 1890's, it reached 241,00,000 pesos in 1898, and 724,000,000 pesos in 1910. In addition to the specie in circulation, bank credit expanded, as much because of the needs of increased production as because of speculation, and the total of foreign loans which were assumed by Argentina—loans used mainly for the construction of public works—reached very important figures.

In the latter regard the chief concern was to extend the railroad network. General Roca told the Congress in his inaugural address in 1880:

Anyone who has attentively followed the progress of this country has been able to notice, as you Honorable Gentlemen know, the profound economic, social, and political revolution that the iron road and the telegraph bring as they penetrate the interior. National unity has been assured by these powerful agents of civilization; they have conquered and exterminated the spirit of the *montonera* and have made possible the solution of problems which seemed insoluble, at least up to the present. Rich and fertile provinces await only the arrival of the railroad to multiply their productive forces one hundredfold by the easy means offered to them to carry to the markets and the ports of the Littoral their varied and excellent products, which include all that nature affords.

This conviction guided Roca's economic policy. The 1,440 miles of railroad that existed when he took office had risen to 3,720 miles when his administration ended in 1886. Four years later, when the revolution of 1890 broke out during the administration of Juárez Celman, the railroad network had increased to 5,850 miles, and it reached 12,200 miles at the end of Roca's second presidency in 1904. In the same period, large amounts of money were being invested in other types of construction—bridges, dams, public buildings, and, above all, the building of the port of Buenos Aires. These cost enormous sums which the State obtained through its internal and external credit, in the certainty that prosperity was a law of Argentine economic development.

Widespread optimism led to the abuse of credit, and the economic situation became serious in 1889. A terrible financial crisis struck the nation, producing innumerable bankruptcies that soon made their influence felt on the government's revenues. In the years immediately preceding the crisis there had been a considerable growth of imports compared with exports, with the resulting impact on commercial balances. In 1887, 117 million pesos worth of goods had been imported, compared with a total of 84 million pesos worth of exports. In 1880 the figures were 128 million pesos as against 100 million, and in 1889 they reached 164 million pesos in comparison with 90 million pesos. In their turn, government expenditures continued to mount out of all proportion to revenues. To meet the expenditure in 1887 of 48 million gold pesos, the treasury had an income of only 38 million pesos. The disproportion was accentuated in 1889 when, with the same amount of revenue the government had to meet expenses totaling more than 55 million pesos. The consequence was inevitable: the government began to issue unbacked currency, and the value of the peso began to depreciate alarmingly. The peso, which in 1886 had been worth .71 of the gold peso, reached a value of .40 in 1890, with a tendency to go lower, which in fact occurred: in 1892 it was worth .30, and in 1894 it was worth .28. But gradually it was brought into equilibrium, mainly because of the steps taken by President Carlos Pellegrini (1890–92), and the currency was finally stabilized at the same time that the financial and economic situation and government revenues became normal. After this crisis, which affected the political life of the country and caused the revolution of 1890, the nation again set out on the road of economic prosperity that it followed until 1920, a period during which the balance of foreign trade was almost always favorable to Argentina.

Even a hasty survey of the economic transformation of Argentina shows the overwhelming effect that these changes were bound to have on society. If the population structure was being altered by the rapid incursion of foreign elements that could not be easily incorporated into the social complex, the new economic developments were also causing a no less profound upheaval in the social system. Of creole Argentina, ethnically and socially homogeneous and economically primitive, there soon remained only a vague memory, preserved melancholically by those who were losing their influence in the nation. Beginning approximately with the year 1880, alluvial Argentina, the Argentina formed as a result of that upheaval, begins to grow, expand, and struggle to find a balance that, obviously, it could not achieve without the aid of time. Meanwhile, the social and political history of Argentina evolved to the rhythm of that attempt at stability, and in a manner that reveals its essential instability.

THE MORAL CONFIGURATION OF
THE NEW SOCIAL REALITY

The social reality created by the flood of immigrants who entered creole society took on the characteristics of a conglomerate mass, that is, of an unformed body in which the relations between the parts, and the nature of the whole, are undefined. The inundation of immigrants added some strange characteristics to the Argentine scene, but the immigrants quickly came into contact with the creole mass, and reciprocal influences that would modify both groups stemmed from their relationship.

The psychology of the immigrants was determined by the motives that had caused them to abandon their native lands to risk the American adventure. The impelling force, above all, had been economic; it arose from the certainty that life in America offered limitless opportunities to those who would make bold efforts, efforts that in areas of less intensive economic development produced only slim benefits. Wealth was thus the decisive motive, and everything that stood in the way of its attainment seemed to have little value.

At the outset the immigrants were in an excellent position to get rich. In the wide-open economy the capacity for individual enterprise among those who were disposed to run the risks was bound to bring success, and their chances were further improved by the habit of hard work that had characterized them in their homelands. They did triumph in most cases, and a moneyed class soon appeared with a psychology marked by excessive esteem for economic success. That was not the only peculiarity, however. The immigrant had simultaneously broken his ties with his birthplace and abandoned the system of norms and principles that had regulated his conduct. Both as a citizen and as an ethical being, the immigrant was a person uprooted, to whom his adopted country, because of its scanty population and level of development, could not offer an explicit, fixed, social and moral structure to replace that of the land he had forsaken. The immigrant began to move between two worlds. His situation led him to adopt an unusual psychological attitude, which Sarmiento described as an early result of Argentina's immigration policy:

The immigrant to South America dreams daily of returning to his homeland, which he idealizes in his fantasies. His adopted land seems to be a valley of toil in which he prepares for a better life. But the years pass; his affairs go on, tying him insensibly to the land; his family binds him indissolubly to the country; his hair turns white—but he still believes that he will return one day to the fatherland of his golden dreams. And when one out of a thousand at last returns to his birth-place, he finds that the homeland is no longer his homeland. He is a stranger there, yet he has left behind in his adopted country the status, pleasures, and affections that nothing else can provide. Thus, living two lives, he does not enjoy one and he cannot enjoy the other. He is a citizen of neither of his two countries, and he is unfaithful to both, failing to fulfill the obligations that the fatherland and the new land impose on those who are born and live in them. He is everywhere a stranger.

The immigrant's disequilibrium could find no resting place except in economic success. The immigrant preferred to feel like a stranger because he could thus appear to assert his superior economic abilities, and in so doing to claim a victory over the creoles, who went on living in their own manner, in poverty but not in degradation, and fully meeting their psychological needs. "In Buenos Aires," Sarmiento commented, "a transformation is worked on the obscure immigrant who lands here beaten down, dressed as a laborer or worse, and frightened by the great city. First, he becomes a man conscious of his own worth; then, he is a Frenchman, an Italian, or a Spaniard, according to his place of origin; next, he is a foreigner, with a position and dignity; and in the end, he who began as a mere laborer turns out to be supe-rior to everyone around."

Such self-satisfaction was understandable. The immigrant was creating an economic system in which he would play a leading role, and he was breaking down the indigenous order in which the creoles were able to retain their humble dignity and their modest pleasures. When the two modes of economic existence came into contact, defeat was inevitable for the traditional order, and the victory of the new system was certain. The result was to awaken hostility, which the creole showed in the quiet contempt with which he referred to the immigrants as "gringos." The fact was that the immigrant was displacing the creole by setting a standard of economic efficiency that put the latter in an inferior economic position and would also soon put him on a subordinate social level.

A rapid intermingling nevertheless began to occur between the immigrant and creole masses. If this was very common at the lower ranks of society, it was no less so among the members of the middle class that was then beginning to appear and was made up to a large extent precisely of the immigrants whose economic success was leading to their rise in society. José S. Alvarez, in his *Cuentos de Fray Mocho* (*Tales of Friar Mocho*), testifies with subtle irony to the social significance of this phenomenon. He describes the Argentine middle class—which was slowly emerging in the alluvial era, and whose characteristics, although still unclear, showed the co-existence of both creole and immigrant ideals —sometimes in conflict, sometimes in a process of fusing, sometimes parallel to each other, but never ceasing to work toward their ultimate mutual adaptation.

The creole minority could not isolate itself from the rising tide of immigration; in a few generations they would be mixed with the descendants of the immigrants. But the creoles made an effort to conserve at least the traditional inheritance of *criollismo* by consciously overvaluing their customs. Their feeling for leisurely living, the absence of concern for economic goals, their rustic habits, and so many other traits that stemmed from the old rural and patriarchal attitude toward life would come to be hallmarks of elegance and be considered indispensable for anyone who aspired to take the final step toward winning social status. In the middle class, on the other hand, the economic and social ideals of the immigrants took root more solidly, while in the less-privileged class (even though the immigrants and their descendants were numerically dominant) creole characteristics survived with some strength, perhaps more as rhetoric, but also with the energy of an elemental tradition founded on natural conditions of existence. In the cities, toward the end of the century, popular dances and songs took on hybrid forms, showing the antagonism between new patterns of daily life and an existence which seemed to spring from the earth itself. Thus the Argentine tango emerged, its rhythmic, melodic, and literary components saturated with creole spirit, but laden also with hints of the vital blends of immigrants and creoles.

Buenos Aires was the backdrop against which the destiny of this human conglomeration was worked out. As Sarmiento asked shortly before his death:

Who are the citizens of this El Dorado that was foreseen by the *conquistadores* of long ago? It is a city without citizens. The most industrious and progressive of its 400,000 inhabitants are strangers who, the more one recognizes them as the artisans of its transformation, themselves remain unchanged in their roles as instruments, makers, builders. Cities are built as cloth is woven, for the use of those who need them; thus a great city of America is produced, a city that is for rent, one in which few have any stake, a world on the march, created by people who leave Europe as ripe fruit separates from the branch, to be carried to these shores by the trade winds. Growing and expanding, we shall build, if we have not already built, a Tower of Babel in America, its workmen speaking all tongues, not blending them together in the task of construction but each persisting in his own, and thus unable to understand the other. And so the world's great hope for the future against a new cataclysm and flood will be dissipated by the winds of vulgar events—prolonged drought or foreign or civil war. One does not construct a homeland without patriotism as its cement, nor does one build as the soul and glory of nations a city without citizens.

So Sarmiento, one of the proponents of immigration and of unlimited economic progress, lamented the gross manner in which his plans were being implemented, to the peril of Argentine nationalism. Another of the artisans of progress, Roca, roundly affirmed that Buenos Aires was not part of the nation, "because it is a province of foreigners." But neither he nor other members of the oligarchy who long ruled the country were able, or wished, to do anything to direct a larger number of the immi-

grants into the interior. To do so would have required alteration of the agricultural system and the creation in the interior of
new centers of economic activity to assist permanent settlement
by those who arrived in Argentina to find that their only opportunity was to go to work as peons at low salaries on the immense
estates of the wealthy. None of these changes was made, and the
immigrant took his revenge by remaining in Buenos Aires to try
his luck, not in productive labors but in those of distribution, thus
multiplying the numbers who aspired to gain wealth by subsidi-
ary economic activities. "The city was growing as a rival of the
republic," Ezequiel Martínez Estrada points out, and the rivalry
deepened day by day, aggravated by the social composition and
the constant struggle between the rivals: Buenos Aires, amorphous, moving toward grandeur but not yet great; and the rest
of the country, made up largely of the rural creoles, rigid and
intractable in areas remote from the influence of immigration.
This duel conceals, and in great part explains, the lack of definition in our society, and the defects of our political life.

THE NEW SOCIAL AND POLITICAL GROUPS

The conglomeration formed by the flood of immigrants and the
creole population seriously altered the social order and posed
grave political issues. Up to this time the elite had tried to keep
in close touch with the masses as a result of the experience acquired under Rosas. It attempted to lead the people toward economic and social development, while drawing them away from
certain practices that were considered dangerous. Now, faced by
the new reality created by the movement of the immigrants, the
elite became perplexed about the stand it should take. The process of social transformation began to appear to be unmanageable,
and the upper class discovered that the new social mass was act-
ing with a degree of autonomy that was leading it toward its own
objectives, which the elite did not share.

In fact, the elements comprising the creole-immigrant mass,
endowed with more vigorous economic and social drives than

those of the old creole populace, were slowly making profound social adjustments and creating a proletariat and a middle class with definite characteristics. The incentive of riches, the opportunity to exercise initiative, the new possibilities in agriculture and ranching, the expansion of trade and industry, the growth of financial speculation—all contributed to the impulse felt by the new masses to attempt any kind of economic adventure. Among the immigrants many were reduced to the condition of hired hands, while others prospered and climbed high on the social ladder. These changes made a sharp impact on the elite. Up to this time its members had comprised no more than a republican aristocracy: they owned the land, but within the primitive Argentine economy they had made only limited profits, which sufficed to maintain their status in a society that was generally at a low level. The situation was now changing rapidly. Economically, the labor and exertions of the creole-immigrant mass began to benefit the elite to a hitherto unsuspected degree, and the elite turned out to be the owner of the capital that these productive forces needed in order to live and to fulfill its aspirations. As a result, the elite was converting itself into a wealthy oligarchy, through its ownership of the means of production, even before the rise of the masses in society was noticed. The same process that was shaping a middle class and a proletariat out of the amorphous creole-immigrant mass was transforming the former austere, republican elite into a capitalistic oligarchy.

By 1880, the outlines of Argentine society were being defined more and more sharply along those lines. Socio-economic groups began to evolve in response to the new situations in which they found themselves, and they adopted characteristics that were at first imprecise but tended to become defined with the passage of time and with the difficulties that accompanied their development. By the end of the century, the new group had become highly conscious of its role and its opportunities.

More homogeneous, and scarcely altered in their social attitudes, the elite promptly defined its position and reacted categorically to the new terms of Argentine reality. A feeling of social

superiority—an aristocratic outlook—began to burgeon among the
men of the ruling generation of 1880. They were conscious of
the chasm that separated them from the inferior, heterogeneous
mass, and this awareness reinforced the certainty felt by the
leaders that they were different, that they were true sons of the
country and the lords of the land. The conviction swelled in them
that they had an unquestionable right, as the patrician class, to
benefit from the wealth that the creole-immigrant mass was creating, which was multiplying the opportunities for the elite to
enrich itself from its hitherto unproductive properties. Wealth
was the new ambition. The austere habits of a Mitre or a Sarmiento began to seem inappropriate to the material greatness that
the country was achieving. A fever for luxury, ostentation, and
economic power began to torment the elite, which increasingly
turned away from the hard demands of republican virtue. On
the climb to riches the country could not produce enough to satisfy the elite; it seemed imperative to try one's luck in any kind
of economic adventure, many of which quickly turned out to be
shady "deals," which compromised the sovereignty of the nation
and alienated its wealth.

Indissolubly united, the sense of aristocracy and the desire
for enrichment shaped the political attitude of the elite in the
alluvial era. Although they firmly maintained their liberal convictions, which they regarded as the mark of European civilization, the members of the new oligarchy tended to close their ranks
and rally to the defense of their privileges. Liberalism was a de-
sirable and convenient system for them, and now it seemed to be
compatible with a resolutely conservative attitude. In effect, the
members of the oligarchy believed that political power belonged
to them by right and, furthermore, that it was patriotic not to
surrender it to the men emerging from the creole-immigrant
mass. Conservative liberalism showed itself to be strongly antipopular. It maintained a kind of enlightened despotism that increased the natural public skepticism in critical situations such as
the country was experiencing, in which there were contradictions
between theories and facts. Increasingly isolated from the masses,

who were the flesh and blood of the country, the oligarchy saw its prestige decline, until in the end it abandoned power with the same elegant indifference of the good loser's parting with his money at Auteuil or at Epsom Downs.

The numerous creole-immigrant mass, composed of diverse elements and renewed by the constant influx of new immigrants, followed a wavering and contradictory course, neither gaining nor losing much ground. Some of the creole traits acquired by these people involved them more or less effectively in the existing social situation, but the avalanche of immigrants tended on the whole to detach the creole-immigrant populace from the immediate problems of working out their common existence and to submerge that class in the struggle for money. The sentiment of social inferiority that pervaded the creole-immigrant mass contributed to this attitude; their natural reaction was to try to compensate for their status by getting rich, an objective that would mean a corresponding rise in their social position, if it could be achieved.

The aspiration for success was the mainspring of the mass man's conduct. The goal was not difficult to reach in a developing society that was full of opportunities, and in which restraints and prejudices were only then hardening. Money was the master key that permitted these men, by their own bold efforts, to move ahead to victory for themselves and their descendents. But this process brought with it a tremendous moral crisis, similar to the one that was occurring for other reasons in the oligarchy. Since the goal was to attain certain positions by breaking through determined opposition, it was all too often believed that moral scruples could be cast off in order to reach the objective.

As the nature of the popular mass very slowly became more defined, its political attitudes began to emerge. Only the negative elements seemed to come into play: the mass that was taking shape did so as a reaction to the elite, and showed itself to be anti-oligarchic, antiliberal, and refractory to European civilization. And soon the people would assert their vigorous, democratic tendencies and stress their own ideas, even to the point of

overvaluing anything that the elite belittled. Faced with the resistance of a class that was clinging to power, the mass continued
to develop its ideas of democratic reform.

This Argentina, in which tradition was clashing and mixing
with the elements brought in by the flood of immigrants, was
bound to differ from creole Argentina. Slowly the process of
homogenization began, stimulated by a capacity for absorption
that marked Argentine life. But the process has not yet ended,
and it cannot be predicted when it may end, given the long span
of time demanded by the phenomena of social fusion. Meanwhile, the reactions of the mass continue to demonstrate the imprecision appropriate to its changing structure, and its predominant political tendencies, especially that of popular democracy,
seem to flow in wide channels, out of which lead side channels
that divert the tide or even turn it backward. This is Argentina
today—uncertain, enigmatic, but full of opportunity, promise,
and hope.

VII

THE COURSE OF CONSERVATIVE
LIBERALISM

The old republican elite, now raised to the category of an oligarchy not so much by its own exertion as by the pressure applied from below by the creole-immigrant mass, began to fix its position and course of action, having discovered that in its hands lay the instruments that could assure to it the enjoyment of great privileges. The newborn oligarchy was not unaware of the inadequate social basis of its leadership role and of its instability as the class that was monopolizing power and the economic advantages obtained from it. Roberto J. Payró, with his acute critical sense of social problems, has one of the characters in his book, *Las divertidas aventuras del nieto de Juan Moreira* (*The Diverting Adventures of the Grandson of Juan Moreira*), say: "We are all descendants of tradesmen or of ranchers—this we know very well. But everyone tries to forget it, and the one who is furthest from his grandfather—who might have been a country storekeeper, a clerk, a shoemaker, or a shepherd—is the most aristocratic." But precisely for this reason the oligarchy believed that it was necessary to redouble its efforts to fortify its position and to prevent the flood of immigrants from snatching away the advantages it had gained. Joined to a narrow, spirited egoism of class, this conception of Argentina's social and political problems also reflected an attitude that was considered to be patriotic. The oligarchy believed that it represented the country with greater fidelity than did the newcomers, who were scarcely a part of the nation.

Yet certainly the elite's negligence in assisting and accelerating the process of assimilation and in settling the immigrants and converting them quickly into advocates of the national destiny was not patriotic. It adopted a class outlook and a program in which liberal principles were accommodated to opportunism; in short, the elite oriented itself politically toward decided conservatism.

This attitude, with all its limitations, had some value, but it was deprived of its virtues by increasingly narrow and rapacious policies. The country gained, but much, very much more was gained by the beneficiaries of power, and soon the ideas upheld by the elite on a doctrinal level were dirtied by the gross activities that those principles were intended to conceal. Thus the so-called "Organization" fell, but in falling, it also dragged down a liberal tradition that was worth saving. Gradually the political force that destroyed the regime was obliged to recognize that there was something in the tradition they had to restore and incorporate into their own set of values. From the opposition emerged men and parties who would later, in different ways, embody the defense of the liberal ideals that survived the wreckage of the political group that was once the incidental vehicle of those principles.

THE PRINCIPLES

The evolution of the republican elite toward an increasingly oligarchic organization was rapid. From Sarmiento to Avellaneda and from Avellaneda to Roca, power passed from hand to hand—thanks to favoritism—without any serious rift in the system of political inheritance. However, considerable deviation occurred as far-reaching changes took place in the economic and social life of the country, beneath the surface of merely political events.

The support that Sarmiento gave to Avellaneda and that Avellaneda extended to Roca certainly reflected their belief in a continuing political tradition. To some degree this was a fact: some elements of the liberal tradition were perpetuated, but it was no less true that great variations were introduced by the changing rhythm of social and economic reality. And the old representatives of the republican elite, men like Mitre and Sarmiento, led the opposition to these changes.

The men of the generation of 1880 had been shaped in the tradition of the ideas that had served as the basis for the organization of Argentina, and they had absorbed the spirit of liberalism. Eduardo Wilde, who was one of the most typical men of that generation, alluded to the formative years of his generation when he said: "Those were times of continuous dispute over opinions, reputations, and ideas. We all agreed on only one thing —that we were ultraliberals and revolutionists in art and in politics. It was imperative to reform beliefs, to institute socialism (liberal, intelligent, enlightened socialism), and to reorganize the republic—even more, to reorganize America, and to make out of all this a great nation." Nonetheless, with the passage of time, circumstances caused this liberal tendency to follow another road. Now it became necessary to transform the country, but from above, without allowing the avalanche of immigrants to tear power from the hands of the patricians. This attitude created an internal contradiction between liberal and democratic ideals. "We have the same conservative spirit," Manuel Quintana said to General Roca when the former succeeded the latter in the presidency in 1904; thus he defined the essence of the shift that liberalism had undergone since the year 1880 at the hands of the new oligarchy. The fact was that liberalism resolutely adopted a conservative position when faced by the pressure exerted by the flood of immigrants.

Without renouncing its progressive ideals, the oligarchy attempted to evade the process of social reform at work in the country. Henceforth, the intent of the elite was to draw a line between politics and economics, emphasizing reform in the latter field while restraining any attempt to change the former. Roca stated his thoughts in a famous phrase at his first inauguration, in 1880: "Peace and administration." Peace, to Roca, meant not only severe repression of all revolutionary attempts like those that had brought bloodshed to the republic in 1874 and in 1880, but also the determined elimination of any fair and open struggle for power, which might be considered dangerous for a country in the process of being transformed—and even more dangerous for his own class. Administration, on the other hand, meant the fulfillment of liberal ideals of progress and enrichment; that is, the realization of the program laid out by the men who had organized the nation. So it happened that the dual highway the oligarchy would follow was clearly marked out: the one, liberal to the end as far as the economy and administration were concerned; the other, strictly conservative in politics.

Yet the principles of liberalism were unable to endure in their traditional forms. In the eyes of the emerging oligarchy it was necessary to put the country abreast of the economic progress then characterizing Europe. International capitalism was reaching its peak, and Argentina was an economic region whose exploitation attracted capital seeking profitable investment. Nothing was easier than to guide the Argentine economy into this channel, even though it might be necessary to modify principle to some extent, or perhaps even to select the phase of liberal thought that preferred material progress.

The oligarchy was also fundamentally concerned with achieving liberal ideals in the field of the organization of the judiciary and the government. Modification of the colonial form of the State and of its juridical principles was necessary in order to bring Argentina up to the level of the progressive nations that were the oligarchy's models. The achievement of this program, joined to the plans for economic reform, cast into relief the opinions that motivated the men of 1880, whose only blind spot with respect to the liberal tradition was their skepticism toward the popular masses out of which the nation was being formed. An attentive observer, Pedro Goyena, indicated from his Catholic point of view how a new mentality was appearing in the oligarchy. "Contemplate modern civilization," he said in 1883. "What is it but the all-absorbing domination of material interest? Is it possible for man to evolve satisfactorily as an intellectual and moral being in the midst of such a pompous display of human industry, wealth, and abundance? The reply cannot be in the affirmative. If it is certain that man has progressed materially, it is not certain that he shines by the splendor of his virtues." And, in fact, this preoccupation with putting the country on the road to economic and social progress was matched by a profound moral skepticism.

In serving economic progress, the oligarchy discovered that it suited the interests of the nation and its own interest as the ruling class to offer opportunities to foreign capital for making productive investments in the country. Granted that it might be necessary to assure high returns and to offer somewhat excessive guarantees: none of those considerations daunted the men of 1880, who were utterly optimistic about the nation's destiny. Nor did they have any doubts about possible threats to national sovereignty that might result from the voluntary surrender of the country's riches. If they felt any doubt, they salvaged their last scruples with the assurance that these economic adventures were contributing to the benefit of their own class interests. Everything, therefore, seemed to favor a policy that should soon modify the economic and social structure of the country.

With regard to the ideas for governmental reform, the oligarchy conceived the audacious plan of giving Argentina a juridical system that would reflect the nation's social heterogeneity. To replace the antiquated, semicolonial forms of government that had lasted until 1880, there was an urgent need to create a modern, vigorous administrative system provided with the legal instruments that would facilitate the full use of the human resources the country now possessed in order to achieve its dreams of material greatness. All moral resistance and any force that might compete with the State had to be swept aside; all the tools of government, on the other hand, had to be perfected and concentrated within the State. But it seemed no less important to the men of the ruling class that the State should remain totally in their hands, even at the risk of having to abandon the political principles that were the essence of liberalism.

CONSERVATIVE POLITICS

It was in politics that the old ideals of liberalism fell victim to class interests. As early as the first days of the struggle for economic aggrandizement, the oligarchy learned that if it should succeed in retaining power, it might hope for important benefits and attractive privileges. But the rulers realized that no political instrument should slip out of their hands, and they prepared to do whatever might be necessary, with or against principle, to strengthen their positions. From this political attitude, fed by its easy justification as patriotism, was born what would be called shortly after 1880 the "unicato" (one-party rule), and still later, the "Organization."

Julio A. Roca and Miguel Juárez Celman were the pre-eminent leaders of the *unicato*. This was an elemental political system in which one could distinguish the former tendencies toward native authoritarianism, now restrained by the strong brakes of constitutional order; and it was a system that led to both a solemn affirmation of juridical principles and to their constant, systematic violation by fraud and violence. The core of the system was an absolutist conception of the executive branch, determined perhaps by the political instability of the country, but strengthened by the desire for centralization shown by Roca and Juárez Celman and, to a lesser degree, by those who followed them in the presidency, such as Pellegrini, Quintana, and Figueroa Alcorta. Within this concept, republicanism was negated in various ways by the decisive influence exercised over politics by the president of the republic. Voluntarily or involuntarily, all the devices for controlling the institutional life of the country were in his hands, not excluding those that ought to have ensured a federalist form of government. As Congressman Olmedo wrote in a letter to Juárez Celman, referring to the kind of authority that General Roca was already exercising in 1882:

Yesterday it was the province of Corrientes; Entre Ríos followed; today it is Santiago del Estero that is falling or will fall under the sword of the Consul, who aims to hold undivided power, no doubt in order to be Caesar, at least for six years. An error! A fatal error! It is not possible for a government to exist without public opinion and legal machinery, but only his personality and power are keeping General Roca in office. What is the point of this boss rule, which is full of peril, makes his friends uneasy, and worse yet, renders his authority useless against the day when he will need it? If he wishes power, is it not his in its highest and most ample form, that given him by the laws, that with which he is armed by the constitution? Must he be the cause of soldiers taking up their *machetes*? Does he need the cheap words of mercenary reporters to prop up his authority, which no one disputes and which we all wish to fortify legally?

If a co-regionalist, ashamed of the obsequiousness demanded by the president, could make such complaints, it is not strange that opponents painted the situation in still darker colors. Some years later, during the troubled days preceding the revolution of 1890, Joaquín Castellanos would tell a meeting of the Civic Union:

National life is paralyzed as far as the functioning of its established organs is concerned. An all-encompassing centralism such as could not have been imagined by the most fanatical defenders of the Unitarian regime has been substituted for our constitutional forms of government. The president of the republic is exercising *de facto* total public power. He has in his hands the reins of municipal authority, the keys to the banks, tutelage over the provincial governors, control of the voices and the votes of the members of congress, and he even manages the judicial machinery. Furthermore, he has become what is called the boss of the ruling party, a party whose members are passive bodies who neither deliberate nor decide anything nor exercise public functions, and who have become accustomed to begging as favors from the boss the positions they rightfully should attain at the polls. The president makes *de facto* use of the Special Executive Powers which were placed in the constitution because of earlier, notoriously unhappy events of our political life, despite the fact that the document provides that those who wield these powers in favor of any one provincial governor should be considered as infamous traitors to the nation. No one has expressly asked him to exercise the Special Powers, but without intent they have been surrendered to the head of the executive branch by the tacit renunciation which other branches of the government have made of their attributes and prerogatives.

These complaints and diatribes reveal the interior dynamics of the *unicato,* which not only established itself as a centralized regime to the degree required by the defense of its privileges, but became more and more exclusive, as though moved by a blind force that impelled the oligarchy to confide *de facto* dictatorial power to a savior capable of containing the threats that loomed in the distance. Thus, against all logic, the elite began to demand unanimous support from its own followers in the legislatures, even to the point of humiliating the representatives, which, at the same time, humiliated all representative assemblies. As Osvaldo Magnasco said in 1891:

The Argentine congress, during two administrations and throughout the last ten years, has let itself become a vassal to the pernicious influence of the chief executive. Congress has accepted political slavery and has worked to bring about its current loss of prestige, which demeans a body that, in these hours of unparalleled trials, could have rallied support and the force necessary to make it a focus of resistance, as in other times it has been the solid and unmovable bulwark against the excesses of insolent and autocratic executives.

And who could be surprised at this situation if the most enlightened men were corroded by skepticism and if there was none among the oligarchy to preserve the traditional devotion to the people that had nurtured the republican fervor of Sarmiento or of Mitre? Eduardo Wilde, a liberal *por excelencia,* did not hesitate to write these revealing words: "The candidate whom General Roca designates will be the president. The General has made himself responsible for this course and he must accept the honor with a clear conscience: he has gained it legitimately. . . . It seems as though General Roca must have an oracle hidden some place, which puts the most patriotic ideas into his head every night and places the most just and proper words in his mouth." And once when he was asked to define universal suffrage, Wilde replied: "It is the triumph of universal ignorance."

This opinion of the right to vote explains the imperturbable boldness with which the government and party officials arranged and carried out electoral frauds. Mitre, who had remained on the margins of the oligarchy as an illustrious member of the old republican elite, said at the political meeting of April 13, 1890: "Since the lists of registered voters are falsified and the polling places are closed by fraud as the result of this plot by administration officials against popular sovereignty, the people are divorced from their government, excluded from public life, and expelled from the protection of the constitution." A full-scale system was rigged up to dominate the political situation in every part of the country, and no method was left unexploited to ensure victory. Venality, tricks, fraud, and force were all exercised both by hired thugs and by government forces. The popular Argentine folk-figure, Juan Moreira, was in reality nothing more than one of the bravos who put themselves at the service of the government in order to win elections. While public faith was being insolently violated in every hamlet and city ward, government circles continued dreaming about the uncontainable progress of the country, the unending growth of national wealth, and the perfecting of the juridical devices needed for orderly national life. Nor were solemn and emphatic declarations lacking, such as that made by President Quintana, the most autocratic of the leaders produced by the oligarchy, when he took office in 1904: "Far from being timid, I vehemently desire peaceful, democratic activity for my country, and one of my greatest ambitions is to evoke debate between opposing doctrines and to preside from the presidency with impartiality over the encounter of two great, organic parties."

Surely nobody was confused by these words: the convictions behind them were notorious. The oligarchy was certain that it was not facing an organized opposition but, rather, a heterogeneous mass that had scarcely begun to outline its vague aspirations. Juárez Celman maintained that a party fit to govern could not be created by the masses, and Mitre himself declared that the Radical Civic Union lacked the characteristics necessary for such a function. The attitude reflected in this conviction could therefore be only that of ensuring the monopoly of power to the oligarchy, which was convinced that it comprised a "party of government," that is, a group of men who knew what they wanted and what suited their interest.

DEFENSE OF THE OLIGARCHY'S INTERESTS

If, in politics, the oligarchy displayed blind conservatism—blind and suicidal—it maintained only a portion of the dignity of its principles in accomplishing its ideals of economic progress and reform. Before long, the oligarchy saw that the enrichment of the country and of its own members could get out of hand, but it lacked the austerity to orient its steps toward the sole objective of the general welfare of the country. Thus it pursued its policies with cool calculation, and it did not waver in disowning its traditional principles in order to benefit its new privileges.

The oligarchy's great treasure, its starting point in the race to riches, was the land, of which its members possessed vast expanses. By 1880, almost all usable public land had been taken up, but the landowners were obtaining only slim returns from their property. It should be said that the enormous task that the oligarchy accomplished through the government toward modernizing the country and incorporating recent technical advances was stimulated and guided by the intention to obtain the increment of wealth from these expanses of land. It was not only essential to import laborers who would work the land; it was imperative to make it productive, and above all to bring it near to the centers of distribution. Thus the oligarchy began to stimulate immigration and to construct numerous public works, seeking to have the benefits of such measures redound on their lands.

The immense majority of the immigrants remained localized in the Littoral region, and the public works doubtless benefited the areas where the return was greatest. But to achieve those results the oligarchy dispensed with systematic planning and did not hesitate to concede to foreign capital immoderate advantages, which compromised the national patrimony. While it may have been necessary to grant concessions for the construction and exploitation of specific services, the terms offered to the consortia that agreed to do the work were usually extremely advantageous, even when there were no equivalent risks. The construction of certain railway lines brought awards of enormous tracts of land to the concessionaires; even so, the generosity of the capitalists who were risking their money seemed to be admirable.

In 1887, General Roca, speaking in London after a banquet that was offered to him by the investment house of Baring Brothers, said: "I have always had the greatest affection for England. The Argentine Republic, which will one day be a great nation, will never forget that its present state of progress and prosperity is due, in great part, to English capital, which does not fear distance and which has flowed into Argentina in substantial quantities in the form of railroads, streetcar lines, settlements of colonists, the exploitation of minerals, and various other enterprises." But these English capital investments took the form of loans on which it was necessary to pay interest. Argentina's foreign debt quickly reached fabulous figures that threatened the financial stability of the State and its very autonomy. In 1896, Juan Bautista Justo, the founder of the Socialist Party in Argentina, wrote in an article in *La Nación*:

English capital has done what their armies could not do. Today our country is tributary to England. Every year many millions of gold pesos leave here and go to the stockholders of English enterprises that are established in Argentina. No one can deny the benefits that the railroads, the gas plants, the streetcars, and the telegraph and telephone lines have brought to us. No one can deny to English companies the right to possess vast expanses of land in our country, since the Argentine lords of the land have the right to live on their income wherever it most pleases them. But the gold that the English capitalists take out of Argentina, or carry off in the form of products, does us no more good than the Irish got from the revenues that the English lords took out of Ireland. The money might as well be blown up or sent to the bottom of the sea. We also suffer from absentee capital; without opposing its coming, we ought not to regard as a favor the establishment in the country of additional foreign capital. It is this capital that largely prevents us from having sound money and obliges our financial market to submit to a continuous drain of hard currency. May capital come in all good time—but the capitalists ought to come with it.

Justo's observations reflected the long-held fear inspired by the State's large investments, particularly in public works. President Roca advanced his own point of view before congress in 1885:

If the State has spent a great deal of money, it is as active capital of the nation: in railroads that have been completed or are going to be completed, in telegraph lines, port installations, bridges, in the thousands of miles conquered from the savages, in buildings and other public works demanded by the evolution of the country (which has made the permanent capital of the nation out of this city, which belonged to the viceroys and to the regional governments that proclaimed their American independence), in the rapid increase in agricultural production, in flocks and herds of livestock whose quality is improving and who are multiplying endlessly, in the immigration that increases daily, and in the thousand industries that are being born and are vigorously developing throughout the country.

But it is certain that despite the activity of this capital in the country, the servicing of the loans increasingly unbalanced the financial structure, while at the same time the abundance of money rapidly created a climate favorable to business deals, especially to financial undertakings whose expansion was shown by the speculative enterprises entered into by large segments of *porteño* society. During 1889 and 1890 the stock exchange was the scene of feverish activity. "There," Julián Martel wrote, "the cream of Buenos Aires society was mixed, so to speak, with the dross of the foreign newcomers, who were trying to disguise their origins." The speculative fever had in fact penetrated all levels of society, and it was not long before it led to the economic cataclysms that could be foreseen as a consequence of sudden enrichment in the uncontrolled "game of the millions." The State and private persons suffered grave losses, which, of course, had an impact on the entire economy. The oligarchy, on the brink of disaster, tried to ride out the storm by protecting foreign credit, in defense, certainly, of the good name of the nation, but also with the hope of being able to count in the future as in the past on the support of foreign capital. Carlos Pellegrini, to whom fell the arduous task of leading the country after the crisis of 1890, said later:

When I became president of the republic, I was certain that with the resources which the country possessed at that moment, and as long as no new sources of income were obtained or developed, it would not be possible to service the foreign debt. But I believed that the credit of the nation was worth any sacrifice. Many people criticized me then for what I did. In the midst of the financial anguish, when there was not even money to pay government salaries, I sent the last peso to Europe to pay the interest on our debt for the period from October 1, 1890, to January 1891. Along with the money to pay the interest—which pointed up what sacrifices the government was capable of making in order to maintain its credit—I sent Doctor de la Plaza to meet with the committee of the Bank of England, which at that time had been constituted under the name of the Baring Committee and was headed by Baron Rothschild.

After some harsh lessons the country entered on a moderate course. Without completely abandoning its program, the oligarchy tried not to exceed the national economic potential, but since it was important not to cut off foreign capital, the leaders wished to strengthen confidence in the seriousness of the government and planned, during the second presidency of General Roca, to unify the nation's debts by putting up the customs revenues as security. Without any doubt, the plan was too much of a compromise of national rights, since it authorized foreign intervention in the supervision of national finances. It was violently rejected by the public, and the government soon had to withdraw the proposal. From then on, it became a mark of sound policy to try to limit borrowing. In the end, prosperity began to return, and foreign capital, sure of obtaining huge profits, began to flow in again. In 1908, Figueroa Alcorta was able to say:

The balance sheet from our last harvest, our trade statistics and those representing the growth of our industries, in general, every factor relevant to the material progress of the country, demonstrate that the prosperity we have attained exceeds the most favorable forecasts, and that these labors to build a great nation, which are founded on the efforts of a hard-working and progressive people, have an unshakable foundation and an extraordinary future.

In the same year, when announcing the slate of Socialist candidates, Justo said:

Many of the great landlords do not even know where their properties
are located—land they bought at the laughable price of four hundred
pesos per square league, which today is worth more than two hundred
thousand pesos per league. The work of the bourgeoisie has been to
increase the value of their lands by means of concessions and guarantees
for railroad construction. They have propagandized for immigration
by paying agents in Europe with public funds in order to attract laborers
who would cultivate their fields and keep salaries down, a condition
made possible only by the increase of available workers.

The accusation was valid. The oligarchy was working for the
country's material progress, but its objective was to satisfy its own
interests.

The oligarchy's conservatism was made categorically clear
with the appearance of the first organized labor forces. In 1902,
mindful of the spread of resistance to low salaries and to the sur-
plus of workers, congress approved the Residence Law, basing it
on a plan drawn up years earlier by Miguel Cané, the subtle
humorist of *Juvenilia*. The law gave the government authority
to expel foreigners who were active in provoking social conflict.
At the same time, police repression increased. Demonstrations
by workers were violently broken up, and the police furiously
pursued the laborers who took part in the strikes that occurred
frequently after 1904. In 1909 and 1910 labor agitation was
renewed, and severely repressed. The anarchists' answer was to
attempt to assassinate the chief of police of Buenos Aires, and a
short time later they placed a bomb in the Colón Opera House.
The government reacted immediately; in June 1910, congress
voted the so-called Law of Social Defense, which applied severe
measures to organized labor. Nonetheless, the men who made
this answer to such a natural social development were the same
men who had contributed toward endowing the country with
legislation that was in other respects modern and progressive.

ANTI-CLERICAL LEGISLATION

After 1880, a definite intent could be observed in the oligarchy
to reform and reorganize the State juridically, an intent so vigorous and so defined that the traditionalists affirmed that it

amounted to a specific plan. As José Manuel Estrada said in 1884 at the closing session of the Catholic Congress:

Gentlemen, whether or not there is a conscious conspiracy at the highest level of the government to put into effect a Masonic program of anti-Christian revolution is not a matter for discussion. We would not be here if the apostasy of those who govern us had not aroused popular indignation! Whether or not this has been a premeditated, dictatorial usurpation of the rights of God and of the nation, I can tell you the tale of a year in which an unfeeling government has trampled simultaneously upon the immunity of the Church, the honor of the teaching career, freedom of conscience, the faith of parents, the innocence of children, the freedom of suffrage, and the independence of the provinces—all our rights as Christians and Argentines.

Estrada was not mistaken. Despite its antidemocratic attitude and zealous defense of its privileges, the oligarchy was thoroughly liberal in some respects. It was characterized by what Miguel Cané defined as "a spirit open to the powerful, evolutionary forces of this century, with faith in science and in human progress." This tendency caused the religious problem to be specifically raised. In a short time, solutions were found to serious issues of Church jurisdiction, and that institution, not without resistance, lost important positions in Argentine life. In addition to the Law of Civil Registration, the Law of Public Education was approved in 1884, and was debated at length, gravely dividing Catholics and liberals. The former defended the need for religious instruction, maintaining that the State's educational capacity was too limited to provide the moral training proper to the Catholic tradition of the people. Pedro Goyena, one of the most fiery Catholic spokesmen, said:

To entrust exclusively to the State the formation of the school children would be to make the State a factory for producing people who were carbon copies of whatever model suited the official of the State—that is to say, its governor. That action would deprive future citizens of all original and independent character; it would mean the accumulation of mechanical units, of beings who would lack the inspiration the father of a family wants his children to receive, and to attain which he eagerly seeks a school in which the teacher may communicate those sublime yet simple ideas that enlighten the mind, strengthen the will, and assuage the heart—schools in which the instructor teaches that the supreme law is the law of God, of God who assists us in this world and rewards us in eternity. . . .

The school without religion, the school from which the idea of God has been proscribed, the school in which His name is never invoked— that school is condemned, and no one defends it directly and openly. Schools must be religious in their nature. I tell you that it would be enough to admit that schools should provide moral instruction if we recognize by the same token that they must provide religious instruction.

The liberals, who opposed the Catholics, defended the principle of state education and freedom of conscience, summarizing their ideals in the motto "secular, compulsory, and free schools." As Delfín Gallo said in congress:

The Church has not forgotten its old theories about its predominance over all temporal authority. As the Decretals state: "All men, even the princes of the earth, must bow their heads before the priests." And Saint Bonaventure, one of the great Church fathers, said: "As the body is subordinate to the spirit, so too the temporal powers must be subordinate to the spiritual power, which is the highest, the most noble, the nearest to God." These are the doctrines that the Church has proclaimed, by virtue of which the priest, under the leadership of the Supreme Pontiff, and as the representative of spiritual power, must exercise immediate, direct, and omnipotent domination over all the temporal powers on earth.

I do not believe, Mr. President, that this objective will be achieved, given the state of world civilization; but I do fear that some people, who are not very advanced on the cultural scale—for example, the people of Ecuador, and others of our race who still find themselves submerged in semibarbarism owing to the instability of their institutions and to countless revolutions—may fall into this hidden trap. It is my desire that we not lay even the smallest brick that might contribute to the erection of that edifice. It seems to me that after all the advances that humanity has made, no one can claim the desirability or the utility for the Argentine Republic to have the spiritual power, from which the popes have derived their secular authority, dominate the temporal power, that is to say, the sovereignty of the people, which today is the basis of all political government.

The two positions collided violently throughout the debate, and the conflict echoed widely outside congress. If the Catholics were aggressive, the government of General Roca was no less decisive, not hesitating to take such severe measures as dismissing José Manuel Estrada from his teaching posts and expelling the papal nuncio from Argentina. The oligarchy displayed pride in its attitude, in its intellectual superiority, in its independent character. A little later, during the government of Juárez Celman, emotions were again stirred up by the proposed law on civil marriage. Eduardo Wilde, a skilled writer and man of the world, who was then the Minister of the Interior, supported the law in the chamber of deputies, affirming that its approval was necessary "for the advancement and evolution of our society," especially, he said, "since we are a country of immigration." Filemón Posse, the Minister of Justice and Religion, supported the proposed law in the senate with the assurances that the bill was "the genuine expression of the holy freedom of conscience, of that freedom, won by civilization, which today makes it impossible for a man to be marched to the stake because he does not believe in Jesus Christ."

In opposition to these men the most competent Catholic spokesmen—Estrada, Goyena, Funes, Pizarro—again raised their voices. The polemic aroused public opinion and to some extent contributed to the serious disturbance that occurred in 1890, which was motivated in part by the new and restless democratic spirit and in part by the strong antiliberal movement that had appeared as a reaction to the oligarchy's decision to impose modern legislation upon the nation.

VICISSITUDES OF LIBERALISM

The widening breach between liberal principles and democratic principles led the oligarchy to a crisis. Because of its attitude toward the creole-immigrant mass and because of its marked tendency to pull in and close its ranks, the oligarchy gradually weakened its foundations without most of its members noticing that fact. But not all of them failed to see the portents. Mitre deserves credit for having kept up the struggle against the antidemocratic trend; he saved his own reputation and, with him, other men later saved their names—men who once belonged to the oligarchy and were eminent representatives of its principles, but who came to have sharp insights into the formless political and social panorama of the republic. Possibly the most significant among these men were Carlos Pelligrini and Joaquín V. González.

Pelligrini had been one of the most typical representatives of liberal, antidemocratic policies. His declarations concerning the desire of some of the people to obtain electoral freedom revealed an audacious contempt for the principles of democracy. However, the changing political conditions had an effect on his generous character, and he began to modify his convictions. In agreement with Roca, and more particularly with the latter's cabinet minister, Joaquín V. González, Pelligrini advocated an important alteration of the electoral system in order to establish a new procedure of counting votes for persons rather than for parties—a change that was later abolished by President Quintana. And when Pelligrini returned to Argentina after a trip to Europe, he maintained with powerful conviction the need for honesty and principle in Argentine politics, a view that he stated with rugged sincerity in the speech he gave in the senate in 1906, when he was discussing the amnesty law for the members of the Radical Party who had launched a revolution in the preceding year:

The past will be forgotten, peace will reign, and we will have re-established the unity of the Argentine family only when the day comes on which all Argentines possess equal rights, the day when they are no longer confronted with the saddening choice of giving up their privileges as citizens or appealing to arms to vindicate the rights of which they have been despoiled. I utter these words in order to call our leaders to a sense of duty and to tell them that we are not going to cure these ills with fine phrases but only with the strength of our wills, with energy, and with practical acts, with something that will raise up spirits, with something that will drive away the storm clouds and permit our citizens to have hope in the effectiveness of their rights, and to give up methods of violence. I am not abandoning the principles that I have always professed. I condemn and I shall always condemn acts of violence. But it will be a sad day when I have to convince myself that my sincere appeals to patriotism and to duty have been sterile, and that we must abandon the future to its fate.

The death of Pelligrini prevented him from witnessing the triumph of his ideas; perhaps it also saved him the humiliation of witnessing the fall of the regime to which he had belonged. Yet there is no question that his words had profound influence on Roque Sáenz Peña, the artisan of the reform that Pelligrini had advocated in his last years.

Joaquín V. González also belonged to the oligarchy, and he was also, for a time, a zealous defender of its interests, which he regarded as identical with the nation's interests. But he was a man of high character and he possessed the virtue of serenity. Faced with the social problems that were unleashed at the beginning of the twentieth century, his first reaction resembled that of other men of his class, but soon he began to discover the hidden motives behind the agitation among the masses, and he began to counsel prudence to his peers. He himself, as one of General Roca's ministers, undertook to prepare labor legislation, and when in 1910 he published his examination of the national conscience, which he entitled *El juicio del siglo* (*The Judgment of the Century*), he wrote these words, which are especially notable if one recalls that they are contemporaneous with the most violent labor repression in the nation's history:

Those who control opinion in this country have felt surprise at the appearance in our midst of the spectacle of violence, although our national existence is never more disturbed and bloody than when we quarrel and dispute over control of the government and its key machinery. Now the controlling group is offended by the violent and aggressive forms that the working class has sometimes adopted in its propaganda and in its struggle to raise itself in the social and economic life of the country. Confronted with such tactics, the traditional and dogmatic criteria of the governing class led them to resort to a system of defensive and repressive penal laws. The oligarchy began by imagining that protest movements, collective petitions, and even the passive attitude of strikes, taken as defensive measures, were crimes. Later, calmer and more objective standards judged those acts to be the organic evidence of a permanent condition, a stage in the social evolution of humanity. Preference was given to seeking the causes of agitation and their legislative remedies in order to contain and to direct the ideas and desires of such a numerous and influential class and to cure the masses of any unhealthy or abnormal attitudes they might assume. New labor legislation in Europe, Australia, New Zealand, and the United States has attained the status of a rational system, and these ideas have also begun to spread among us, inspired as they are by the humanitarian principles that feed and nourish the cause of labor. To the extent that the ignorance and prejudices of the upper classes give way to a more enlightened understanding of the scientific aspects of collective living, the severity of their rule will disappear, and in place of measures of exclusion or of violent repression aimed at punishment or extermination, they will seek juridical solutions—forms of justice that may reconcile issues and conflicts between men and classes. Our constitution has opened the doors of this land to all men and to all civilized ideas that imply material or moral progress for Argentine society. Unless it is proven that the social ideas of the working class are a backward step or a crime or a source of disturbance to public order, it is impossible to draw from the letter or the spirit of the constitution a single sentence that would permit the exclusion from the bosom of this nation of those ideas. Such ideas are conserved in the laws and the international treaties of the most civilized European nations, and they spring from the immanent spirit of love, charity, and fraternity which inspires the sublime code of the Gospels, the soul and support of all modern institutions.

Thus liberal ideas—generous, humane, full of democratic understanding—flourished again in the oligarchy. And this trend influenced many men of strong moral fiber, to whom the divorce between progress and democracy had begun to be insupportable.

With its class consciousness weakened, and a breach opened in the ideological structure that supported it, the oligarchy lost its impetus and agreed to its own surrender. There was a unanimous demand for a law that would rectify the electoral system, and when Roque Sáenz Peña came to power in 1910, he prepared to satisfy the demand, the justice of which was no longer doubted. He promptly sent to congress the draft of an electoral law establishing the secret, compulsory ballot, with representation for both majority and minority groups. At that time Sáenz Peña stated in a document of great significance:

At this unique and decisive moment we are balancing the present and the future of our institutions. We have arrived at a point where our road divides into two distinct routes. Either we must proclaim ourselves incapable of developing a democratic system, which depends totally upon free suffrage, or we must do our job like Argentines, by solving the chief problem of our times despite the temporary special interests that now promise only unlimited arbitrary rule without future solutions to our ills.

Sáenz Peña well knew that the interests of the oligarchy were doomed by the approval of the law of secret and obligatory voting. But his appeal to patriotism was backed by threatening public opinion, while the oligarchy, for its part, had begun to lose faith in its exclusive right to govern a country that was growing and changing from moment to moment. So it happened that there was no force able to oppose approval of the law, which in 1912 was added to the institutional framework of the country as an effective instrument for perfecting its democracy.

As soon as the new electoral machinery began to function, the oligarchy lost its political strongholds. In 1916, the Radical Party candidate, Hipólito Irigoyen, became president of the republic. The conservative groups continued to hold some of their positions in certain provinces, but their strength decreased visibly before the drive of the new, free forces. The ideology of the elite was by this time only a shadow of its former liberal conservatism, impoverished as it was by the narrow, limited ambitions of the most reactionary groups. From this ideological posture it was not difficult to make the transition to what was called "nationalism" —the adaptation of the fascist ideology that began to take root among some of these people after 1922.

Nonetheless, the liberal tradition was not entirely lost; it was included in parts of the diffuse program of the Radical Party and was embodied principally in some men who repudiated the excessive personalism that could be noted among the Radicals after they came to power. But it was among other men and other parties that liberalism again bore fruit and regained constructive force by being adapted to new demands and new realities. It was

Lisandro de la Torre, the continuer of the inspired work of Aristóbulo del Valle and the founder of the Progressive Democratic Party, who became the bold leader of the march toward material progress and civic betterment. And in the end it was Alfredo L. Palacios who tried to infuse into Socialist thought whatever could be preserved that was at the same time alive and creative in the liberal tradition and compatible with basic Socialist ideology.

VIII

THE COURSE OF POPULAR DEMOCRACY

Another political line began to appear after 1880, frankly divergent from conservative liberalism: popular democracy. Imprecise at first, it slowly took on direction and distinct qualities; it was even influential at a crucial moment in 1890. After that date, popular democracy split into various currents, but it continues to prevail today, in differing guises, on the Argentine political scene.

Popular democracy was born as an aspiration of the creole-immigrant mass. It acquired the form and direction of a political movement through the efforts of other groups that joined in the struggle against the oligarchy by taking the leadership of a mass that was still shapeless and insecure in its convictions and ideals. Nothing contributed as much to the political awakening of the new mass as the severe political and economic crisis that broke over the regime during the administration of Juárez Celman. The incompletely formed ideals, latent in the popular mind, erupted—even though they did not manifest themselves completely—in the rebellion of July 1890. They took concrete form in the demands made by the Civic Union, a party from which men and groups soon split, which strengthened various other political movements with increasingly well-defined objectives. One of these, the Radical Civic Union, received the largest share of popular support. It attained power under the guidance of Hipólito Irigoyen (and thanks to the existence of the new electoral law of 1912) after a long period during which the party had engaged in both revolutionary activity and political boycott.

The Radical Party held power from 1916 to 1930, and tried

to realize some of the ideals that had given it life as a party of the people. Meanwhile, other political movements, some popular, others reactionary, developed and grew. Finally, in 1930, a conservative revolution put an end to the Radical era and returned power to an outworn oligarchy that was profoundly antidemocratic and whose intentions showed the influence that fascism had exercised in its ranks. Thus the Radical Civic Union fell from power, in part because of its own errors and in part as a victim of the ferment of reaction that characterized postwar world politics.

POLARIZING THE POPULAR MOVEMENT

Scorned and forgotten by the oligarchy, the popular mass that came into existence as the result of the fusion of the lower-class creoles and the immigrants began to feel in its own flesh the consequences of the policies of the conservative regime. Now there were new Argentines—the children of the immigrants—who aspired to take part in public life, spurred on not only by civic spirit but also by the no less justified if less noble ambition to climb to a more glittering social status than that promised by their origins. Yet all of them, even those who were indifferent to political problems, felt the impact of the serious economic situation that arose during the government of Juárez Celman.

Brought on partly by the maneuvers of international capitalism, the crisis of 1889–90 was aggravated in Argentina by the unwise economic policies of the oligarchy. In addition to overextending its own speculations, the elite stimulated the passion for speculation among the less solvent classes. If some of the wealthy were ruined financially, there was not a person in the proletariat and in the middle class who did not suffer the effects of the dizzying rise of the price of gold and the decrease of the buying power of the peso. Although salaries had increased, the proportion of the increase was always less than what was necessary to make up for the devaluation of the paper money. The railroad strike of 1888, during which the workers asked to be paid their daily wages in gold, was the result of that condition, which also caused the strikes that broke out, with the same objective, in the following years.

The misfortunes of the people were, despite all, only one of the symbols of the grave economic situation through which the country was passing. The national treasury felt the results of the crisis quite as intensely, and the government made desperate efforts to rout the depression, but its remedies did not gain support from independent sectors of public opinion, which regarded these efforts as new maneuvers by the oligarchy bordering on the criminal. In June 1890, Senator Aristóbulo del Valle, the embodiment of hostility toward the dominant oligarchy, launched a relentless attack against the government because he had confirmed the existence of secret issues of paper money. Del Valle said:

The facts I have described have been aggravated by the latest event of which this chamber most certainly does not have knowledge and which is going to surprise it as it has surprised me. The fact is that subsequent to the debate that took place in the chamber over the tax on gold, in which this question was discussed, still another secret issue of four and one-half million pesos has been made for delivery to the National Bank, not because of pressure from depositors crowding the doors of the bank and possibly endangering its existence, but to meet obligations whose nature I cannot appreciate, but which would be part of the routine operation of the bank. . . .

The chamber ought to understand that when I present these facts, and thus commit my reputation as a man and as a senator, I must have enough data not only to make a judgment but also to speak with all the moral certainty of which a man is capable. From the moment when this information was revealed to me, I sought to adopt all the procedures that prudence counsels in order to ascertain the truth. When in complete honesty and good conscience I became convinced that this was an actual fact, then I did not feel a flicker of hesitation. Between the so-called demands of the administration and those imposed by the honorable conscience of a man in public life in fulfilling his sworn duties, there was no vacillation by me. I cannot justify any of the secret issues of public money, stamped with the great seal of the nation, that have been made by the national government; nor can I justify the money put in circulation by the public treasury; nor can I justify the issues that have been made to save the National Bank, or to save the Provincial Bank, which was in danger of having to close its doors. Before seeing the seal of the nation falsified by the government of my country, I would prefer that the National Bank and the Provincial Bank should fail. I am not among those who believe that ills are cured by measures that poison society. We are being eaten away by the sickness of moral corruption, a great moral corruption that has fastened upon our bodies like leprosy. There is no way to save ourselves except to burn out the evil by acts of justice.

Del Valle's demands not only shook parliament and the government but also had enormous repercussions among the public. For some time there had been a growing restlessness on the political front. The "organization" increasingly displayed its cynicism and voracity, and the court followers who surrounded the president did not hide their obsequiousness and their firm resolve to continue the narrow, group politics that marked their regime. By 1889, public indignation had begun to boil over. Francisco Barroetaveña said in an article published in *La Nación*, under the heading, "Tu quoque, juventud":

The designation of the president of the republic, who constitutionally cannot be a party head, as the boss of the National Party; the docility of congress; the applause that is directed to it from all the provinces when it perpetrates outrages such as closing the Stock Exchange; the suppression of the electoral system; the unconditional support given, as it is tonight, by a group of Argentines protesting against civic decadence: are these not symptoms that demonstrate to us a profound moral regression of the people and a complete perversion of ideas?

Nevertheless, Barroetaveña's article was itself evidence of a healthy, vital reaction by public opinion, which would not be long in making itself felt. A popular movement began to be organized, motivated by a keen civic spirit, which quickly acquired vast proportions.

The first public expression of this awakening of a political conscience was the meeting held at the Jardín Florida (Florida Gardens) in September 1889. From then on, the activity of the opposition groups was feverish. Their energy attracted lively sympathy to the new movement, which was demonstrated in the meeting of April 13, 1890, in the Buenos Aires Frontón. A high optimism pervaded the words of the orators, now faced by the evident awakening of the citizens, who had been lulled to sleep for so many years by the harmful acts of the regime. "The very depths of my patriotic feelings are shaken," said Leandro N. Alem, the president of the new and growing party, "as I contemplate the resurrection of civic spirit in the heroic city of Buenos Aires." A few months later, Lisandro de la Torre expressed the same sentiment, when he said in Rosario:

I do not say, gentlemen, that the battle has been won, but I say and I maintain that now there are soldiers who will fight it, minds that radiate enthusiasm, hearts and blood that will not shirk. I tell you that this listless people has become an aroused people, and that when faced by the awakened giant, the decadent tyrants can no longer find support and shelter in their unworthy intrigues, which the people despise and disdain.

The leaders of the popular movement, which was beginning its cycle in Argentine political life, were not in error. The majority of the people were arising to defend their rights; they were disposed to redeem them from the minority that had usurped them to its own benefit, for the majority had indeed remained on the margin of the organization created by the "unicato" for the enjoyment of power. Mitre said as much to the meeting at the Frontón:

The whole society is truly represented here. Here are men who represent the past and the present, men who, divided at times by passing issues, are united now in a single end and a single idea, with no other aims than the common good. Here is youth, the hope of the fatherland, to whom the government of the nation will be entrusted in the near future by the law of time. Here are all those who do not unconditionally abdicate their conscience as free men and who raise high the conservative principles that preserve peoples and reinforce good governments.

Mitre was indicating precisely some of the social elements that were joining the ranks of the popular movement. There were segments of the old elite, represented by Vicente Fidel López, Aristóbulo del Valle, Bernardo de Irigoyen, and Mitre himself—

men who had not gone over the precipice with the oligarchy, per- haps because some of them belonged to the *porteño* party, which had been defeated in 1874 and in 1880. Also at the meeting were the youths of Buenos Aires who had not bowed down to the pro- vincial politicians who had held power since the time of Avel- laneda, youths who aspired to open a breach into public life with- out self-compromise or obsequiousness. Also present were other social elements that Mitre perhaps did not discern from his lofty position. The popular masses were there, taking on new sub- stance through the addition of immigrants and by the mixture of Europeans and creoles. Out of this complex a middle class was being formed that was becoming more numerous, and it was mo- tivated by ambitions. The laboring groups were also present, class conscious and unionized to gain their specific demands, not dis- daining to lend their support to the struggle for the triumph of formal democracy. Finally, the Catholic groups formed part of the popular movement; these, while defending their democratic ideals, protested energetically against the liberal reforms intro- duced by the regime.

This heterogeneous social mass fervently embraced the ban- ner of the Civic Union. The Civic Union had been organized as a political party in 1889 and speedily acquired considerable size, especially in the early months of 1890. At the meeting held in April in the Buenos Aires Frontón, Alem was named president of the party. Soon the Civic Union branched out into the interior of the country, where groups were beginning to collaborate in the enterprise that the party had undertaken from the day follow- ing the public meeting in April: revolution.

With strong support among the military and warm public backing, the revolution was rapidly prepared and broke out in July 1890. The government succeeded in repressing it, but had to guarantee total amnesty to the rebels. Nor could Juárez Cel- man be kept in power. He was deserted by many of his erstwhile faithful followers, and he resigned after a few days. Senator Pizarro summed up the result of the revolutionary movement in a famous phrase: "The revolution is conquered, but the government is dead." Thus there suddenly emerged on the Argentine political scene a party which, at that moment, united all the aims of popular democracy.

CHANNELING THE POPULAR MOVEMENT

Following the brief coalition of popular forces against the regime, the groups that had temporarily united followed their own tendencies and organized as specific political units. Despite this, there was considerable agreement on the basic ideas of formal democracy and the struggle against the oligarchy.

In the letter in which he had extended his support to the meeting of September 1889, Mitre had defined the fundamental objective of the political struggle that was about to take place as the mission of the new, civic force: "It is to normalize public life by vindicating free suffrage; to guide the future of our fatherland along the honest road of constitutionalism, reconciling facts with rights in order to improve our government by peaceful means and to cause it to be loved for the benefits it will bring in the midst of the liberty of all and for all the people." This general principle seemed to be a point of agreement for all sectors; it was affirmed by almost all of the articles of the Proclamation issued by the Civic Union in 1889, and it was implicit in the announcement in 1896 of the first political platform of the Socialist Party, which advocated "universal suffrage and the representation of minorities in all national, provincial, and municipal elections." This was not the only area of agreement. The Socialists and anarchists categorically asserted their position of conflict with the oligarchy from the point of view of proletarian interests, and the Civic Union showed a similar tendency from the point of view of the interests of the inorganic mass that constituted the democratic majority. "We are not overthrowing the government in order to reform men and to substitute others in command," said the Proclamation of the Revolutionary Junta of July 1890; "we overthrow it in order to return the government to the goals for which the people constituted it, on the basis of the national will, and with the dignity of former times, and thus destroying this ignominious oligarchy of upstarts that has dishonored the institutions of the republic in our own eyes and in the eyes of foreigners." However, differences between the various groups quickly appeared, dividing the former Civic Union into several parties, each with its own tendencies. And all of the factions were soon to be mutual enemies.

In 1891, the bloc had split into two distinct parties: the National Civic Union and the Radical Civic Union. The former, headed by Mitre, accepted the possibility of trying to reach an understanding with the ruling oligarchy, and limited its political ideals to a short-range formula: national reconciliation under a rule of legality and honor. This led to the "Accommodation" with an oligarchy that at the moment, on the eve of the elections of 1892, seemed to be repentant. Mitre defended this position with clarity:

There are some men who want to pursue a relentless struggle that would exclude all peaceful discussion and be deaf to reason; others protest against the Accommodation in order to remain where they are, left behind by social advances; and still others pursue the course of mere expectation, which is the passivity of impotence, when it is not cowardice. You of my party are in favor of what has been called the Accommodation, in order to eliminate a sterile conflict that would be a waste of vital forces. The Accommodation promises to normalize institutional life in peace and in liberty, and to unite all our brothers in a plan to redeem and reconcile people and governments on legal grounds. You possess the relative truth that seeks final truth; you use your own judgment and intelligence.

This was the most conservative thesis within the reform movement. Its partisans were satisfied with having forced the oligarchy for once to give ground in its narrow ambitions. Yet this accomplishment was possible only because conservative elements had joined the popular movement through the force of circumstances; for these conservatives there was no problem of rising socially and politically as there was for the classes that until then had been looked down on by the oligarchy.

"Relentless struggle" was, on the other hand, the motto of

the Radical Civic Union, headed by Leandro N. Alem. He had expressed his specific opposition to the Accommodation. "We will not accept," he said, "compromises of any kind that imply the continuation of this disgraceful regime that has victimized individuals throughout the republic." Some years later, in 1897, Hipólito Irigoyen restated this thesis: "When one places faith in the cause for which one has struggled, one preserves above all else the power of principle, with the conviction that victory will come in due time." Intransigency was an established political device, but it was also the product of a fixed conviction that the people had aspirations the oligarchy was unable to satisfy and demands that could only be fulfilled by total victory. The idea gained momentum that the Radical Civic Union was an exceptional political movement—the true embodiment of the popular majority and, therefore, its authentic political representative. "Your party's cause is that of the nation itself, and it represents the power of the people," Irigoyen said. "Thus the party will be judged," he added, "and thus it will pass into history as the origin and summation of the heroic resistance of the Argentine people to a most despicable oppression."

Received with mounting acclaim as the only authentic Argentine party, the Radical Civic Union refused to make any arrangement with the oligarchy, or involve itself in the prevailing electoral system, which was based on fraud and on the violation of popular sovereignty. The party proclaimed revolution as the justifiable and necessary answer to illegitimate authority. As Irigoyen said in 1905: "Revolutions are part of the moral law of society. It is possible neither to create them nor to detain them, except by making reparations that are as extensive as the causes that engendered the revolts are deep." And while the party awaited its triumph, which was possible only by a legal instrument that would assure the free expression of the general will, it abstained from electoral activities so that it would not contribute by its presence at the polls to the legitimizing of intrinsically illegal situations. Revolution and abstention were the fundamental principles of the Radical Party up to 1912, when the law of secret and obligatory suffrage was passed, and the Radicals took pride in maintaining their position. As Irigoyen said: "We have been called revolutionists and abstentionists by prejudiced, incompetent people. That is precisely the most accurate and complete definition of the beliefs we have flaunted as our supreme duty."

The Radical Civic Union limited itself to the defense of the principles of formal democracy, believing that this was the common aspiration and the core of the unanimous wish of the entire population, except the oligarchy. Irigoyen had repeatedly expressed this belief and he stated it again concisely when he was elected president. "The Radical Civic Union," he said in a message in 1916, "is not with anyone or against anyone, but with all for the good of all." But this was a faulty evaluation. As long ago as the time of the heroic struggle against the oligarchic regime, the principles of radicalism had been denounced by the Socialist Party as insufficient from the point of view of the claims of the proletariat, which it advocated in accordance with the basic principles of Marxist doctrine. The founder of the party, Juan B. Justo, pointed out that the Radical Civic Union, like the oligarchy, was preoccupied only with attaining power and that it lacked the capacity to confront fundamental economic and social problems. In 1898 Justo said:

Some people, arrogant because they have not completely ruined the country during many years in power, believe it is essential that they continue to rule. Others believe mainly that the country needs something they have called civic virtue—but they will prescribe for the country whatever they wish once they have taken over the government. Finally, still others personify virtue and, in deprecating the virtue of their fellows, sometimes arrive at a point of intransigence, believing that their own accession to power is the great public need of the moment.

Socialism, in turn, considered the political problem to be secondary, while not ignoring it, because it saw embodied in the principle parties the economic and social interests that worked against those of the proletariat. In 1896 the first proclamation of the party stated:

Until now, the wealthy or bourgeois class has had the government of the country in its hands. The followers of Sáenz Peña, Mitre, Irigoyen, or Alem are all alike. They fight among themselves because of their appetites for power, or from hatred or out of personal loyalties, or because of cheap, shameful ambitions, and not for a program or for an idea. This is demonstrated in each party by the sorry picture of their internal dissidences. If the public still goes along with this political farce, it is because the people are confused by the phrase-making of paid charlatans or because they are shamefully selling their votes for a miserable pittance. All the parties of the wealthy class in Argentina are alike when it comes to increasing the benefits of capitalism at the cost of the working people, even though this may be done stupidly and by compromising the welfare of the country. The Socialist Worker's Party does not claim that it is struggling out of pure patriotism, but only for its legitimate interests; it does not pretend to represent everybody's interests, but rather those of the working people against the oppressive, parasitic, capitalistic class; it does not make the people believe they can attain well-being and liberty at any time, but it assures them victory if they commit themselves to a tenacious, persevering struggle; it expects nothing from fraud or from violence, but everything from intelligence and popular education.

The Socialist Party was founded at a convention held in June 1896 and, impelled by these ideas, ran a ticket in the election of that year. From then on it worked with persistence, winning its first victory in 1904, when Alfredo L. Palacios was elected as a representative to congress. The party produced studious men who critically analyzed the national political scene—men such as Juan B. Justo, Enrique del Valle Iberlucea, and José Ingenieros, who was the author of important essays on our political and social development, namely, *Evolución de las ideas argentinas* and *Sociología argentina*.

However, socialism was not the only route taken by the workers' movement. Anarchism began to develop almost simultaneously, at first adopting the individualistic form; later, with Pedro Gori's arrival in the country, it began to swing over toward anarchistic socialism; finally it lined up with Kropotkin's faction, which was known as anarchistic communism. This was the orientation followed by the strongest of the anarchistic organizations,

FORA, or the Argentine Regional Workers Federation, established in 1901, which later split off in order to follow an exclusively syndicalistic policy. Refractory on principle to any form of organization, anarchism clashed physically with socialism, just as these political groups clashed over theoretical approaches to social and political questions.

Of all the factions that emerged from the popular movement that erupted about 1890, the one that made the most rapid gains and attained the greatest influence was the Radical Civic Union. A party of vague ideals, motivated more by emotion than by thought, it promptly attracted the largest number of creole-immigrant supporters, whose interests and aspirations it eminently represented. Its first leader was Leandro N. Alem, a popular orator who gave masterful, electrifying speeches. He had belonged to the Autonomist Party in the time of Adolfo Alsina, and, like Alsina, he tried to win the people—the "slumdwellers," as the oligarchy called them with some reason—among whom persisted more than a trace of the tradition of Rosas. Some of the men who had joined the Radical Civic Union had also belonged to the Rosas party, such as Bernardo de Irigoyen; and Alem himself was tied to the Rosas regime through his family.

Alem became the undisputed head of the Radical Party at the time of the revolution of 1890, of which he was the civilian leader, and his authority was confirmed after the withdrawal of the Mitre group in 1891. But there were some men of great moral authority and political strength, such as Aristóbulo del Valle and Hipólito Irigoyen (a nephew of Alem), who continued to exercise influence. Beginning in 1889, secret hostility developed between Alem and Irigoyen; it came out in the open in 1893, when they headed unrelated revolutionary plots: Irigoyen in the province of Buenos Aires, and Alem in Santa Fe. When both movements failed, the Radical Civic Union entered a period of crisis. The hostility between the two leaders divided their followers and weakened the party, about whose destiny Alem made a notable prophecy in 1896: "The conservative members of the Radical Party will go along with Don Bernardo [de Irigoyen]; other Radicals will become socialists or anarchists; the Buenos Aires rabble, led by that perfidious traitor, my nephew Hipólito, will come to an agreement with Roque Sáenz Peña, and we intransigents, we will go to ——." Aside from its emotionalism, the prophecy was partially fulfilled. The party crisis was serious, and Alem understood that he had lost influence and authority, a circumstance that appears to have led him to commit suicide that same year. "I have ended my career; I have concluded my mission," he wrote on the night of his death. "It is preferable to die rather than to live a life of sterility, uselessness, and humiliation. Yes, a man may break, but he must not bend. I have fought so hard in recent years that I cannot bring myself to speak of it; but my energy, perhaps already spent, has been incapable of holding back the mountain—and the mountain crushed me." Thus the *caudillo* confessed his defeat at the hands of the man who was then climbing toward the front rank of the Radical Civic Union: Hipólito Irigoyen.

Introverted and subtle, Irigoyen imposed his decisions by moving party wires from behind the scenes. These tactics brought about in the following year the separation from the party of a man who was destined to play a brilliant role in Argentine public life. Lisandro de la Torre proclaimed his dissident stand in a revealing document published in 1897, when he resigned as a member:

From its origin the Radical Party has had in its midst a hostile and disturbing influence that has slowed its progress, deflected its best policies, and converted every patriotic act into a cheap altercation full of rancor and personal ambition. This influence has been that of Señor Hipólito Irigoyen, an unrelenting, hidden influence that operated in the same manner before as after the death of Dr. Alem; a negative but terrible influence that with cold premeditation aborted the revolutionary plans of 1892 and 1893 and that at this moment is destroying the great plans for a party coalition by placing low, petty sentiments ahead of the good of the country and the wishes of the party.

De la Torre was referring to Irigoyen's resistance to a new accommodation between the Radical Civic Union and Mitre's party, a plan against which Irigoyen had renewed his stand of noncollaboration. His attitude allowed General Roca to be elected president for a second time and brought about the near-disappearance of the Radical Civic Union for some years.

But its disappearance was merely an illusion. Irigoyen soon began secret preparations for another revolution, employing without haste or hesitation his delicate technique of conspiracy. After long labor, the revolution, laid almost exclusively within the army, broke out in 1905. It failed to accomplish its objectives, but from then on the conservative oligarchy began to realize that the course of noncollaboration and revolution which the Radical Party had decided to follow was a constant menace that had to be removed. The Radical Civic Union was growing and becoming stronger, and the oligarchy reached the point of convincing itself that the party indeed represented the majority of the people. Many of the best men of the elite began to repeat Irigoyen's belief that only an honest suffrage could restore peace to the nation.

In 1907 and 1908, Irigoyen had two meetings with President Figueroa Alcorta to discuss amnesty for the revolutionists of 1905, and the need to establish an electoral system that would assure the secret and obligatory vote to the citizens who were registered on the national military rolls. Irigoyen later discussed this second point with his old friend, President Roque Sáenz Peña; out of this instructive meeting there came shortly afterward the draft law, which the president sent to congress and which was approved in 1912. This prerequisite having been fulfilled—"the first step in the longed-for redemption that will make our inheritance fruitful," Irigoyen had said—the Radical Civic Union went to the polls and won control of the government in 1916, with the election of Irigoyen as president.

THE RADICAL ADMINISTRATION

A new epoch in Argentine politics was inaugurated with the attainment of power by the Radical Party. In general, the members of the traditional oligarchy were ousted from office and the seats were filled by new men who were for the most part not linked to conservative interests. At the same time, there were signs of the rise of the middle class to respectable levels in various aspects of national life—the final phase of a process that had begun many years earlier.

Nonetheless, the oligarchy was neither conquered nor did it remain totally removed from control of the State. In the ranks of the Radical Civic Union were many men who were connected to the agricultural and livestock wealth of the country—the true representatives of their class interests who inevitably would temper the economic and social action of the new government. Furthermore, it quickly became apparent that political concerns were placed ahead of all others and that there was no plan for social and economic transformation of the existing order. In politics, on the other hand, there was clear-cut direction, marked out unequivocally by the president of the republic, who was recognized as the head of the party.

During the fourteen years of administration by the Radical Party, some continuity in fundamental principles was noticeable; in other ways, however, the presidency of Marcelo T. de Alvear (1922–28) was a modification of the policy that Irigoyen had followed during the period between 1916 and 1922, and that he instituted, even more emphatically, during his second, brief presidency (1928–30). The fact was that Alvear and the Radicals who gathered around him, who were known as "antipersonalists," abandoned certain lines of Radical policy, of which Irigoyen was the outstanding representative, and oriented themselves toward a new form of conservative liberalism. But without doubt it was the policy of Irigoyen, with its successes and its errors, that represented the political beliefs dominant among the people who comprised the Radical Party following, and who considered themselves to be the majority in the country.

The first objective of the Radical Civic Union on attaining power was to carry out what Irigoyen had called the policy of "reparation," that is, to correct the political and administrative vices identified with the conservative regime. As the president said in his message of 1922:

We have held public office in obedience to the popular mandate and inspired by the duty to make reparation, within our abilities and to the extent that time permits, for all the injustices, moral and political, collective and individual, that have long dishonored the country. For this reason, and under no circumstances, must we shun those sacred obligations, which constitute the moral and physical health of the fatherland.

Devoted to his cause, and motivated by a messianic spirit, Irigoyen believed—as Juan B. Justo had pointed out many years before—that the mere fact that the Radical Party had come to power meant that it would fulfill its aim of reforming Argentina. But the practical activities of the party were not motivated by any clear and organized system of ideas, and its political enemies, especially Lisandro de la Torre, a frequent opposition candidate, pointed out that the Radical Party lacked a program, that is, a categorical statement of the solutions it proposed for the various national problems. Irigoyen had already answered this objection by stating that the significance of the Radical Civic Union, which he considered to be the expression of the nation, was in itself a program:

Only those who are confused would ask this movement of national redemption for its program. As pretensions to legality and norms of justice, these appeals affect me in the same way as those of the subject who asks for a reckoning from his ruler, or the criminal who questions and judges his judge. It is the same as trying to operate institutions that have not been established or to apply a constitution that has not been written.

This view was open to censure as being antidemocratic, and that is the way de la Torre put the case during the presidential campaign of 1916. Yet it may be more just to see in it traces of the antiliberal feeling that lay behind the uncertain posture of radicalism.

The fact is that Irigoyen personified, and brought into his administration, the old Radical hostility toward the oligarchy; and that hostility was shown not only by repudiation of the "fraudulent and discredited" regime of the latter, but also by opposition to the liberal tradition and, to a certain extent, by loyalty to some of the attitudes that had prevailed during the era of Rosas. Faced by the offensive that foreign imperialism had un-

leashed upon the country, Irigoyen asserted the principles of economic nationalism and the urgent need to defend the patrimony
of the nation. "During his term of office," Irigoyen said in 1920,
"the president will not alienate an ounce of the public treasure,
nor will he cede an iota of the absolute dominion of the State over
those riches." This line of thought led him to establish strict controls over the exploitation of Argentine oil resources under a
system that granted to the State "monopoly rights over the production and sale of petroleum." This attitude was not merely
circumstantial, nor was it motivated solely by forebodings about
the economic policies of the United States (an apprehension that
in fact was felt by Irigoyen and by many prominent Radicals);
a further motive was a deep-rooted conviction of the need to expand the intervention of the State in economic life. Irigoyen expressed his belief in a message he sent to congress in 1920:

The State ought to acquire day by day a position of greater authority
in the industrial enterprises that provide public services; and there
should be a substitution of existing private capital in some of those
businesses in countries like ours, which are undergoing constant, progressive development, and in which public service must be considered
primarily as an instrument of government.

Irigoyen also brought to the government a concern for the
defense of Catholicism. When the legislature of the province of
Santa Fe approved a provincial constitution that reduced the importance of the Church in relation to the State, Irigoyen pointed
out to the governor of the province, who was also a Radical, the
unsuitability of such a policy; shortly after, the constitution,
which had been inspired by Lisandro de la Torre, was vetoed.
In the same manner, Irigoyen opposed the approval of a divorce
law, and he more than once tried to entrust important public
functions to members of the clergy. But he displayed his antiliberal feeling most clearly with respect to the use of presidential
authority, an authority that he carried to the extreme by establishing a regime that was publicly defined as "personalism."

There can be no doubt that Hipólito Irigoyen had a vigorous
and persuasive personality that deeply affected those around him;

it is equally clear that he proposed to bend to his will, without violence, but stubbornly, those who opposed him, and to constitute with his followers a solid mass whose actions could only sap institutional freedom. In spite of his mystical respect for republican government, in spite of his genuine devotion to constitutional order, Irigoyen demanded of his partisans in public office a loyalty bordering on the sycophantic. The prompt result was an increasingly centralized system of government. To the degree that the Radical Party continued to win provincial governorships and seats in congress, the majority of those who held public office seemed to depend even more closely on the president of the republic, whose influence was customarily invoked wrapped in unmistakable terminology such as "the high party authorities." The wishes of the president were almost always influential in settling matters that, according to law, were the concerns of existing agencies that had been established specifically to counterbalance the authority of the president, whose suggestions were equivalent to orders. Thus a strongly personal government grew up, and those who supported it in the provincial legislatures and in the national congress were called "the regimented majority."

As a result of his desire to reform Argentina, Irigoyen did not hesitate to intervene in the provinces for political reasons. There can be little doubt that he had some administrative justification for his acts, since almost all the provincial governors and legislators had been illegally elected. The president intended to cleanse the political atmosphere of the country by removing those officials, and by offering to the people of the provinces the chance to express their wishes. "There was no human force that could have made me desist from reorganizing all such illegitimate governments, the usurpers of popular sovereignty," he asserted in an important document in 1918. Later he said that he would ensure the most absolute honesty in the new elections, but there were ample opportunities to engage in political maneuvering aimed at putting in power men of the party who obeyed the president's wishes.

Motivated by the desire to eliminate the representatives of

the oligarchy from any positions they continued to hold, the Radical government strongly backed the student movement that began at the University of Córdoba in 1918 and touched off a general reform of all the universities. Unpremeditated and inspired by noble ideals, the students sought to renovate university life. The first manifesto of the reform movement, drawn up by Deodoro Roca, stated:

Up to the present the universities have been the secular refuge of mediocrities, the source of income for illiterates, a safe hospital for invalids and, still worse, the place in which all kinds of tyranny and insensitivity have been expounded from the chairs of learning. The universities have come to be faithful reflections of a decadent society, and they persist in presenting a sad spectacle of senile immobility. That is why wisdom passes silently by these mute and shuttered halls, or enters, distorted and grotesque, into the service of bureaucracy. When on a fleeting impulse, the universities open their doors to men of lofty intellects, their officials later repent, and make life impossible for those scholars within their walls. Thus it happens that under this system instinctual forces work to vulgarize teaching; finally, the vital expansion of university functions does not become the product of organic development but depends instead on the inspiration of periodic revolutions.

Although the Radical government, because of its militant opposition to the oligarchy, supported the university reform movement, and consented to modify the statutes regulating the institutions of higher education, the party was nonetheless remote from the true spirit impelling the young students who sensed the revolutionary restlessness of the day. The Russian Revolution of 1917 had aroused a lively preoccupation with social issues, which was reflected in student circles. The effects of the Russian upheaval were felt in other areas; before long, and because of the pro-Allied position of its members in the national legislature, a split occurred in the Socialist Party. In January 1918, the dissident group founded the International Socialist Party, which changed its name to the Communist Party in December 1920, when it joined the Third International. A new revolutionary fervor began to appear among the working masses, as was demonstrated by some serious strikes that put to the test the social convictions of the Radical government.

Early in 1919, a conflict that started among the metallurgical workers led to a serious strike. Up to that time, the government had tried to act with moderation toward the laboring movement, but on this occasion its repression was violent. The government not only resorted to the use of force, but also tolerated the activities of private gangs, organized by the employers, who committed absolutely irresponsible acts in the streets. The expulsion of foreign workers and the imprisonment of Argentine workers put a fitting end to this task of oppression, which deserved the name, "the Tragic Week," by which those days came to be known.

Nevertheless, the Radical government was not the systematic enemy of the workers, whom it tried to benefit by certain protective laws; it was, rather, indecisive, moderate, and contradictory, as a result of the mixture of diverse elements within the governing party. Because of this moderation and diversity, the Radical Party was unable to create either a Radical bourgeoisie, which might have been able to eliminate the oligarchy, or a vigorous, organized, Radical laboring mass. The conservative parties maintained their strength in several provinces; the Progressive Democratic Party became powerful in Santa Fe; the Federal Capital was little by little won by the Socialist Party. Under these conditions it was no surprise that Irigoyen's successor, despite the fact that he had been selected by Irigoyen himself, should promptly receive a warm welcome from the anti-Irigoyen elements, which nurtured the hope of stripping the popular Radical boss of his prestige and altering his political course.

As soon as he had taken over the presidency in 1922, Marcelo T. de Alvear lost no time in putting distance between himself and Irigoyen. Alvear was not disposed to tolerate control by the party leader over and above his own constitutional authority, and the methods which were followed by his predecessor in dominating all branches of the government were repugnant to the new president. Furthermore, by conviction and background Alvear was an heir of conservative liberalism. He soon gathered around him the

Radicals who did not share in the idolatry of Irigoyen, and many other sympathizers who, without being openly active in politics, shared the conservative outlook. The Radical Party quickly split: the "antipersonalists" backed the president; the "personalists" continued to support Hipólito Irigoyen with tenacious devotion, to the point that they more than once seemed to represent a danger to the government. And it was during Alvear's presidency that the oligarchy began to react energetically. Foreseeing Irigoyen's victory in the elections of 1928, the leading conservatives and some ranking army officers began political conversations. But circumstances did not seem ripe to prevent Irigoyen's accession to power for the second time, and, indeed, he won the election from the antipersonalist candidate by such a margin that his victory could be described as a plebiscite.

Irigoyen's second presidency ought to have been the culmination of the first; now he should have been able to carry out a more resolute policy, since the opposition was weaker. However, when the president took office he was aged, and around him he found only self-serving obsequiousness. His political course was in general the same as that of his first administration, perhaps more emphatic in certain aspects, for example, in its economic nationalism, which was displayed in the forceful yet dignified words on intervention that Irigoyen addressed to the President of the United States, Herbert Hoover. But Irigoyen's use of power accentuated political and administrative vices, and popular discontent was added to the old, inflexible opposition of the oligarchy. In 1932, Ricardo Rojas, who was then being persecuted by the dictatorial government of General José Evaristo Uriburu, wrote:

Perhaps the great sin of the Radical government has been not so much its administrative disorganization as its violation of the Sáenz Peña electoral law in Córdoba, in Mendoza, and in San Juan; in having nullified the collaboration of the cabinet and control within the legislature, because of a misconceived sentiment of party solidarity; in having been careless in selecting political appointees; and in having put pressure on the opposition by means of certain demagogic techniques. All this signifies forgetfulness of historic Radicalism, of its doctrine of free suffrage, of its constitutional program, and of its democratic ideals. Maybe that is why the government fell without a struggle in 1930.

The revolutionary movement which had appeared to be inopportune earlier, during the presidency of Alvear, broke out in September 1930. Now it developed that the conservative groups, in whose ideology the influence of Italian fascism could be traced, together with military leaders of similar tendencies and politicians of different parties who wished at any price to bring about Irigoyen's fall, were allied. Out of the alliance had come a military conspiracy that executed the revolt on the assumption of having support from the public, which, for its part, had also repudiated the indefensible administration of Irigoyen. However, the people did not understand what was hidden behind their presumed saviors: on September 6, 1930, they lined the streets of Buenos Aires to see the revolution, which was not much more than a military parade headed by General Uriburu, but they soon showed their aversion to the oligarchic, reactionary, and fascist elements within the movement. Thus began the era of bitter problems that are still corroding Argentina's political conscience.

IX

THE COURSE OF FASCISM

Following the revolution of 1930, a fascist pattern was firmly imprinted on Argentine political and social life. Although the fascist line was sometimes uncertain, it occasionally took on vigor and definition; then one day, despite its meandering course, the modification of its true colors by the diverse influences that came into play and by the indefiniteness of its goals (the result of the contrary forces at work), it succeeded in imposing itself on all the other currents of opinion, and it prevailed for a time, until it was swept away by the weight of its own ignominy.

The existence of this political line began to be noted on the eve of the revolution of 1930, when the influences of European fascism initially found soil suitable for cultivation in Argentina, partly by chance, and partly because of national and world conditions. Only a very short time before the outbreak of the military movement headed by General Uriburu, voices began to be heard that were different from the voices expressing the sentiments of conservative liberalism or of popular democracy. Leopoldo Lugones let himself be seduced by the glitter of forceful solutions to social problems, and on the anniversary of the victory of Ayacucho he proclaimed that "the moment of the sword" had come for Argentina. He blazed a wide trail that was followed by some small groups that feared more than anyone else the results of a popular democratic government, possibly because they knew at close quarters the fallacies and flaws in the remnants of conservative liberalism. Besides, democratic government had once been pure and vigorous, but it was now corrupt and menacing; behind it they saw the specter of Communism, which awakened un-dreamed-of terror among the advocates of the use of force.

The magazine, *La Nueva República,* brought together, among others, Rodolfo and Julio Irazusta, Ernesto Palacio, César Pico, and Juan E. Carulla, the original core upon which great influence was exercised by Charles Maurras and Benito Mussolini. Among minority groups, which to an extent had aristocratic pretensions, these men spread ideas of the need for a government of force "which would maintain," as Carlos Ibar-guren wrote, "social order, a hierarchical system, and discipline, in order to escape the menace of Soviet Communism." Such words permit one to define these groups as the first to lay down the line of Argentine fascism, which popularly went under the name of "nationalism."

The leader of the revolution of 1930 kept in close touch with these elements, and it is undeniable that fascist doctrine came to be more or less influential in Uriburu's thinking. The traditional Germanophile concepts then prevailing among officers of all ranks in the army also met with his approval, as did the commonly held opinion that the defects of the second Irigoyen admin-istration were inescapable in a democracy. Finally, Uriburu had the idea that what had happened in recent years was only a detour in the nation's political path, and that the backwardness of con-servative liberalism could somehow be ascribed to the inexperience of popular democracy in exercising power. All those influences converged upon the man who had sufficient audacity to attempt a movement that was eminently antipopular, a fact realized by the country in general a few days after the new government took control.

FASCISM AND FRAUDULENT DEMOCRACY

The antipopular revolution began as a result of an uneasy feeling that had spread among the Argentine people in the preceding years. In November 1931, Ramón Doll, who later joined the nationalistic ranks, gave his explanation of the revolution:

Whether we have a government by political machine or a government run for an ideal, in our history they end up the same: sterile, inefficient, and apathetic. The first is a little more informed; the second, a little more patriarchal, but both are equally remote and disconnected from the great national problems. In other words, both machine rule and rule for an ideal create the inert, empty caricature that in Argentina today passes for government and politics.

To meet the crisis that began in 1930, several different approaches were attempted, which finally reduced to two: one was typically fascist; the other we may call fraudulent democracy. They were antithetical positions: the first was held by a minority, the second was more acceptable to the liberal majority, which, once the Radical Party had been eliminated from honest electoral competition, sought refuge in the hope of victory under the government-sponsored system of presidential voting.

There had been much discussion whether or not Uriburu, before launching his revolution, had explicitly stated that he intended to lead the country toward a para-fascist organization. Whereas it is true that the politicians who participated in the regimes that emerged from the heat of the September revolution denied that there had been any commitments of that nature from the General, the nationalists associated with Uriburu asserted that plans of that kind were clearly defined in his mind but were perhaps not expressed to the politicians because an exclusively military revolution had been planned. It is certain that the documents that date from the early days of the revolution resolutely affirmed that the new government would submit to "the revolution and the basic laws."

The express revelation that the movement concealed a corporative design was not long in coming. On October 1, General Uriburu issued a public proclamation in which, among other subjects, he stated:

The impatience of certain political groups, especially the fact that they invoke agreements we have not made and words we have not spoken, have compelled us to break our silence and to interrupt for the moment the primary and most urgent task the country demands we fulfill: the reorganization of public administration. . . . If the revolutionary government restricted itself simply to replacing the men who have held political offices, certainly its action would win the applause of all the parties that might benefit. But the revolution was not made to change the electoral structure. Placed above the parties, we do not seek to impose our ideology, but we have the duty to make it public so that it may be considered and discussed. . . . We do not regard either the constitution or the existing basic laws to be perfect or untouchable, but we declare that they cannot be reformed except by the methods set forth in the constitution itself. . . . We believe it is necessary to reform the constitution in a way that would harmonize the national and provincial revenue systems, give effective autonomy to the federal states, assure the functioning of congress, provide for the independence of the judiciary, and perfect the electoral system—all these so that the constitution may take into account the social needs of the people and the *fuerzas vivas* (the dynamic elements). We are of the opinion that when those elements can be brought to bear in an effective manner, it will not be possible to reproduce the evils that the revolution has extirpated. When the representatives of the people cease to be merely representatives of party committees, and take their seats in congress as workers, ranchers, farmers, professional men, industrialists, and so on, democracy for us will have come to be something more than a beautiful word. But it will be a congress elected by the Sáenz Peña law, which will state the need and the extent of these reforms, in accordance with the provisions of Article XXX of the national constitution.

The principles enunciated by the leader of the revolution provoked resistance, above all, among the politicians who threatened to make the government an orphan in terms of public opinion. It was perhaps to assuage alarm and to affirm those principles that Carlos Ibarguren, who shared or perhaps inspired Uriburu's views, gave a speech in Córdoba in which he confirmed the intention to make a revolution in depth, although he modified the scope of the corporative policy stated in the manifesto of October 1. Ibarguren said:

Public opinion may also be represented in parliament in the same way that representation is extended to the unions and to corporations that are solidly organized. Society has evolved profoundly from the democratic individualism that is based on universal suffrage to the collective structure that responds to general interests that are more complex and organized in coherent form within the social framework.

It thus became evident that a more or less well-defined movement of a fascist type existed, and that it was vaguely trying to resolve the contradiction between conservative liberalism and popular democracy, provided that the solution was not too prejudicial to the former. This new-born fascism had elite pretensions; in spite of the fact that it talked about social problems, it concentrated on the problems of the State, without paying attention to the ones created in the social order by the existence of privilege. An armed militia, the Argentine Civic Legion, was organized to support the movement. Like the nationalist movement itself, this militia did not recruit its members from among the common people but from the sons of conservative families, and it practiced small-scale terrorism with discreet police backing.

A few years after the advent of Mussolini, a complete parody of fascism had thus appeared in Argentina, but it was a copy made by *aficionados* who had no contact with the masses and who tended toward what might be called "enlightened fascism." Their words had reached the ears of General Uriburu, who was well prepared to receive them because of his old authoritarian and pro-German inclinations. And even though the leader of the revolution was unable to obtain from his advisers or from his own ponderings an acceptable program for directing the work of government, an attitude was established that was hostile to the activities of those who were called "the politicians."

Some nationalists have pointed out that nationalism coincided in its aims with radicalism, and that the revolution was transformed into a movement against radicalism only by chance. Be this as it may, the first steps of the fascist revolution were frustrated by the acts of the politicians of whom the nationalists thought so ill. Perhaps that was why Uriburu maintained in a speech at the end of 1930 that the movement had been carried out by the army "without making any sort of agreements with the political parties," which, he claimed, considered themselves "to be chosen to divide the spoils of the party that had fallen from power." This claim was made repeatedly both by the leader of the revolution and by the nationalists.

Nonetheless, the parties that had opposed Irigoyen were gaining strength little by little, thanks partly to the support they received from some of the military leaders, headed by General Agustín P. Justo, who were not satisfied with the prospect of a fascist dictatorship. This development raised the problem of determining what had been the objective of the revolution, especially after the proclamation of October 1 and the speech by Ibarguren in Córdoba on October 15. Federico Pinedo of the Independent Socialist Party described the background of the movement in the newspaper *Crítica* on October 10, pointing out not only the corporatist inclinations of General Uriburu but also the efforts that had been made by the parties opposed to Irigoyen to prevent those inclinations from becoming the main object of the revolutionary government. Referring to a conversation he had with Uriburu, Federico Pinedo wrote:

Not everything he told me gave reason for optimism and tranquillity. During the course of the conversation, the General did not conceal the political and social ideas that he cherished and that I had known about for a long time. The General did not believe in the suitability for our country or for nations in general of certain institutions that the majority of Argentines considered essential in a democracy. He did not believe that citizens ought to have the vote simply as citizens, that is, without any distinction based on their activities, their economic interests, their social functions, their standing or rank. He believed that grouping men according to the goals of political organization in a purely geographical way by mixing all the citizens within each district, without distinction between them, and with one vote for each man— in other words, the electoral system prevailing in all the democratic countries—was and would continue to be pernicious.

He maintained that an immensely superior system would be the one that would base political power on grouping citizens in categories— unions, professional bodies, and corporations, divided according to interests. Only thus was it possible to escape domination by the committees of the political parties that, according to him, were the only arbiters of the destinies of countries organized on the basis of the individual and equal ballot for all men, simply as men.

The objections I made to all these ideas can be imagined. The General listened with deference to my defense of our legal electoral system, which is similar to that of all other countries except Russia and

Italy. He listened to me express my firm conviction that the prevailing democratic system not only permits but assures control by public opinion rather than by political committees, because the latter, although they are able to influence elections, are obliged to submit to the dictates of the masses. I told him that even if the prevailing system had no other merits to make it worthwhile, it had decisively in its favor the fact that there is no way to replace it, since the country would never agree to having a group of people decide to declare themselves superior to their peers and try to impose their rule by diminishing the political power of the rest of the people by means of conditions and limitations on the right to vote. The General expressed the view that he had no intention of depriving anyone of the right to vote, and that everyone would be able to vote, even women, but that the people should exercise their vote within their group, category, union, or corporation. I made the observation that in this case elections would lack meaning, because it mattered little whom the workers, farmers, industrialists, merchants, and property owners were going to elect if it were known beforehand from the organization of the electoral system that congress would have such and such number or representatives of the workers, so many from the farmers, so many from the property owners, etc. I referred to the publications written on this point by the liberal German, Mises. The General declared that he would take into account with pleasure those and any other observations, objections, and arguments, since he did not hold rigidly to his own opinions and was not trying to impose any set system on the country. He said he was only suggesting the ideas that he considered useful, that he tolerated and respected fully the rights of others to make their points of view prevail.

A variety of arguments was also employed by orators who spoke in Córdoba on October 25 in reply to Ibarguren, attacking the propositions he had advanced ten days earlier; and Alfredo Palacios expressed similar ideas on December 6. But not all of the positions taken against the fascist offensive had the same implications. The Socialists, the Progressive Democrats, and some of the other parties insisted—as Palacios expressed their views—that they were not opposed to considering a possible constitutional reform once a legal government had been established, if the aim were to enlarge democracy, not suppress it. The parties that formed the National Democratic Federation (and later those of the so-called "Concordance") claimed that under the existing circumstances it was necessary to defend democratic institutions but at the same time to suffocate the Radical Party, which without doubt was supported by the majority of the electorate. This was an admission that the reign of fraudulent democracy was near, because everyone was aware of the resources, both in leadership and among the people, that were still possessed by the party that had been conquered in the military revolution.

So the dilemma was posed. Either the revolutionary government would opt for a fascist course, or it would give in to the advocates of a democracy based on electoral fraud. Events forced General Uriburu to choose the second course. Nonetheless, it was stained with the colors of fascism.

THE PERIOD OF FRAUDULENT DEMOCRACY

Events moved on with measured pace. When General Uriburu saw his plan for basic reforms vanish, he agreed to support the presidential candidacy of General Justo, who had no chance of winning except by fraud. Not without melancholy Uriburu observed the creation of the Democratic Socialist Alliance, whose ticket was headed by his intimate friend, Lisandro de la Torre; and he further noted the strong comeback of the Radical Party, whose candidate for the presidency, Marcelo T. de Alvear, had been prohibited by the government from running for office. When the leader of the antipopular revolution turned over the seals of office to General Justo, he left to the latter his old profascist plans, along with the hope that they might be initiated by constitutional means.

The epoch of fraudulent democracy began. The circumstances of its origin shaped its destiny and the thinking of the men who served it, and it is important to observe those conditions carefully. In essence, the old duel between popular democracy and the oligarchy was being renewed, but now with shades of meaning that fundamentally altered the situation. The first of the conditions was the renewed predominance of the oligarchy after its many years in opposition, an assertion of power now complicated by various factors such as the adherence of some Radical groups that were called antipersonalists and were of typically conservative mentality, together with the more or less stable support of certain nationalist groups. The latter served as spearheads for the oligarchic cause by their spectacular and chauvinistic patriotism and by their extemporaneous mobilization of the ideas of the old conservatism—as if those ideas were suited to the times. The second new factor was the division in the Radical Party, which was deepened gradually by the influence of the group led by Marcelo Alvear, an influence that was undeniably democratic, but was less sensitive to popular social unrest. Other sectors in the party reacted more positively toward the needs of the people and toward the issues represented by a more advanced group who created *Forja,* a center for economic and political studies. Meanwhile, the alliance of socialism with the Progressive Democratic Party had also forced the Socialists to swing a little to the right, so that the political panorama within the country during this period of fraudulent democracy revealed a diminution of civic virtue and a retreat by all the progressive forces capable of stimulating social progress.

In this way a political situation developed that was based on fraud and supported by a predominantly conservative coalition that had the backing of the army and the Church, and within which fascist groups served as the catalyst. These groups were inspired at the outset by Maurras and Mussolini and were swept along by the principles of Hispanidad as understood by Ramiro de Maeztu; they were seduced later by the Wagnerian arrogance of Hitler.

The apologists for fraudulent democracy claim that theirs was not a continuation of Uriburu's government but, on the contrary, was inspired by the political thinking of men who, as Federico Pinedo said,

saw that it was impossible to avoid a military revolution, and therefore threw themselves into the struggle to make sure that the movement would follow a democratic path. They sought to restrain the revolutionary leaders from their proposed imposition of the corporative or fascist ideas of reform that the head of the movement favored and that he had the sense of honor not to conceal. It may be that some, or many, of these men and these parties later sinned in electoral matters: I will speak of that in due course, and these words are not written to excuse them. Yet the fact is that in the most difficult times through which Argentine republican and democratic institutions have passed—which did not come when frauds were being committed and concealed, but when there was the definite, confessed intention to change the bases of public power by creating a system of corporations or guilds or other more or less fascist bodies—it was the men and the parties in the coalition, and not the ones who refused to join, who waged the battle to limit all of the extravagant revolutionary ideas and who maintained as the foundation of the Argentine State the will of its citizens, reckoned simply as citizens.

Pinedo's opinion, naturally, was not shared by those who actively opposed the regime. From the center parties to the extreme left, the unanimous opinion held of the men who were running the government or who were in the legislature was that they were seeking to retain power either to restore or to extend the privileges that the oligarchy had long enjoyed. The Radical leader, Enrique Mosca, spoke of this period as "these somber and chaotic days that, beginning on September 6, have witnessed the revolt of the barracks against the citizens." The leader of the Progressive Democrats, Lisandro de la Torre, courageously criticized the entire era by analyzing the government's economic policies. The Socialists, Palacios and Bravo, launched fierce campaigns in the senate against the acts of the dictatorship that in their judgments warranted reproof.

The government made no answer except to maintain what Pinedo called "half-way democracy"—that is, the system of fraud that was carefully organized by the Governor of Buenos Aires province, Manuel Fresco, and lauded as "patriotic" by its representatives. Electoral fraud corrupted the authority of the government and opened the way for absolute irresponsibility, particularly in the handling of political problems. The administration of General Justo believed that the crisis that had affected the whole world since 1929 involved deep danger for Argentina, and the government became still more alarmed by the results of the

Imperial Conference held in Ottawa in 1932, at which Great Britain agreed to give preferential treatment to imports from its dominions. The consequence of this alarm was a policy of exaggerated concessions to Great Britain, combined with a reform of the banking structure and the first attempts at State intervention in economic matters by agencies charged with regulating the production and consumption of certain products. Anything seemed preferable to losing the English market, which so greatly benefited the old and the new oligarchy, whose privileges were being guarded by the government.

Fraud and privilege were the characteristics of the era. Frequently it seemed that the constant public accusations directed against the government would end in awakening the sensibilities of the men who were abusing power; but all was in vain. The results were serious, above all because industry was beginning to develop, a new alignment of the popular masses was taking shape, and the people were slowly succumbing to the most acute political skepticism. These were the signs of the turbulent days of the "infamous decade," as one of the nationalists called it. President Roberto Ortiz, who came to office through fraud, aroused hope that an end might be in sight to the illegal political system by which the country was being drugged; his statements, his acts, and the election of some of his associates seemed to imply that the free ballot would be restored. However, illness forced him to give up the presidency in 1940, and that hope was lost. The people again fell into dark pessimism. Thus the way was prepared for the eruption of fascism.

THE RISE OF FASCISM

The ground for fascism was prepared especially among small minority groups. The political bankruptcy of the nationalists who had tried, in the person of General Uriburu, to seize control of the September revolution fragmented the views and activities of that movement: some were disposed to come to an understanding with the regime; others were pushed into underground conspiracies or strategic regrouping.

Organizations with fascist tendencies multiplied. To the "Legion of May" and the "Civic Legion" were added the "Argentine Nationalist Action," headed by Juan T. Ramos, the "Argentine Guard," led by Leopoldo Lugones, the "Military Legion of the Schools," and the "Nationalist Civic Militia." But the most significant organization, as Carlos Ibarguren points out, was the "Argentine Civic Legion," which was later transformed into the "Alliance of Nationalist Youth," headed by General Juan Bautista Molina. At the same time, within *Forja* a current of Radical nationalist thought developed; and the philo-fascist groups, led by Raúl Scalabrini Ortiz, were also strong.

After 1933, and especially after the arrival in Argentina of the German Ambassador, von Thermann, the influence of Hitler's doctrines and methods began to dominate among the groups that had formerly drawn their inspiration from Mussolini and Maurras. In some civil and military circles the overpowering prestige of Nazi Germany blinded the proselytes of the "New Order," who, furthermore, were used and generously compensated by the German Embassy.

Ibarguren, who in a sense was the leading theoretician of the movement, has complained that nationalism in the period from 1933 to 1943 has been badly understood and malevolently confused with the fascist and Nazi movements; but his own career demonstrates the continuity of ideals between these groups and the similarity of goals between the underground movement of that decade and the unmasked, pro-Nazi revolution of 1943, to which is owed the final coming of fascism with the government of Perón.

Ibarguren himself expounded on various occasions what he called "the doctrine of Argentine nationalism." The fact is that his is a moderate fascism, colored by the same observations about "true democracy" that fascism has used everywhere as arguments. But it is enough to recall the connection between those ideas and Perón's so-called "Justicialist Doctrine" to demonstrate the beliefs implicit in the declarations of the man who had inspired the Civic Legion. Here are some of the points of what Ibarguren has called the "Statute of the Nationalist State":

1) The interests of the Nation comprise the supreme public order for Argentina; the State must guarantee, disseminate, and develop those interests. No one may assert rights against Argentine public order.

2) It will be necessary to endow the State with a structure by which, in place of the State's being an expression of the political parties and of their committees, as is the case at present, it may represent society in all its integral, organized parts. This entire structure ought to be consecrated by the will of the Nation as expressed in assemblies that derive from the enrollment or registration of social groups, in conformity with the functions that those groups fulfill in Argentine life in the economic, spiritual, professional, and laboring order.

3) The State recognizes and guarantees all the liberties and rights of man as a human being, and of the citizen as a political element of the Nation, in accordance with the order established in this statute.

4) The national economy, made up of the totality of production and trade, must have as its prime goal the well-being of the collectivity and the potential of the Nation.

5) The State, thus integrated by all the organized social forces, will be their authentic expression and will have the obligation of coordinating and rationalizing all production and distribution within the economy of the country.

6) The State must protect and assure labor its just return, and firmly establish social welfare to such a degree that each laborer may have a decent existence fitting to his level of living, which will be verified periodically in the different regions of the country. By means of the respective organized social groups—guilds, unions, corporations, professions—the State will coordinate and regulate the interests of employers and of labor on a basis of parity. It will approve the collective contracts that are agreed upon and resolve questions that may arise. For this purpose the State will establish labor tribunals, and thus avoid conflicts and the so-called "class struggle."

To complement nationalist thinking, Ibarguren believed it opportune to publish, in 1948, a book entitled *La reforma constitucional*, whose principles in good measure inspired Perón's "Justicialist Constitution" of 1949, a document that was not, however, as corporative as Perón asserted it to be. However, the constitution of the Chaco province (1951), and various laws that at the time created "Organizations of the People" throughout the country, reveal the continuity of the same type of political thought.

The outbreak of World War II was a critical date in the

growth of the fascist movement in the decade from 1933 to 1943. The propaganda and activities of the philo-Nazis were intensified soon after the war began. Periodicals and magazines were published in order to serve the German cause; the information services and espionage and counterespionage organizations sought sympathizers to collaborate in their tasks. Nationalists of all shades seemed most suitable for such jobs, although some of them, out of a sense of honor, refused to collaborate, whereas others accepted, on the principle of uniting for a cause. The nationalists, a great majority of whom were members of the oligarchy, attacked the imperialist powers from the outset, particularly Great Britain. German sources contained abundant materials for ascertaining the character and measuring the rate of penetration of British capital into Argentina, and there was no lack of investigators to study the data, and thus feed the anti-imperialist zeal of the nationalist groups. With that material, and with less substantial data, nationalism forged the belief that it was necessary to shake off the English yoke. To accomplish this, Great Britain and the entire democratic world would have to be smashed by the German forces. These ideas had unity, and nationalism was pro-Nazi by virtue of these beliefs.

The international policy of President Ortiz leaned toward a neutrality that was faintly benevolent for the democratic powers and seemed to be a serious obstacle to the nationalists. But beginning in 1940, when Vice-President Ramón S. Castillo succeeded Ortiz, that orientation began to change slowly. Castillo, who was certainly favorably disposed to the nationalists' point of view, began to feel the pressure from the pro-Nazi groups, and the government switched its course. The neutralists, who scarcely concealed their totalitarian sympathies, redoubled their activities, despite evidence that public opinion—even anti-British opinion—was by no means favorable to the Germans. Soon the entire apparatus of public power came to be an instrument of pro-Nazi policy, which in foreign affairs favored the Axis and in internal affairs led to decided gains for totalitarianism. The then Colonel Juan D. Perón was counted in the ranks of those who served the

Nazi cause. Faced with the drive toward internal totalitarianism, which now was prudently cloaking the fraudulent old framework of our democracy, the political skepticism and despair of the masses grew deeper. Thus the country moved down strange roads toward the triumph of fascism.

THE REVOLUTION OF JUNE 1943

In spite of his sympathy for the Axis, President Castillo at heart continued to be a typical representative of fraudulent democracy, which became more and more corrupt with the passage of time, and was increasingly committed to defending its own privileges. Here is the way in which Carlos Ibarguren described the social situation in a letter to Robustiano Patrón Costas, the oligarchy's nominee for president:

As an Argentine and as your sincere friend, I strongly hope that you may have the greatest success in your government, and that you will cleanse the public scene of the present actors, who are nothing but a gang of professional politicans striving to hold onto their jobs and their private interests. May you win the complete economic independence of our fatherland, liberating it from monopolies and from the pressure of international capitalism that now choke many of its vital organs. May you bring morality into the public administration, which today, in spite of the personal rectitude of Doctor Castillo, presents such a lamentable spectacle of venality that any part that is examined spurts out the pus of corruption, staining even the highest officials. I am confident that in our foreign relations you will know how to manage effectively Argentina's needs and interests, and that you will defend proudly and valiantly our sovereignty and our traditional honor.

Caught between the need to defend the interests of those who supported his policies and the claims of the pro-Nazis and nationalists who demanded that he support the Axis countries (with the corollary of promoting internal totalitarianism), President Castillo was obliged to juggle his decisions. The year 1943 brought indications of the weakening of the Nazi-Fascist offensive. The president turned again toward his faithful followers, who preferred to resort to the illegitimate tranquillity of fraudulent democracy and sacrifice the glad hope of being part of Germany's lebensraum. It was then that Patrón Costas was nominated as the conservative candidate for the presidency, but he did not satisfy the toughest and boldest defenders of the Axis. Out of the barracks emerged the mysterious GOU—the Group of United Officers—a collection of pro-Nazi military men who, one way or another, had to perpetuate the existing situation because of their commitments.

The traditional political parties that opposed fraudulent democracy—the Radicals, the Socialists, and the Progressive Democrats—continued to confront the suspected pro-Nazi plotters and the reactionary forces who were trying to establish in Argentina a totalitarian regime or a hybrid government made up of a German-type totalitarianism and North American capitalism. At the same time, the GOU went on working in the greatest secrecy to prevent the country from escaping a system that would guarantee the security of the groups that were heavily involved with the Reich. A committee set up by congress to investigate Nazi penetration found substantial reasons for alarm, and public opinion was put on the alert, but the administration responded with increased pressure to prevent its own situation from becoming critical.

Meanwhile, the GOU was closing its ranks and preparing to use force; at the same time, it was trying to present its views as though they were ideals for the government of Argentina. From the secret document that Carlos Ibarguren said he possesses and that appears in his book *La historia que he vivido* (*The History That I Have Lived*), one may extract some suggestive paragraphs that define the characteristics of the GOU:

The Work of Unification seeks to bind together the officers of the Army, in spirit and in fact, understanding that in such a fusion lies the true solidarity of all the ranks, from which is born unity of action, the basis of all national, collective effort. The order of the day is to create a single body animated by one ideology and possessing a single will. It is impossible to protect the Army against all its internal and external enemies if one does not place its interest above all personal gain and if all of us do not feel the same holy pride in being its servants.

We face the danger of war at a time when our home-front is in complete collapse. Two enemy courses of action may be clearly seen: to bring to bear powerful pressure by the United States or by its agents, or to threaten a communist revolution of the Popular Front type. . . . Confronted by these hostile political forces, the nation shows only a dispersion and division of the elements of order.

In international matters, we follow the orientation of our government. We choose to fight for our country and to die for it, if necessary, doing so in defense of its honor and its interests, no matter who may try to compromise them. . . . Internally, political instability may soon lead either to the victory of existing tendencies (but only with a change in the present international situation and, as a result, in the war), or to the triumph of the Popular Front, disguised as a Democratic Union, which will immediately seek to make a communist revolution, as in the case of Spain. . . . The Popular Front must be destroyed in order that we may avoid a civil war, which we do not fear but which we have the patriotic duty to shun.

Today it is necessary not only to grasp the political problems that in the end may occasion the serious disturbances with which we are familiar, but also to prepare the army so that it may in good time avoid those problems. That objective will be achieved only when military men are guided by a single ideal and share a single doctrine and, resolved to labor with the greatest unity of action, find each other resolute to impose order, from the moment when stability is first threatened. In our country we have long upheld the concept of exaggerated respect for the Law, which puts us above any suspicion of political activity. This will serve us as a shield when the time is ripe for us to set to work. If that moment arrives, it will be necessary to proceed rationally to do our job: the Chief of the Army will make the decisions and we will execute them.

Evidently this plan aimed at reducing the civil life of Argentina to its narrowest bounds and enclosing it within rigid military limits. This attitude was incomprehensible unless one assumed that the military leaders were trying to justify something in which the public ought not to share, and about which the public should know nothing. Indeed there was something hidden behind the plot that broke out in revolution on June 4, 1943, which in itself was only a salvage operation by the group involved with Nazi infiltration, and which also sought to prevent the Castillo government from swinging toward the United States.

The revolution began as a profoundly unpopular military dictatorship, and it laid the basis for a totalitarian regime, especially after the elimination of the last moderate revolutionists in mid-October 1943. Its methods were unequivocal: the activities of the political parties, of the unions, and of the universities were hobbled; simultaneously, obligatory religious instruction was established by the minister of public instruction, Martínez Zuviría. Perhaps in order to strengthen its weak position, the government turned for support to groups of workers who collaborated with the police. In a vast attempt to compromise the free consciences of the workers, the sub-secretary of war, Perón, was named director of the department of labor. Fully committed to its organizational tasks, fascism was on the march.

THE COURSE OF "PERONISMO"

This entire process was nothing less than the genesis of a fascist regime, but, as events developed, certain peculiarities appeared that derived from the personality of the principal proponent of the movement. There can be no doubt that Perón was the most active leader among the pro-Nazis in the revolutionary government, and he began to utilize methods typical of those counseled by Nazi-Fascist tradition and by the political views prevailing in military circles. The tenets of the military men are summarized in a proclamation issued to the army by pro-Nazi officers shortly before the revolution of June 4. The last paragraphs of the proclamation referred to the manner of using power after it had been seized:

Once we have conquered power, it will be our mission to be strong—stronger than all the other [South American] countries together. We must arm ourselves and remain armed always, triumphing over difficulties, battling against internal and external conditions. Hitler's struggle in peace and in war will be our guide.

Alliances will be the first step. We already have Paraguay; we shall have Bolivia and Chile, and it will be easy for us to put pressure on Uruguay. Then the five united nations will easily draw in Brazil, because of its form of government and its great nuclei of Germans. The South American continent will be ours when Brazil falls. Our tutelage will become a fact, a grandiose and unprecedented fact, achieved by the genius and heroism of the Argentine Army.

Mirages! Utopia! people will say. Nevertheless, we turn our eyes once more toward Germany. Conquered, she was forced in 1919 to sign the Treaty of Versailles, which would have kept her under the Allied yoke as a second-class power for at least fifty years. In less than twenty years she traveled an amazing road. Before 1939 she was armed as was no other nation, and in the midst of peace had annexed Austria and Czechoslovakia. Later, in war, all Europe was bent to her will. But this was accomplished only by hard sacrifice. An iron dictatorship was necessary, to impose upon the people the renunciation essential to that formidable program.

So it will be in Argentina. Our government will be an inflexible dictatorship, although at the beginning we will make the concessions needed to put it on a solid basis. The people will be attracted to the cause, but they must work, deprive themselves, and obey—work more and deprive themselves more than any other people. Only thus will it be possible to effect the armaments program that is indispensable for the conquest of the continent. Following the example of Germany, we will inculcate into the people by radio, by the controlled press, by films, by books, by the church, and by education a spirit receptive to understanding of the heroic road that must be followed. Only thus will the people succeed in renouncing the pleasant life they now lead. Our generation will be a generation sacrificed on the altar of the highest good—the Argentine fatherland, which will shine with un-equaled light for the greater benefit of the continent and of all hu-manity.

To reach this goal, Perón used a tool of inestimable value—his ability as an orator capable of employing the tone, the vocabu-lary, and the ideas most appropriate for swaying the Argentine masses, especially the people of the urban working districts. This factor, whose value was multiplied by the use of the radio, came to have immeasurable significance in Argentine politics.

Little by little, this unpopular revolution began to become popular, although the politicians and the middle class did not notice what was happening. A natural orator, who had a monop-oly of the radio, Perón began to gather around him more or less dissatisfied labor leaders and worker organizations that were jus-tifiably disenchanted by the conservative policies which had pre-vailed since 1930. His master stroke was to include all the political parties of the country in the blame for the existing situation, while in fact the responsibility belonged only to the groups on the right. On October 15, 1944, Perón stated:

> Everything had been falsified: liberty, the rights of citizenship, political leadership, justice, and morality. As a result, our people were on the point of losing their most important resources—hope and faith.
>
> The most secretive and venal of oligarchies, holding the State in its power, had rigged an electoral machine that gave the people the right to vote but never allowed them to elect their leaders. As if this were not enough, the oligarchy even split its gains with the party bosses who were apparently in opposition.

With such arguments, supported by the instruments of power, Perón succeeded bit by bit in planting his fascist slogans in the minds of the politically inexperienced masses.

These themes were partially or completely expounded on different occasions. "We seek to suppress the struggles between classes, and supplant them by a just agreement between workers and employers—that is to say, the people—under the sheltering justice that emanates from the State," Perón said on May 1, 1944. "We do not divide the people into classes in order to set them to struggling, one against the other; we try to organize them so that they may collaborate in the aggrandizement of the Fatherland," he added on August 11. "All sympathy for the bourgeoisie has died; a new era of the world is born; the rights, the responsibilities, and the role of the People in providing basic solutions to their problems must be asserted daily," he stated on July 19, 1945. These preachings, revolutionary and reactionary at the same time, like all fascism, kept on gaining vitality; they ended by striking root in the consciences of certain social groups that belonged to the category that has been technically described as the *lumpenproletariat*. On the other hand, Perón's implicit and explicit doctrines alarmed many people in the middle class and among the capitalists, but they continued obstinately to reject the social reality that was emerging before their eyes, rejecting it as if it did not exist, just as they had been doing since 1930.

An attempted military revolution in October 1945 forced Perón to retire briefly from power, but it gave him the opportunity to organize meticulously his return to public life, which took place under extraordinary circumstances that demonstrated how deeply his policies and plans had penetrated. On October 17, 1945, with the unconcealed collaboration of strong elements of the army and the police, a march was organized that led out from the suburbs and the workers' districts and converged on the center of Buenos Aires to demand "liberty" for Perón. This movement had, on a grand scale, the same internal structure as others that had been organized previously by the police so as to give a little popular "warmth" to the acts of the revolutionary government of 1943; but this time there could be no mistaking the spontaneity of the mass movement of people for whom the name of Perón had become a symbol of social reform. Perón himself defined the special nature of the movement in the speech which he gave on October 17 from the balcony of Government House:

May this historic hour be dear to the republic; may it create a bond of union that will lead to an indestructible brotherhood between the People, the Army, and the Police. May this union be eternal and infinite, so that this people may grow in spiritual unity within the true and authentic forces of nationality and order. May this union be indestructible and infinite, so that our people may not only possess happiness but also be worthy of understanding it.

What could this rare identification between the people, the army, and the police signify except a dictatorship of the masses, controlled, supported, and directed by the apparatus of power? Everything indicated that the political plans of the new leader were only an imitation of fascism, as Perón had outlined them in the speech that he had given as minister of war at the University of La Plata on June 10, 1944.

THE NEW ORDER

Perón triumphed on February 24, 1946, in presidential elections that were controlled by the army and preceded by an electoral campaign in which the forces of the State and of the government-backed gangs systematically attacked the opposition. He was inaugurated some months later, on June 4, 1946, and took up his tasks of government. It could be noted that he was preparing to make substantial modifications in the organization of the State. Everything favored him: he had a great majority in the chamber of deputies and in the senate, and his party—or, rather, the conglomeration of parties and groups that had gathered around him—had won in all but one of the provinces. With the universities placed under government control, the press censored, the labor unions controlled, and the administrative machinery and the military and police forces unconditionally at his service, Perón began to lay the foundations for a "New Order" for Argentina.

The fact is that he did not make excessive innovations, but limited himself to implementing, with variations and additions, the old aspirations of the nationalist groups. Perón, who now presented himself as the leader of the Argentine people and the standard-bearer of the proletariat, using very modern formulas to solve economic and social problems and talking about anti-imperialism and atomic energy, said in a speech on June 28, 1944:

The Argentine Republic is the product of the Spanish conquest and colonization, which brought to our shores the cross and the sword, joined together like brothers with a single will. And in these present times it seems as if that extraordinary conjunction of spiritual forces and of power will again be created, representing humanity's two greatest symbols: the Gospel and the Sword.

Perón did not in fact deny his ideological inheritance. He had the open backing of the Church, the army, and the police; these comprised a grid into whose openings he inserted the support that was given him by the proletariat groups. On that basis he began to erect his government organization, threatening the army with the popular masses and with the specter of a general revolutionary strike, while intimidating the workers' organizations with the apparition of the army and of military dictatorship. Fascism was fulfilled in Perón because of the unusual circumstances that surrounded his appearance in public life, conditions that favored the co-participation of forces from divergent political traditions. The "New Order" had to have two ceremonials, two different masks. The stern posture of an army trained on the Prussian model had to be alternated with the crude, chaotic exaltation felt by the mass of the *descamisados*—the "shirtless ones" —whom he tried to inoculate (vainly, as it turned out) with brutal sentiments of violence. And Perón learned the art of tireless speech-making in two distinct styles: one, that of the severe and laconic military man; the other, that of the agitator at the barricades.

The diverse aspects of the "New Order" gradually fell into place. For some time, the dictator reserved to himself the serene exposition of the constructive labors of his regime, while leaving to his wife, Eva Perón, the apparently revolutionary vehemence of speeches delivered amid clamorous approval. In both cases, radio oratory was a key technique of government: the virile voice of the president and the throaty voice of Eva Perón had a profound effect on the politically inexperienced masses, far different from anything to which they were accustomed. They carried the people to the zone of instinctual reactions. The influence of Eva Perón brought support to the "New Order" equal in strength to that produced by the lofty and severe discourses, full of manly expressions and noble arrogance, which the president delivered to his military comrades on official occasions and in the garrisons. And by means of this abundant oratory, the president kept on introducing ideas that spelled out the real and achievable dimensions of the long-standing program of Argentine nationalism.

One of the fundamental problems of the "New Order" concerned the economic basis of the new State. Strangely, two currents of ideas coincided in the plan proposed by the president: on the one hand, there was a generic design adapted to the principles of the General Staff, which in turn was inspired by German theoreticians from von der Goltz and von Clausewitz to Goerlitz; on the other hand, there was a specific plan for the Argentina that the nationalists were glorifying in accordance with the fascist variation of anti-imperialism.

The first trend was categorically revealed by Perón, then

minister of war, in the speech that he delivered at La Plata on June 10, 1944. After referring to the demands implicit in "total war," as described by Ludendorff, he dealt with the problems of "Industrial Action" in the following terms:

When we examine the problem of industrialization with specific reference to our country, we can state that it constitutes the critical point in our national defense. The cause of the crisis must be widely sought in order to be able to solve it.

Over a long period of time, Argentina's production and wealth have been of an almost exclusively agricultural and ranching character. This is due in large part to the fact that our population growth by immigration has not been as great as was hoped, owing to the high return from this type of production in relation to the number of workers needed. When world markets became saturated, production was automatically limited and, consequently, so was entry into the country of the laborers required in that production.

Argentine capital, invested in this secure but scarcely brilliant way, showed reluctance to find outlets in industrial activities, which were long considered to be reckless adventures and, although this may seem laughable, not suitable for gentlemen.

Foreign capital dedicated itself especially to commercial activities in which all profits, no matter how quick and excessive they might be, were always permissible and legitimate; or it, too, sought security in the establishment of public services or basic industries, often with a minimal return guaranteed by the State.

The economy of the country rested almost exclusively on the products of the earth, which were processed in a most inferior manner; later, when these products had been transformed in foreign lands, to the benefit of those economies, we acquired them again as manufactured goods.

Foreign capital showed little interest in establishing itself in Argentina in order to develop our natural resources; a policy of that nature would mean benefits for our economy and would aid our growth, but it would be prejudicial to foreign interests, since our products would compete with those made abroad.

It is evident that the recovery of our economic freedom must be undertaken by Argentine capital; at the very least, the State should stimulate capital, leading it and pointing out the road to follow.

The scarcity of foreign manufactured goods, brought on by the World War of 1914–18, fortunately impelled the boldest capital to throw itself into the new adventure, and a great variety of industries was established, demonstrating our true possibilities. When the war ended, many of these industries disappeared, some because they were artificial; others, which ought to have been maintained, because they lacked government assistance, which they needed in order to maintain themselves. Yet many emerged magnificently from the trial by fire of foreign competition both within and outside the country.

But this industrial transformation was carried out on its own, by the private initiative of some "pioneers" who had to overcome innumerable difficulties. The State did not possess the foresight that ought to have guided and instructed capital: directing the rational utilization of energy, facilitating the training of laborers and executive personnel, coordinating the exploration for and extraction of raw materials with the need and possibilities of processing them, guiding and protecting the sale of products in national and foreign markets. All of these would have considerably benefited the national economy.

To support these statements, I shall refer to only one of its aspects. We have spent great sums of money abroad in acquiring war materials. We have paid seven times their value because seven is the coefficient of security in war industries. All that money has left the country without benefiting our economy, our industries, or the working masses whom it could have fed. An intelligent policy would have allowed us to build the factories to make those goods in Argentina, and now we would have the factories, as well as substantial industrial experience, and the invested capital would have passed from hand to hand—Argentine hands.

What I say about war material can be applied to farm machinery and to equipment for transportation by land, river, or by sea, and it can be extended to any other type of activity.

Argentine technicians have demonstrated that they are as capable as foreigners, and if anyone believes that they are not, then we should bring the foreigners here so that we can promptly assimilate all they can teach us.

The Argentine worker, when he has been given an opportunity to learn, has shown himself to be as capable, or more capable, than foreigners. If we do not have machinery in sufficient quantity or quality, we can manufacture or acquire as much as necessary.

The raw materials are offered to us by the bowels of our land, which waits only for us to extract them. If we do not possess them all, we will acquire them wherever they may be found, doing the same as the European countries, which also do not have all such resources.

The present conflict, which has caused foreign manufactured goods to disappear almost completely from our markets, has caused our industries to flourish again, and in a way that causes admiration even among the leading industrial countries.

The theory to which we long clung, that if the day came when danger threatened our Fatherland we would find in foreign markets the materials of war that we would need in order to complete the initial equipping of our army and to assure its resupply, has been demonstrated to be utopian.

National Defense demands its own powerful industrial establishment, not any sort of industry, but heavy industry. In order to achieve such industrialization, official action by the State is undoubtedly necessary. This will solve the problems that I have cited, and it will protect our industries, if need be. Nor do I refer to artificial industries, established exclusively for profits, which have recovered from their invested capital many times over, but to those that dedicate their activities to this lasting work, which will contribute to the good of the economy and will assure National Defense.

This typically General Staff conception dealt with the material goods of the nation, with its wealth. The doctrine aimed at national self-sufficiency. But the generalization of such requirements brings one inexorably to a totalitarian concept, which the dictator expressed in his "National Doctrine" in this forbidding phrase: "The defensive action of the nation extends inward from its geographic frontiers to include the ideological formation of the people, in the person of each and every one of its inhabitants." And the entire country, which had not undergone any war or sighted any enemy, was put in a condition of internal defense or, as the dictator later established it, a "state of internal war," a situation in which he could experiment with his political theories.

The idea around which the dictator revolved was that of organization. The State must be organized; the government must be organized (if this goal were attained, the government would be personified in the figure of "the Leader"); and the masses must be organized (then they could call themselves "the People"). Each facet of Perón's political views took on extraordinary characteristics, but none was as singular as the image that the dictator formed of himself as "the Leader."

Conducción—"leadership"—a term transferred to the political lexicon, but of military origin—was, to Perón, an art. *El con-*

ductor nace, no se hace—"the Leader is born, not made"—he frequently said. At the same time, he denied to the masses the opportunity to lead themselves. "When the mass has no sense of leadership, and no one takes it by the hand, it is incapable of proceeding alone, and it ends in political catastrophes," he said on March 15, 1951. But if the masses can count on a skillful leader—a circumstance presumed to be providential—they can attain all their ambitions, since *como él sea, será la masa* ("as he is, so will be the mass"). The Leader, therefore, is an artisan, an artist. He is different from the *caudillo,* because the Leader plans and executes; like the artist, his task is "to create, always to create, always to be ready to create."

This notion called for a bridge between the masses and the talented Leader. The dictator imagined that the chasm would shrink if the masses were organized into the People, and if the People would give themselves up to their vocations, grouped in great organizations—workers, students, businessmen, professional people—which would facilitate the artist's task of molding them. But even so, he believed it essential—another reflection of his barracks training—to create what he consistently referred to as "staffs" of intermediate directors. "It is necessary to teach those at the intermediate levels about leadership, because leadership cannot be accomplished by only one man and the people; if this mass is not held together tightly, it will dissolve."

The theory was put in practice, and the dictator succeeded in creating all of its forms that his fertile imagination could conceive, but this was accomplished only on the basis of a powerful apparatus of force that increasingly demanded intellectual immobility from the country. The dictatorship practically choked the free expression of ideas, precisely because all the heavy armor that sustained the government could not withstand the slightest critical inspection. Perhaps the dictator believed in the efficacy of his Argentine version of decrepit European fascism because, in his egoism, he used to say that he would never commit what he called "Mussolini's mistakes." It was his misfortune to commit even worse errors; and one day, ingloriously, he fell from power. In a short time nothing remained of the vast corporate structures he had created; soon his words echoed hollowly, except for some, which were prophetic. Listen to his pronouncement of October 21, 1946: "We are not in the least the enemies of capital, and the future will show that we have been its true defenders." The fact is that during the last months of his rule, he prepared to concede vast oil-bearing zones to a foreign enterprise.

THE FORCES IN RESERVE

While the fascist movement that dominated Argentina from 1943 to 1955 was being born and was developing, the traditional political parties maintained and refined their theoretical positions. The vast social movement that had been evolving in Argentina since the crisis of 1929 and the revolution of 1930 forced the parties to accentuate their concern for social problems.

That concern was by no means new for the Socialist Party, which had been fighting the privileged classes since the end of the nineteenth century, and which, since 1930, had not only energetically defended political liberty, but also had struggled actively to uphold the principles of social justice, insofar as these could be defined in the light of Argentine reality. For this reason, Américo Ghioldi was able to say at a Socialist Party congress in June 1948:

Finally, I want to assert that we are the Left in this country. There is no movement more advanced than ours, because we link together in admirable alliance three ideas that dispute for supremacy among themselves but that must live in harmony: democracy, equality, and liberty. Political democracy was dominant for a time, but it weakened because it did not satisfy the demands for equality which are the profound requirements of a society in need of social justice. Under the present government there may exist a trend toward the predominance of the egalitarian principle, but it lacks the feeling and the creative sense of liberty without which human beings atrophy and the living nucleus that creates and re-creates is extinguished.

Nor was the Communist Party unaware of the tensions within society; it condemned the policy of the oligarchy and it labored in its own way to create strong and disciplined groups within the working class in order to spread its revolutionary principles.

On the other hand, concern for social conditions had been less intense among the other parties, but all of them now began to feel the need to take a stand in the face of the portents that were daily becoming more visible. The problem was most severe within the Radical Party, a popular party by definition, and the one that had traditionally regarded itself as representing the majority of the people. It was profoundly shaken by the defeat of February 24, 1946. As a result of the election, the reform ideas of a faction of the party, which adopted the name of "Intransigent," began to gain strength. Its main objective was to bring some definition into the vague general principles that Radicalism claimed to uphold, but those principles went through constant changes when presented to the electorate. As Arturo Frondizi wrote in his book, *Petróleo y política*:

We have affirmed that we must accomplish our revolution by an "absolute change, as much in the internal as in the external order of our society"; that this revolution is historically linked to our past; and that it is also linked at this moment to the course of events through which Latin America is passing. We must now specify some of the fundamental facts that will give being to this revolution in order to transform the old social order into a new one, consonant with the real needs of the people. This revolutionary content is tied to basic changes in the socio-economic structure, which embrace at least three concrete and essential aspects: (a) agrarian reform; (b) industrialization; (c) economic democracy.

In succeeding Intransigent Radical Party publications, sharper focus was given to solutions of long-standing national problems that the Perón regime had pretended to solve but had only deepened. And because of the astute and sustained effort of this group, one could note a progressive winning over of minds, as if to the increased deepening of problems there corresponded a progressive clarification of their solutions.

Such were the positions taken by the popular parties, among which one must not forget the Progressive Democratic Party that —following the inspiration of Lisandro de la Torre—made every effort to clarify its liberal doctrines. Concern for social problems arose even among the conservative groups that had divided into different political entities during the era of fascism. Despite the early warning by Marx, the theme of social reform had been ignored by the privileged minorities, and even by the parties that represented popular democracy. The violent seizure of the country by fascism was the sign that the problem existed. At the close of the cycle of Argentine fascism—an epoch of twenty-five bitter years—Argentine political thought began to show enough maturity to perceive the truth that always hides behind political alternatives.

BIBLIOGRAPHY AND SELECTED READINGS

I. BIBLIOGRAPHY

(THE AUTHOR'S LIST OF ARGENTINE WORKS IN SPANISH)

Alberdi, Juan Bautista. Bases y puntos de partida para la organización política de la República Argentina. 4th ed. Buenos Aires, 1952.
——. Fragmento preliminar al estudio del derecho. Buenos Aires, 1942.
Alvarez, Juan. Las guerras civiles argentinas. Buenos Aires, 1914.
Alvarez Suárez, Agustín Enrique. Adónde vamos? Buenos Aires, 1915.
——. South America; ensayo de psicología política. Buenos Aires, 1918.
Ayarragaray, Lucas. La anarquía argentina y el caudillismo. Estudio psicológico de los orígenes argentinos. 2d ed. Buenos Aires, 1925.
Azara, Félix de. Descripción e historia del Paraguay y del Río de la Plata. 3d ed. Buenos Aires, 1943.
Canal-Feijóo, Bernardo. Constitución y revolución, Juan Bautista Alberdi. Buenos Aires, 1955.
Carbia, Rómulo D. Historia crítica de la historiografía argentina (desde sus orígenes en el siglo XVI). La Plata, 1939.
Cárcano, Ramón José. De Caseros al 11 de septiembre (1851–1852). 2d ed. Buenos Aires, 1918.
——. Del sitio de Buenos Aires al campo de Cepeda (1852–1859). Buenos Aires, 1921.
Castiñeiras, Julio R. Historia de la Universidad de la Plata. 2 vols. La Plata, 1939–40.
Celesia, Ernesto H. Rosas; aportes para su historia. Buenos Aires, 1954.
Chanetón, Abel. Historia de Vélez Sársfield. 2d ed. Buenos Aires, 1938.
——. Retorno de Echeverría. Buenos Aires, 1944.

Cúneo, Dardo. Juan B. Justo y las luchas sociales en la Argentina. Buenos Aires, 1956.

Echeverría, Esteban. Dogma socialista. La Plata, 1940.

Estrada, José Manuel. Lecciones sobre la historia de la República Argentina. Vols. II and III of Obras completas de José Manuel Estrada. 2d ed. 12 vols. Buenos Aires, 1898–1927.

Frondizi, Arturo. Petróleo y política; contribución al estudio de la historia económica argentina y de las relaciones entre el imperialismo y la vida política nacional. 2d ed. Buenos Aires, 1955.

Gálvez, Manuel. Vida de Hipólito Yrigoyen, el hombre del misterio. 2d ed. Buenos Aires, 1939.

García, Juán Agustín. La ciudad indiana; Buenos Aires desde 1600 hasta mediados del siglo XVIII. Buenos Aires, 1953.

García Mérou, Martín. Alberdi; ensayo crítico. Buenos Aires, 1916.

González, Joaquín V. El juicio del siglo ó cien años de historia argentina. Buenos Aires, 1913.

———. La tradición nacional, con una carta del general Bartolomé Mitre. Buenos Aires, 1957.

González, Julio V. Filiación histórica del gobierno representativo argentino. 2 vols. Buenos Aires, 1937–38.

Groussac, Paul. Estudios de historia argentina: el padre José Guevara.—Don Diego de Alvear.—El doctor don Diego Alcorta.—Las bases de Alberdi y el desarrollo constitucional. Buenos Aires, 1918.

———. Los que pasaban. José Manuel Estrada.—Pedro Goyena.—Nicolás Avellaneda.—Carlos Pellegrini.—Roque Sáenz Peña. Buenos Aires, 1919.

———. Santiago de Liniers. 3d ed. Buenos Aires, 1952.

Gutiérrez, Juan María. Origen y desarrollo de la enseñanza pública superior en Buenos Aires. Buenos Aires, 1915.

Ingenieros, José. La evolución de las ideas argentinas. 4 vols. Buenos Aires, 1937.

———. Sociología argentina. Buenos Aires, 1946.

Justo, Juan B. El socialismo argentino. Buenos Aires, 1910.

———. La teoría científica de la historia y la política argentina. Buenos Aires, 1898.

Korn, Alejandro. Influencias filosóficas en la evolución nacional. Buenos Aires, 1936.

Larra, Raúl. Lisandro de la Torre; el solitario de Pinas. 6th ed. Buenos Aires, 1957.

Levene, Ricardo. La anarquía de 1820 en Buenos Aires, Buenos Aires, 1933.

———. Ensayo histórico sobre la Revolución de Mayo y Mariano

Moreno; contribución al estudio de los aspectos político, jurídico y económico de la revolución de 1810. 4th ed. 3 vols. Buenos Aires, 1960.

————, ed. Historia de la Nación Argentina (desde los orígenes hasta la organización definitiva en 1862). 2d ed. 10 vols. Buenos Aires, 1939–47.

López, Vicente Fidel. Historia de la República Argentina; su orígen, su revolución y su desarrollo político hasta 1852. 4th ed. 10 vols. Buenos Aires, 1926.

Lugones, Leopoldo. Historia de Sarmiento. 2d ed. Buenos Aires, 1961.

Luna, Félix. Yrigoyen, el templario de la libertad. Buenos Aires, 1954.

Martínez Estrada, Ezequiel. Muerte y transfiguración de Martín Fierro; ensayo de interpretación de la vida argentina. 2 vols. México, 1948.

Mitre, Bartolomé. Historia de Belgrano y de la independencia argentina. 2d ed. 4 vols. Buenos Aires, 1960.

————. Historia de San Martín y de la emancipación sudamericana. Buenos Aires, 1952.

Oddone, Jacinto. Historia del socialismo argentino. 2 vols. Buenos Aires, 1934.

Orgaz, Raúl Andrés. Alberdi y el historicismo. Córdoba, 1937.

————. Echeverría y el saint-simonismo. Córdoba, 1934.

————. Vicente F. López y la filosofía de la historia. Córdoba, 1938.

Palacio, Ernesto. Historia de la Argentina, 1515–1957. 3d ed. 2 vols. Buenos Aires, 1960.

Palacios, Alfredo Lorenzo. Esteban Echeverría; albacea del pensamiento de mayo. 3d ed. Buenos Aires, 1955.

————. La justicia social. Buenos Aires, 1954.

Palcos, Alberto. La visión de Rivadavia; ensayo sobre Rivadavia y su época hasta la caída del triumvirato. Buenos Aires, 1936.

Paz, José María. Memorias póstumas del general José María Paz. 2d ed. 3 vols. La Plata, 1892.

Piñero, Norberto, and Eduardo L. Bidau. "Historia de la Universidad de Buenos Aires," *Anales de la Universidad,* I (1888), 5–431.

Probst, Juan. Juan Baltasar Maziel, el maestro de la generación de mayo. Buenos Aires, 1946.

Quesada, Ernesto. La época de Rosas. Buenos Aires, 1950.

Ramos Mejía, Francisco. El federalismo argentino (fragmentos de la historia de la evolución argentina). Buenos Aires, 1915.

Ramos Mejía, José María. Las multitudes argentinas. Buenos Aires, 1934.

————. Rosas y su tiempo. 2d ed. 3 vols. Buenos Aires, 1907.

Ravignani, Emilio. Historia constitucional de la República Argentina. 3 vols. Buenos Aires, 1926–27.

Rivero Astengo, Agustín. Juárez Celman, 1844–1909. Estudio histórico y documental de una época argentina. Buenos Aires, 1944.

Rojas, Ricardo. Historia de la literatura argentina. 6 vols. Buenos Aires, 1948.

————. El profeta de la pampa; vida de Sarmiento. Buenos Aires, 1945.

————. El radicalismo de mañana. Buenos Aires, 1932.

Saldías, Adolfo. Historia de la Confederación Argentina. Rozas y su época. 3 vols. Buenos Aires, 1951.

Sánchez Viamonte, Carlos. Historia institucional de Argentina. México, 1948.

Varela, Luis Vicente. Historia constitucional de la República Argentina. 4 vols. La Plata, 1910.

Vedia y Mitre, Mariano de. Roca. Paris, 1928.

Yunque, Alvaro. Leandro N. Alem, el hombre de la multitud. Buenos Aires, 1953.

II. SELECTED READINGS

(WORKS IN ENGLISH SUGGESTED BY THE TRANSLATOR)

Alexander, Robert J. The Perón Era. New York, 1951; London, 1952. Labor and politics during Perón's first presidency.

Backhouse, Hugo. Among the Gauchos. London, 1950.

Blanksten, George I. Péron's Argentina. Chicago, 1953. A political scientist examines some of Perón's theories and practices.

Bradford, Sax. The Battle for Buenos Aires. New York, 1943. Appraises Nazi penetration of Argentina and Argentine–United States relations.

Bruce, James. Those Perplexing Argentines. New York, London, Toronto, 1953. Views of a United States ambassador.

Bunkley, Allison Williams. The Life of Sarmiento. Princeton, N.J., 1952.

Burgin, Miron. The Economic Aspects of Argentine Federalism, 1820–1852. Cambridge, Mass., 1946.

Cady, J. F. Foreign Intervention in the Río de la Plata, 1838–50. Philadelphia, 1929.

Davis, Thomas B., Jr. Carlos de Alvear, Man of Revolution. Durham, N.C., 1955.

Defense of Freedom. By the editors of *La Prensa*. New York, 1952. Editorials from a great Buenos Aires newspaper reveal the fight for liberty under the Perón dictatorship.

Ferns, H. S. Britain and Argentina in the Nineteenth Century. London, 1960.

Greenup, Ruth and Leonard. Revolution before Breakfast: Argentina, 1941–1946. Chapel Hill, N.C., 1947.

Hanson, Simon G. Argentine Meat and the British Market: Chapters in the History of the Argentine Meat Industry. Stanford, California, and London, 1938.

Haring, Clarence H. Argentina and the United States. Boston, 1941. A short but useful introduction.

Hernández, José. The Gaucho, Martín Fierro. Adapted from the Spanish and Rendered into English Verse by Walter Owen, with Drawings by Alberto Güiraldes. New York, 1936. A superb translation of the most famous Argentine poem, which also documents the close of the age of the gaucho and of the open range.

Herron, Francis. Letters from the Argentine. New York, 1943. Perceptive reports on life in Argentina, particularly in the interior.

Hudson, William Henry. Far Away and Long Ago; A History of My Early Life. Many editions. One of the masters of English prose describes life on the pampa in mid-nineteenth century.

James, Preston E. Latin America. 3d ed. New York, 1959. The chapter on Argentina maintains the high level of this study of Latin American geography.

Jefferson, Mark. Peopling the Argentine Pampa. New York, 1926.

Johnson, John J. Political Change in Latin America: the Emergence of the Middle Sectors. Stanford, California, 1958. Argentina is one of the countries examined in detail.

Kennedy, John J. Catholicism, Nationalism, and Democracy in Argentina. Notre Dame, Ind., 1958.

Kirkpatrick, F. A. A History of the Argentine Republic. Cambridge, 1931. A British view, stressing the colonial period and the War for Independence.

Lieuwin, Edwin. Arms and Politics in Latin America. Rev. ed. New York, 1961. Consideration is given to Argentina in this general analysis.

Lynch, John. Spanish Colonial Administration, 1782–1810. The Intendant System in the Vice-Royalty of the Río de la Plata. Fair Lawn, N.J., 1958.

McGann, Thomas F. Argentina, the United States, and the Inter-American System, 1880–1914. Cambridge, Mass., 1957.

Metford, J. C. J. San Martín, the Liberator. Oxford, 1950.

Nichols, Madaline. The Gaucho: Cattle Hunter, Cavalryman, and Ideal of Romance. Durham, N.C., 1942.

Owen, Frank. Perón, His Rise and Fall. London, 1957.

Pendle, George. Argentina. New York, 1957. Brief description of the land and aspects of society and the economy.

Rennie, Ysabel F. The Argentine Republic. New York, 1945. From Rosas to the rise of Perón.

Sarmiento, Domingo F. Life in the Argentine Republic in the Days of the Tyrants, or, Civilization and Barbarism. Trans. by Mrs. Horace Mann. New York, 1868. First published in Spanish in 1845. Mrs. Mann's translation was reprinted in paperbacks in 1960 and 1961.

Szulc, Tad. Twilight of the Tyrants. New York, 1959. Contains a long chapter on Perón's dictatorship.

Taylor, Carl C. Rural Life in Argentina. Baton Rouge, La., 1948.

Tinker, Edward Larocque. The Horsemen of the Americas and the Literature They Inspired. New York, 1953. Emphasizes the gaucho and *gauchesco* literature.

Whitaker, Arthur P. Argentine Upheaval: Perón's Fall and the New Regime. New York and London, 1956.

————. The United States and Argentina. Cambridge, Mass., 1954. Stresses the twentieth century, particularly the Perón era.

White, John W. Argentina; the Life Story of a Nation. New York, 1942.

Williams, John H. Argentina International Trade under Inconvertible Paper Money, 1880–1900. Cambridge, Mass., 1920.

Willis, Bailey. A "Yanqui" in Patagonia. Stanford, California, 1947. A geologist's experiences in southern Argentina, 1910–15.

GLOSSARY

adelantado: a conquistador-governor named by the Crown.

audiencia: a superior court and also the region of its jurisdiction, in Spain and in Spanish America.

Banda Oriental del Uruguay: the East Bank of the Uruguay (River). This was the name used in the colonial era and in the nineteenth century for the region that is now Uruguay (officially, the República Oriental del Uruguay).

cabildo: the town council. Also, the building in which the council meets.

cabildo abierto: an expanded town council, enlarged by the addition of qualified citizens.

caudillo: local or national politico-military chief.

Charcas: an administrative area of the Spanish empire, including much of present-day Bolivia, Paraguay, and northwest Argentina, under the authority of the Viceroy in Lima.

consulado: a royal corporation of citizens engaged in trade in Spain and in Spanish America.

Cortes: the Spanish parliament.

creole (*criollo*): a person born in the New World of Spanish parents.

criollismo: the way of life of the creoles; the traditional, generally rural attitudes stemming from the colonial and early national periods. In Argentina in the later nineteenth and in the twentieth centuries, a term synonymous with older national values.

encomendero: in the New World, a Spaniard (or other person) to whom an allotted number of Indians owed tribute in labor, goods, or money, and who in turn owed the Indians the obligation to Christianize and protect them.

encomienda: the institutionalized relationship of Spaniards and creoles with the Indians, involving mutual responsibilities.

estancia: a large Argentine land-holding, either for ranching or agriculture.

estanciero: the owner of a large Argentine land-holding.

fuero: a legal right or code of rights pertaining to a group or corporation.

golpe de estado: *coup d'etat*, or the act of overthrowing a government.

hacendado: owner of a large landed estate.

hidalgo: a member of the lower nobility; literally, "the son of someone" (*hijo d'algo*).

junta: a governing committee.

legua: a league; approximately three miles.

litoral: the littoral of the Río de la Plata and the Paraná River.

mestizo: a person of Spanish and Indian parentage.

montonera: irregular *gaucho* cavalry, led usually by a *caudillo*.

Palermo: the suburban estate of Rosas, now a park within the city of Buenos Aires.

patronage: royal patronage (the *patronato real*), by which the papacy gave the crown the right to nominate members of the religious hierarchy and to exercise other controls over Church activity.

peninsular: a person born in Spain but living in America, in contrast to a creole.

porteño: specifically, a resident of the port of Buenos Aires.

Reconquest: of Spain from the Moslems, extending from the eighth to the fifteenth centuries.

reducción: a mission to which Indians were brought to live ("led back").

Santa Cruz: a southern Bolivian province.

INDEX

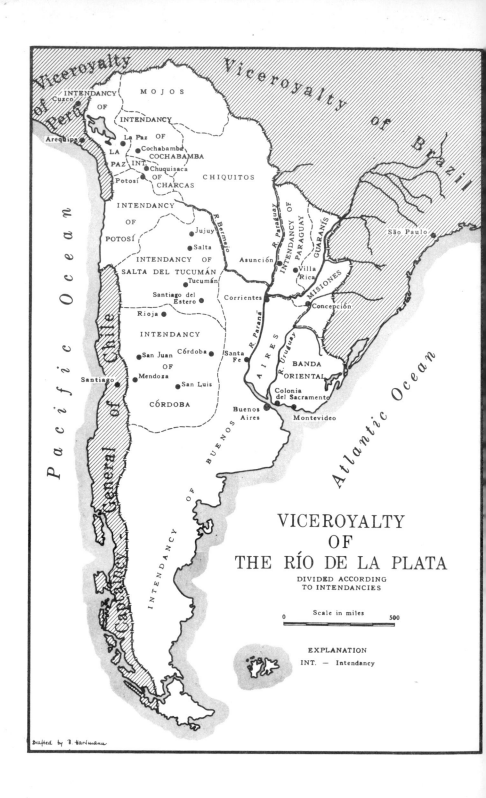

VICEROYALTY
OF
THE RÍO DE LA PLATA

DIVIDED ACCORDING
TO INTENDANCIES

0   Scale in miles   500

EXPLANATION

INT. — Intendancy

Viceroyalty of Perú

Viceroyalty of Brazil

Pacific Ocean

Atlantic Ocean

General of Chile

INTENDANCY OF Cuzco

Arequipa

MOJOS

INTENDANCY OF LA PAZ

La Paz

Cochabamba

INTENDANCY OF COCHABAMBA

Chuquisaca

INTENDANCY OF CHARCAS

Potosí

CHIQUITOS

INTENDANCY OF POTOSÍ

R. Bermejo

Jujuy

Salta

INTENDANCY OF SALTA DEL TUCUMÁN

Tucumán

Santiago del Estero

Rioja

INTENDANCY OF CÓRDOBA

San Juan

Córdoba

Mendoza

Santiago

San Luis

Asunción

R. Paraguay

INTENDANCY OF PARAGUAY

GUARANÍS

Villa Rica

MISIONES

Corrientes

Concepción

São Paulo

R. Paraná

R. Uruguay

BUENOS AIRES

Santa Fe

BANDA ORIENTAL

Colonia del Sacramento

Buenos Aires

Montevideo

INTENDANCY OF BUENOS AIRES

Drafted by B. Hartmann